BRUSHES *with a* STROKE

BRUSHES *with a* STROKE

Sporting Survivors and their Stories of Recovery

NEIL HARMAN

pitch

First published by Pitch Publishing, 2025
1

Pitch Publishing
9 Donnington Park,
85 Birdham Road,
Chichester, West Sussex,
PO20 7AJ

www.pitchpublishing.co.uk
info@pitchpublishing.co.uk

A CIP catalogue record is available for this book from the British Library.

ISBN 978 1 83680 147 4

Typesetting and origination by Pitch Publishing

MIX
Paper | Supporting responsible forestry
FSC® C010615

Printed and bound on FSC® certified paper in line with our continuing commitment to ethical business practices, sustainability and the environment.

Printed and bound in India by Thomson Press

CONTENTS

To Paddy Barclay, who figures in the editorial and very sadly died since we started on the editing process

PREFACE

WHEN A stroke strikes, the victim deals with the consequences in a variety of ways. On 8 May 2023, I was fine one minute and the next in a heap on the bedroom floor, powerless, frightened and with no certainty of what had happened or what was to become of me.

Across the following days, weeks, months, and years (almost two now in my case), life has been a cocktail of conflicting thoughts and emotions, of despair, rage, bitterness and self-pity, interspersed with flickering rays of hope. My mind is full, yet my body is in a bewildering state of pained semi-existence.

Days follow a familiar pattern, striving to see how far I can push myself to improve, desperate for any small sign that I'm getting somewhere, yet resigned to a depressing sameness of frustration and fatigue. It's not a real life, but it's the one I have now.

I know I could not have got through these past two years without the love and dedication of my wife Maureen, our daughters Elizabeth and Kathleen, my extended family, the positivity of friends, and the nursing staff both in Reading and Thatcham, as well as all the marvellous health professionals who have helped me since my release from hospital. I thank them in greater depth in the final chapter of this book.

It would be easy to give in to stroke. It hasn't beaten me yet.

Neil Harman,
February, 2025

STROKE? NAH, NOT ME

I WOULD never know the precise extent of the circumstances that cut me down on May Bank Holiday 2023, which was probably a blessing when all was said and done. One thing was without doubt, if you messed with your brain, the consequence wreaked bloody cataclysm in your life.

My apologies for having resorted to coarse language so early in proceedings though this was increasingly the lot of we stroke victims – a description I grew to loathe – who tended towards aggressive outbursts that were not heretofore in our nature.

To give the awfulness of the attack on me its full description – it was a right intracerebral haemorrhage thalamus and basal ganglia extending into the anterior and posterior horns of the right lateral ventricle. A mind-blowing (literally) and grisly mouthful. But what precisely did it all mean and what could possibly have caused it?

I needed to learn as much as possible because it was embedded in the bloodstream of a journalist of 40 years' experience to need to learn as much as possible about everything.

In the early desperate throes of the trauma, I couldn't determine faces but distinguished voices. I heard one say it was a small bleed, another said significant, while on my return to Wokingham's Corpus Christi church congregation after a six-month absence, the priest announced that my condition had been 'severe' before encouraging a round of applause during Mass which felt both extravagant and faintly embarrassing. In my mind, all I'd done was not die.

I took a deep breath, leaned against the top of the pew behind me and hauled myself to my feet, nodding appreciation towards Canon Simon for what was a characteristically gracious gesture.

I supposed on the face of it, being alive was a cause for restrained celebration. I raised a sheepish right hand while pressing my kneecaps tight against the back of the pew in front, clutching a rosary as tightly as I could in a partially clenched left fist.

When I slumped back, I was reminded how uncomfortable pews without cushions could be especially as the stroke had obliterated my buttock muscles to such an extent that the landing was essentially the crack of raw bone on solid wood.

It wasn't until I saw an image of my brain scan that the precise extent of my dice with death became somewhat clearer. I thought I'd show it to Bassam Alchi, a fellow chorister, and a kidney specialist at the Royal Berkshire Hospital in Reading who, besides my wife Maureen and daughters Elizabeth and Kathleen, was first at my bedside when he discovered I was in residence.

We were in the choir loft – I'd been back singing for a couple of Sundays from the spring of 2024 – and Bassam took a long look at the picture. 'You're pretty lucky to be here,' he said in that matter-of-fact way I had previously admired in the medical fraternity.

The comment caused me to inhale when practising my exhaling diaphragm exercises and led to an onset of spluttering that caused members of the congregation to cast an anxious glance up and over their shoulders.

I had tried for the best part of a year to play down the gravity of my situation because I wasn't that sure of it myself, but I'd been given a taste of the full horror. God had spared me this one and I had every cause to be grateful.

The trouble was, while surviving the initial scourge of a stroke may have been a beautiful thing, living with one was extended torture. How did you deal both effectively and rationally when one half of your body acted independently of the other or rather just went bananas most of the time?

One arm worked, one didn't; one leg worked, one didn't; one half of your face worked, one didn't. And what was worse was that the bits that didn't work openly conspired against the bits that did. That struck me as a particularly unwarranted piling of unfairness upon misery.

I hadn't seen it coming, that was for sure. There had been no warnings, no hints, no 'get ready for something awful' preparedness. In the lexicon of the US sixties TV series *Batman*, it was, 'Whaap!' 'Biff!' 'Oof!' Have some of that, and then a bit more.

One minute alert and bright, the next clinging to mortality with the one good hand I had (the right in this left-hander's case). What had happened? How long would it last? Would I be a stumblebum until my dying day?

If I learned one thing about stroke specialists in several soul-searching months, it was that they had one important thing going for them – they never actually told you anything.

It was all light and shade, there could be no definitive answer because though they were expert at determining the extent of the damage and thus how to seek to rectify it, none could say for sure if it was fixable or offer a time frame or parameters for potential recovery.

The brain wasn't something you could remove, give a robust shake to, shove back in again, tighten the screws and all the circuits would magically reconnect.

A specialist's peer into the future would be no more or less authoritative than mine, so they thought better of going there. They would evaluate the difficult news – if you really wanted to know it – then monitored recovery stage by stage and offered guidance as to how you best prepared for the complete unknown.

Quite honestly, stroke was an utter pain in the arse and several other places besides. The brain – that extraordinary hub of your living network – had gone haywire and needed to reboot by computing which bits of you worked and which required to re-learn the mechanisms you'd started to pick up the last time you were dressed in nappies.

With that, it was over to you and your corrupted body.

***

It was two days after King Charles III and Queen Camilla's coronation and well past the cut-off for completion of a task I should have finished weeks earlier. I needed to sharpen the indistinct edges of the speech for my daughter Kathleen's wedding a few days down the line, one of the most special moments in our family's life.

Being a writer all these years, I believed I did my best work pressed tight against an onrushing deadline. When I had minutes, the words had always come to me, don't ask me how, they just did. The nature of the beast after years of on-the-precipice practise. Having days to play with, I would fidget and prevaricate. It drove Maureen nuts.

Knowing me, then, I'd put the speech on hold until later and prepared instead to walk the dog, catch up with the news, test myself with a samurai Sudoku and see if there was a Championship match on *Sky Football* worth recording to watch later. Just then I was jogged by a particular moment in the coronation ceremony I felt the urge to revisit.

Countless times, I had mimicked Handel's rousing anthem 'Zadok the Priest' in the privacy of the bathroom or in the car and had never quite mastered the breaths required to fully complete the complex semiquaver runs and quaver chords of the 'Alleluia' and 'Amen'.

The rendition by Westminster Abbey's choristers while Charles received his kingly anointing had been so pitch-perfect I decided to replay it before diving back into the mundanity of life post full-time employment – something I had never reconciled myself to in the nine years I'd endured without a clear professional focus.

I was on my sofa breathing deeply and joining in a bracing 'Alleluia' when the left side of my face went disturbingly stiff. Rock hard in truth. My upper left arm followed suit.

I must have slept too long on one side the past night and these pins and needles would dissipate once I got up and paced the living room. Two or three circuits would do it and then I could prepare Arlo, our golden cocker spaniel, for the regular stroll alongside Bearwood Lakes golf course hoping to avoid those owners and their dogs to whom he reacted with a hostility I'd never figured out.

Bloody hell, the stiffness would not relent. I felt beads of perspiration forming on my forehead. Frustration was giving way to real alarm. What was this? Should I just ignore the numbness and hope it would eventually go away or do something about the panic that had begun to mess with any attempt at logical thinking?

I decided to Google the symptoms, the second of that day's acts that may have saved my life (I'd probably have been a dead man had I left home with Arlo in the back seat of the car rather than wanting to listen to Handel's coronation *piece de resistance* one more time).

I typed something like 'sudden numbness in face, left arm' and it flashed immediately as early indication of a stroke. Nah, couldn't be. Not me. Maureen was taking her morning walk and she'd be back soon to tell me I was over-dramatising – a particular habit of mine so she often repeated the accusation.

God knows why but something told me that if I was having a stroke, I'd be taken to hospital and I couldn't go there smelling a bit stale, so I went upstairs for a shower. Upstairs! Bloody idiotic in retrospect, yet a good idea at the time. The dog dutifully followed.

I was emerging still slightly damp from the ensuite and about to reach for some clothes when I went into an uncontrolled tailspin and landed face first on the bedroom carpet, the bottom half of my semi-legless frame on the tiled floor of the bathroom. There was no sharp sensation of pain, in fact no feeling at all except one of floating through the air, and not being able to do anything bar participate in a crash landing.

I dropped my mobile phone in the blur of the fall, but it ended up – quite miraculously – within both confused sight and reach, though getting to it required an ungainly shuffle as half of my body had been liquified.

Nine times out of ten I would have left the phone charging in the kitchen and would not have been able to get at it without sliding in some form or another down the stairs. Had I managed that (hardly likely) I couldn't have stood up to prise it from the charging cord. Bringing it with me to the bedroom was another probable life-saving decision.

As it was, I made a successful grab for the phone, pressed Maureen's number and she picked up, probably thinking on seeing my name that I'd forgotten for the umpteenth time where we kept the dog's poop-bags.

'Sorry to bother you honey but I think I'm having a stroke,' I said in the just-so manner of asking if she might want a biscuit with her second cup of tea before leaving for work. At least she believed me, probably because my words were a bit slurred. There was an audible shriek of 'oh my God' and the distinct sound of her breaking from a walk into a mad dash.

On the way up the lane, she had summoned an ambulance and the operator indicated its arrival in 23 minutes. I had no idea then that every second saved might lessen the seriousness of the stroke's impact on my body, both physical and mental.

It had struck me that had I fallen ten seconds earlier, it would have been in the shower or on the bathroom tiles. Imagine if I had hit my head on an unforgiving, rock-hard surface, the rim of the toilet, say? I would probably have been paralysed or at the very least suffered a far more severe haemorrhage from knocking myself out.

***

I heard the key in the lock, Maureen raced upstairs and said a few things I can't recall before the ambulance pulled up a few minutes later than the prescribed ETA. (1.9 million brain cells died every minute a stroke was left untreated, so I was roughly 47.5 million down at this point.)

The paramedic's initial cry of, 'he's upstairs', was followed with, 'and he's on a tiled floor', expressed with an explicit element of frustration. The visitor introduced himself and I said good morning to his shoes. His name was Dave if I remember rightly. 'Up here,' he called to his oppo. 'We'll need a chair.'

Somehow, without sliding on the still slippery tiles, Dave and his pal winched me up, placed me in the apparatus and managed to get me downstairs without scraping the wallpaper, for which I'd have been held responsible.

'Bloody gravel drive,' Dave muttered. 'Sorry,' I responded.

The paramedics were a little displeased that they'd have to lift me from the front door to the ambulance rather than risk the wheelchair's wheels getting snared in the stones (I'd always hated them anyway but my pleas for asphalt in their place had long since fallen on deaf ears).

I was hoisted into the vehicle, laid on a stretcher, a canula embedded in the top of my right hand and various tubes attached to it. 'I think I've had a stroke,' I said. 'Actually sir, you're having a stroke,' Dave corrected me in a firm West Country burr.. 'Rovers or City?' I asked, guessing Bristol. 'City of course, there's only one team in Bristol,' he replied. Well, at least I was still able to pick an accent.

'Fancy the blue-light treatment?' 'That'd be fun. My first time.' 'Okay, let's do this.'

Next stop was the Royal Berks, seven miles away. Maureen had been informed she needn't break her neck unduly in pursuit of the flashing light as I'd have to be thoroughly examined and would need a CT (brain) scan to evaluate the extent of the bleed before I could be considered equipped to face anyone.

Indeed, I was taken straight from the ambulance, placed in a tube, and watched what looked like the Aurora Borealis inches above my face. I heard someone say brain damage and John Radcliffe, the Oxford hospital that specialised in neurological trauma. Dear God, not that awful please.

On being retrieved from the scanner I first clapped eyes on a dapper, bald man wearing a radiantly green bow tie, which did wonders for sharpening my optical focus. 'Mr Harman,' he said in a gentle, yet striking accent, German I surmised. 'My name is Dr Flossmann.' I was right again.

He began to tell me what had happened and that though I'd had a significant bleed, it was located on one spot on the brain and the damage didn't appear to have spread further. He asked if I had any questions. True to four decades of journalistic training, I managed to muster, 'Will I be able to drink again?' – thinking specifically of a stimulating glass or two of chilled red wine of an evening.

'You're allowed to have one large glass a night but only if it is very expensive,' Dr Flossmann replied. 'No cheap wine, promise me.'

He told me I couldn't be in a better place as the Royal Berks had what was considered one of the most up-to-date stroke units in the country, which was reassuring, as far as it went. With that, I was loaded on to a trolley and wheeled off, walls, ceilings and passers-by merging into one numbing blur.

From there my recollection became a little foggy. Maureen said that in the first instance, as only one section of my mouth functioned properly, I was spouting incoherent drivel (sub-editors who had worked with me on newspaper sports desks across the decades would immediately recognise this description).

I did remember I had no sensation at all down my left side. The arm was useless, as was my leg and malfunctioning mouth, which drooped at one corner. All those sessions spent trying to perfect my Johnny Mathis impression and now it would come naturally. At least my vision hadn't been significantly affected and I knew where I was, but also that I was defenceless, hopeless and clueless.

The wife had brought half a hundredweight of clothes, as if packing for a month on Cape Cod, a long-time favourite Harman holiday destination. Instead, what was before me was a first night of what would become four months of incarceration in places where the likelihood of lobster tail appearing on the menu was decidedly remote.

I supposed I simply had to do what I could, fearful of what else might go wrong but at the same time strangely confident that one day I'd be assured that this was nothing more than a terrible dream from which I'd wake up and be Peter Pan again, or at least an elderly relative of his.

Apart from the removal of some haemorrhoids in the 1980s which were the uncomfortable upshot of sitting twice, often three times a week on damp wooden benches in archaic football press boxes, and having wisdom teeth extracted in the early 2000s, I'd neither been a hospital patient nor taken a sick day in my life.

It was probably when my underpants were peeled away, and a couple of nurses squeezed me into a one-size-fits-all nappy – the first time I'd used the disposable type (in the fifties they were of cotton, washed countless times, and re-fastened with a giant safety pin) – that I realised life would never be quite the same again.

It would be three months before I could get to a toilet without needing either someone's arm or a wheelchair.

And I'd never complete that wedding speech.

***

'Carer! Carer!'

I was the newcomer on A Ward of the Acute Stroke Unit at the Royal Berks, desperately trying to relax but keenly conscious of small shifts in a fellow patient's position, breathing patterns, groans and indistinct chatter from the nurses' station.

I didn't want to pass wind lest it generated a second exceptional bowel movement and the consequent unwanted refilling of my nappy, then realised that the breakdown in my muscle mass – such as it had been – meant controlling any bodily spasm was almost impossible.

My bed was in a corner by the window. The ward was mixed gender and the bespectacled old lady horizontally across from me was banging on the reinforced plastic frame of her bed, demanding attention, and obviously believing she was back at home.

My God, how long was I going to have to put up with this? The poor dear was so confused and no one seemed to be rushing to her aid, so I presumed they'd heard it from her before.

Then a voice was raised, somewhat abruptly, 'Your carer's not here, I'm a nurse. You're not at home, you're in the hospital.' That stilled her for a while but soon she was off again. The lady one down had a tube inserted into her nose and the order NIL BY MOUTH written in black Sharpie on the board above her bed. All she could do was moan, mouth agape. I tried to avert my gaze.

After a couple of days in this woebegone place, I was told I was being moved to D Ward, for men only. I was wheeled to a bed in the same spot, top left-hand corner, with an uninterrupted view of a temporary staff car park in which almost every driver blatantly ignored the one-way signs. I was desperate to get out and remonstrate with them but had to content myself with a few mumbled obscenities and silly arm gestures.

Being by the window was a simple blessing. I could witness life beyond the room in which I was trapped, and promptly asked the nurses to open it a touch (which required the aid of a plastic cup to keep it from slamming shut) for refreshing intakes of real air and to let out the smells and many more stultifying odours from within.

***

I had always been fascinated by the oddities of human nature and didn't doubt that spotting behavioural nuances across 40 years of reporting on public dramas both enhanced my written work and brought occasional employment as a colour commentator for BBC radio sport in the days before its output played havoc with the most able of functioning brains (in my new state, I couldn't take the shrill inconsequence of it anymore).

I was invited to the commentary booth more for my anthropological skills than any express sporting expertise – forever trying to work out what made people tick and why they did the strange things they did. I was good at reading a room if I said so myself.

Tennis players, their coteries, umpires and linespeople had delivered an enriching harvest of peculiarity for as long as I had followed their every moves. I left the boring 'why did Tim Henman go crosscourt rather than down the line with that backhand?' bits to the actual experts.

I scanned my fellow patients in D Ward. What damage had they incurred? What were their recovery chances? Of course, given the obligations for doctor/patient confidentiality, each time I asked a nurse what was wrong with someone they politely told me it was nothing they could share with anyone bar family.

I'd have to try to assess these fellow humans myself while surmising who they were and what they had done to end up in here from the merest snapshot – and a terribly unhappy one at that. The first occupant of the bed directly opposite me was a gentleman I took to be in his late 70s, named Cliff, balding and bespectacled, who gently hummed away to himself most of the day but was able to get up and walk around freely without anyone asking him where he was going or why.

This I found more than a trifle disorienting. No one else in the ward could walk, so why could he, the eldest by some distance? Surely stroke victims were bed-ridden. Cliff would attach one of those bum-bags over his pyjama trousers and stroll nonchalantly about in a flat cap, though he was never out of sight long enough to have ventured outdoors.

It may have been a result of my brain malfunction, but I was finding insignificant things very annoying. Cliff had more than one irritating habit, the incessant humming notwithstanding. First, he kept repeating his home address out loud, to the nursing staff and otherwise simply into thin air.

If one of us managed to escape before him, we would have known exactly where to go to help ourselves to a few valuable trinkets. As I'd lost the ability to write anything down, my short-term memory was compromised and I couldn't walk, I'd at least have been free from suspicion.

Cliff also possessed several books of Sudoku puzzles and – checking no one was looking, but never across at me – snitched the answers from the back to fill in the spaces, all the while sniggering at his own ingenuity.

The great skill of Sudoku is to work out yourself how each nine-number grid is filled. I was addicted to it if truth be told. Copying the numbers surely brought a player zero sense of achievement, but I supposed it helped him cope with confinement in his own corner of la-la land.

'Look, he's doing it again, he's doing it again,' I'd say breathlessly to my family when they visited, pointing across the ward. 'Oh Dad, give it a rest,' was my daughters' response, accompanied by much rolling of the eyes.

Each evening, Cliff emptied his bum-bag of the bronze and silver coins he had stashed around his waist on to his bedside table, counted them out one by one, placed them in stacks and put them back in the bag. He couldn't have spent anything during the day so the number and amount would be the same as the previous night and the one before that. He'd obviously once been a bank clerk.

Later I would see him take coins from a secret compartment in the heel of his shoe and run them through his fingers like Ron Moody's Fagin in *Oliver!* I just found he and his mannerisms both exasperating and compelling at the same time.

Then, without any indication of him being discharged – though he'd counted his coins with particular care the previous night – Cliff was gone and his bed thoroughly washed and swiftly remade for a new occupant. That became the way of it. This was not somewhere you could build a lasting acquaintanceship.

In all, during my two months in the ward, there were eight different patients in that bed. It got to the stage where I'd welcome the latest arrival with a cheery, 'You won't be there long.'

I was trying to give their morale a bit of a boost but, upon reflection, I appreciated why some looked across at me as if they'd just seen a ghost.

***

Each new first name was scribbled on a board on the wall behind the bed so if you were minded to strike up a conversation, you could cut through formality and just say, 'Hi, I'm Neil good to see you X, Y or Z.' There was

Martin (God could he snore), Peter (incommunicado) and, believe it or not, Marc was followed by Anthony.

Some were happy to nod or even chat across the width of the ward, but most seemed lost in their own world and avoided engagement with a stranger, even one with my instinctive affability.

The most sociable was Ernie, a Londoner with a light heavyweight's frame, glasses too big for his face and a distinctively mottled nose. He would venture nearer to a fellow patient's bed than anyone else bar a nurse would dare attempt, though never in a manner that alarmed (well, he didn't scare me).

Ernie marched with the aid of a frame and began every conversation by drawing his face close to yours and saying, 'I've no idea why I'm here you know.' He repeated the same to his wife on her daily call to him and every nurse offering him succour. Whatever he was here for, he had soon departed.

One morning, Dennis the Glaswegian who'd been in the next bed to mine for three weeks was also gesturing goodbye, to be replaced by a much younger lad – I guessed he was in his late 30s – named Steve who the minute he'd been tucked in, and the curtains closed around him, broke into uncontrollable sobs. The rest of us didn't quite know where to look. The nurses retreated but I couldn't just ignore it.

I whispered across the gap between us that he shouldn't be afraid to let go of his emotions, and if there was anything I could do please to let me know. It all seemed rather useless, but I wanted to assure him that whatever was troubling him he shouldn't keep it locked inside. A problem shared and all that.

As time went by, through eavesdropping snippets of conversation, (you couldn't help but hear through the curtain and the old journalist in me hadn't completely died) I learned that Steve, a big, hefty bloke, ran his own company and was petrified that whatever had struck him down might lead to financial ruin, because no one else knew the ins and outs of his business.

He needed to be back on his feet and at his desk as soon as possible and who knew how long that might take?

To these levels of anxiety, I couldn't properly relate. I had all but retired from working life (not my choice) and Maureen was in full-time employment, running a golf club in Surrey that she had turned into a long-lasting success story, which was enormously to her credit.

I knew our finances were sound, but that couldn't stop me fretting about what an uncertain future held, especially as I was marooned in this place for who knew how long and Labour (sure to come poking their noses into everyone's bank accounts), were gaining in public popularity. I kept such anxieties private.

My overriding concern at present was to sustain Steve's spirits and keep pressing home the message that he'd be fine (obviously not knowing if it was true) in the hope he'd quieten down somewhat.

I would gabble on about football to try to take his mind off the personal tribulation, then discovered he was a Chelsea supporter so accepted going there might make things worse. When his wife came in and told him she was learning the business ropes from scratch and was sure she had things under control, Steve dissolved into more floods, his entire body shuddering.

As time went by, he relaxed a little and the night-time sobbing relented. He would end up being discharged from the hospital with me still parked, semi-detached from real life, ready to test my amateur psychology skills on the next poor sod to be dumped into the bed to my right.

It was Arnold as it happened, and he couldn't have been more different to Steve if he'd tried. Arnold was, I surmised, in his early 80s, could barely see and didn't have a clue where he was or what was wrong with him.

When Steve cried, it was full-on, guttural sobbing. Arnold moaned, a low lament as if he was trying to speak but couldn't. The noise went right through what was left of my brain, like someone drawing their fingernails down a school chalkboard.

I told my kids about it, and they thought I had to be exaggerating, so I taped a single uninterrupted ten-minute session of this pitiful noise and played it back to them when I felt he was asleep. Their response was apologetic distress at my situation, dealing on a nightly basis with a sound even my headphones couldn't completely block out.

I tried to chivvy Arnold along, but he either couldn't hear what I was saying or was ignoring me, so I gave up.

His children and grandchildren beat a regular path to his bedside which would temporarily give him – and the rest of us – some respite but as soon as they had gone and the nurses failed to persuade him to take in anything other than his favourite blackcurrant juice, it was back to the whimpering and wailing.

I wondered how much more of that I could take.

MICHAEL JOHNSON

'MICHAEL JOHNSON may just be the coolest man who ever lived.' So read a comment on the social media platform X on 5 August 2024, as the great American athlete appeared on the BBC's Olympic Games output from Paris, hair and beard slightly flecked with grey, and wearing a distinctive, predominantly lilac and mauve, round-necked jumper.

Indeed, Johnson was the epitome of health and wellbeing. He also happened to be the outstanding contributor to our domestic coverage of track and field, mixing a depth of knowledge and silky erudition to perfection. No John McEnroe hard New York edges in this case. It was hard to believe looking at and listening to Michael that he had ever had a day's illness in his life.

In one of the many responses to the 'coolest man' comment, a contributor wrote, 'Back in the day the guy sprinted like Forrest Gump, all chest and quick flat strides, and nobody stood a chance. The undisputed star of Atlanta 1996.'

Others had the more basic desire to know where he bought his colourful, classic tops from.

The effect Michael had on proceedings was perhaps best summed up by one message which read, 'Whoever it was at the BBC who first thought of bringing Michael Johnson on to their athletics coverage deserves a medal of their own. The man is peerless.'

I suspected that few of those drawn to Johnson's calming voice and patterned wardrobe, knew that six years to the month previously he had suffered an attack very similar to my own. His had occurred on the right side of his brain, a thalamic stroke, and had caused the loss of all the immense power in his left arm and leg. Michael was about to turn 51 years old.

Neither of us felt any pain in the initial stage of the stroke's invasion. Mine was measured by a sudden hardening of face and arm, whereas Michael's body started to tingle, and he thought it might be the onset of a cramp.

It was precisely this sense that something isn't quite right, but that it doesn't feel particularly shocking, which makes stroke such an insidious condition. Michael pondered his dilemma for longer than me, almost certainly because he couldn't get his head around how an athlete of his prodigious talents might be suffering anything more serious than a bit of a twinge.

He did at least have the presence of mind to ask his wife Armine to drive him to the nearest hospital, in their case the UCLA Medical Centre, in Santa Monica, California, less than half an hour by car from their home. Michael, like me and many others in the same predicament, initially found clarity hard to come by, which made him even more nervous. Then frightened. Then a bit angry.

He recalled being able to get without assistance on to the stretcher on which he was pushed into the MRI tube but on being removed after half an hour of disconcerting fear and noise, he was unable to stand on his own two feet. There was a greater extent of numbness in his left arm, and he couldn't feel a thing from his left foot.

'At the time you were unable to walk, you were bound to think what's going to happen, because some people made a complete recovery, but some didn't,' he said when we 'Zoomed' across the pond. 'The doctors told me that from everything they had seen, they would be surprised if I didn't make a full recovery.

'That was helpful, but the toughest thing for me was never being able to figure out why it occurred in the first place. I couldn't get to the bottom of that, which made it scarier because there was nothing I could either do or stop doing that might limit the risk of another stroke going forward.

'I went through every test and procedure you could name to try to figure out why, at 50 years old, in great shape, with no family history of stroke, it could happen. I had the help of some of the best experts in the United States and the consensus was – and it wasn't the first time they'd seen this – sometimes stroke just happened, and it probably shouldn't to someone like me, but it did, that one awful time.'

In his case, Michael hadn't had a bleed but rather a clot had formed on the brain, which if not the worst scenario, still had the potential to be dire. 'In those first few confusing days I couldn't walk and couldn't stand, but I went into training mode, did all my rehab, just like I had when I was training for the Olympics,' he said. 'I had a great team working with me who were really encouraging.'

For those from my generation, Johnson was among, if not *the* finest athlete we had seen. His style was individualistic, idiosyncratically upright, but he brought exceptional grace to the track and made running with bullet-like impact appear so gracefully effortless.

For the record, he was a four-time Olympic gold-medallist and thus far the one male athlete to have won both the 200 and 400m at the same Games, achieving this on home territory, in Atlanta in 1996.

He would successfully defend the 400m title in Sydney four years later, a unique achievement. As of the summer of 2024 he still held three of the top 100 times for the 200m, having broken 20 seconds for the distance on 23 occasions. He also bettered 44 seconds for the 400m 22 times, more than twice as many as any other athlete. He was very special.

My conversation with him was among the most uplifting I can recall with anyone about anything. I thought it best to use it here exactly as we spoke, rather than embellish it with my own random thoughts. He was thrilled that the inspiration for me taking on the task of writing this book was to uplift those stricken by this transformational illness and who struggled to come to terms with its impact.

The most obvious first question to pose was why he thought he had been struck down in the first place?

'My physical wellbeing probably prepared me for my stroke episode better than most people,' he said. 'I'd always considered myself very fortunate and appreciated the extent of that good fortune. And so, at that time, though obviously I was really scared this had happened and here I was lying in hospital not knowing if I'd ever be able to walk again, to walk like I used to or do the things I'd always done, at the same time I remembered saying to my wife, "well, why not me?"

'When I thought about what had happened to so many other people through no fault of their own, why would I think I was so special that something like this couldn't have happened to me?

'When I was competing as an athlete, when I was number one in the world, making history and all of those things, I'd often say to myself, "why me? How did I end up the one with this amazing, once-in-a-lifetime kind of talent?"

'So, you had to take the bad with the good. I was 50, about to turn 51, and I'd had an amazing life to this point, so I decided to make the best of it and if I didn't make a full recovery, I still had plenty to be thankful for.

'That wasn't to say that it was easy, but it made it easier because I'd always had gratitude for the life I'd had and kept the perspective that I'd been really, really fortunate.

'I was in good shape when I had my stroke and though my left leg wasn't operating the way that it had before, I could still hobble around a bit. When my friends saw me at the hospital, I was either lying in bed or, because the doctors allowed me to have an exercise bike in my room, I was getting on that a lot, trying to get my leg going.

'It took them [his friends] by surprise that I was able to be exercising so soon, though as one of them said, it shouldn't have, "considering it was you, Michael."'

***

Being able to get back on the horse so soon after it kicked you in the head is obviously not the experience of everyone where stroke is concerned.

Whether or not Michael Johnson was empowered by a reputation he needed to live up to, the inner drive on which his astonishing athletic success was built was correspondingly crucial as he started to put one foot back in front of another.

He had been entirely self-driven as an Olympian, so why should it be any different when he sought to build back to what he once was when there were no medals waiting at the finishing line? Indeed, letting that mask of impenetrable inscrutability slip just a little was just as important. Stroke was a humbling experience.

'When you'd lived a life carried out in public, you clearly had a persona to which people related,' he said. 'I was sure the wider public thought, "Michael Johnson's always been in great shape, he could look after himself and take care of everybody else." That was something I had to deal with internally.

'My wife was very helpful because initially I didn't want anyone to come by and see me in hospital, but she said, "They're your friends, they're here to support you. You've got to let them see you."

'That taught me to learn to be vulnerable and not the person who didn't really need anyone. That was a turning point for me in my life.'

In setting up and inspiring Michael Johnson Performance – the self-styled, 'world leader in athletic sports performance training' he had initially made all the decisions, set all the parameters and governed without delegation.

Now he saw value in 'not thinking you could do all this on your own. I allowed my staff to help and support me more than I had before'.

Trying to be all things to all men brought with it anticipated stresses and strains. Just because Michael could run faster than anyone else in the world over certain distances, didn't mean he was equipped to handle every challenge life threw at him.

The impact of stroke brought with it the realisation that he needed to take things a little easier, on himself especially. 'The only real change that I could make and did make was trying to limit the stress in my life,' he said. 'There was nothing else I could really point to as the culprit [for his stroke].

'Each year I would do a very comprehensive health assessment and examination and my doctors asked me at what level I rated the stress in my life. I always said it was very low because any stress I did have was that I brought on myself because of what I expected from myself.

'I believed I was good at dealing with stress both as an entrepreneur and as an athlete. I chose my work and was able to do what I wanted to do, solving problems and dealing with challenges, which could be stressful. And just because you were good at it didn't mean it was necessarily good for you.

'And because you enjoyed something didn't mean it was good for you either. One of the things I recognised during my own recovery was that there were days when you weren't going to be motivated and weren't going to get better.

'There were even times when I did my training and rehab and felt worse because I hadn't made any progress at all and typically that was what motivated people – they wanted to return to the way they were. If every day you were doing therapy, then typically you'd get better but there would be some days when you didn't.

'Most people didn't understand that and that was when they would start to give up – multiple days of feeling you were not making any progress.

'Having been an athlete, I was familiar with that emotion. There were days I would train real hard and felt I wasn't improving, maybe even going backwards. It was at those times I appreciated the importance of coming back the next day and getting straight at it again.'

The setting of targets – be they genuine or fanciful – was critical in the post-stroke search for a positive ethos. Clearly, the aims that were not of a repeat gold medal Olympian were likely to be more limited, but no less imperative. I pictured myself swinging a golf club without toppling face forwards on to a tee marker. Michael Johnson's horizon was somewhat broader. And, as one would imagine, it involved running a bit faster than other mortals.

'I allowed others to run the company in my absence and just concentrated on the rehab, getting myself as fit as possible,' he said. 'My goal was to get back walking at a certain point, then running and it was the same as when I was competing as an athlete. I was back into that mindset; I had my goals and every day I would wake up motivated to achieve those targets and I did.

'I've tried to use my stroke and recovery to try to encourage others. I recognised that most people aren't as fortunate as I was to have had the background of an Olympic athlete but it was important to take the things that I did know, to help others understand that you had to keep going every day.'

At the age of 56, six years after such a seismic setback, I wondered if Michael believed he was truly back to his old self. 'Yes, I made a 100 per cent recovery in short order,' he said. 'After a few months, I could run again, if rather poorly, but I was able to make big chunks of improvement pretty quickly.

'There was a lingering need to make sure I was walking properly, keeping it symmetrical, but regaining coordination completely in my arm and in my fingers, all of those things still took some time.

'If I hadn't gotten that last little bit of improvement it wouldn't really have affected my life. Nor would it have allowed me to get back to doing all the things I'd done before, but I kept at it. I was 90 per cent for a good year and then it took another year before I was truly 100 per cent.

'Recovery is very individual, each person had a different timetable, a different attitude, a different approach, a different motivation, a different goal. Everyone had to figure out for themselves the best way to go about it. It was about understanding who you were as a person. And be in no doubt, recovering from a stroke required you to get the absolute best from yourself.

'That was more important for me in my stroke recovery than it was standing on the blocks before an Olympic final. I didn't have any lingering upset physically or emotionally from stroke, but it made me much more conscious of things, dealing with stress and pressure and making sure I managed them much better than I did before.

'People tended to associate pressure with something negative and that you didn't like, but that wasn't the case for me. I liked pressure. I was the person who chose to wear gold shoes at the Olympics, I chose to try to make history and become the first man to win the 200 and 400 at an Olympics in my own country. These were *my* choices, no one else's.

'I was very good at managing that pressure, and I ran my best times and had my best performances when I was under the most pressure. I didn't run away from pressure, but that didn't mean it was always good for my body or for my brain.

'You did your best to control the things that you could but there were certain things you had no control over. I'm never going to know why I had the stroke, so all I could do was keep doing the right things and believe with my whole heart that because I was in such good shape when I had my stroke, it helped with my recovery and gave me my best chance of a better life moving forward.'

***

Within a week of the Paris Olympics' closing ceremony, Michael was announcing the latest challenge of his many since that ill-fated day in 2018. He unveiled a blueprint for a new athletic league called Grand Slam Track, with the hope it would launch sometime in 2025.

In a column for *The Times*, he wrote, 'The Olympics have always proved there was an appetite for athletics, but you needed the same rivalries, high stakes and storytelling we saw in Paris and fans needed to know where they could find it in between the Games.

'And they needed to know that when they were watching it, they were watching the best athletes. That's what we are focused on delivering. How would this work? We envisaged a league in the mould of the tennis Grand Slams, four high-level annual events in the same location with the best athletes competing head-to-head.

'Grand Slam Track athletes would be under contract and so they were guaranteed to be there. The focus would be on speed and the fastest athletes so we'd only go from the 100m to the 5,000m.

'We'd have eight athletes in each of 12 groups – six men's and six women's – so we'd need 96 athletes. We'd contract 48 Grand Slam Track athletes so the top four in each group signed long-term, multi-year contracts. They were guaranteed to be at all four meetings. The other four would be called 'Challengers' and would sign for a race based on who was hot at the time. If someone popped up mid-season and clocked an amazing time, we could bring that person in.

'I think this would be a way of making the sport relevant outside of the Olympics and World Championships. In the past we have asked fans to buy a ticket and they found the best athletes were not there or they had pulled out because they weren't obligated. That diminished the sport, and the earning potential of athletes, too.

'Track and field isn't going to go anywhere. We can say it's unsustainable, but it's been sustaining itself under the same model for years. Is it optimal? No, it's not. It's fraught with problems and it has been for a very long time.'

As 2024 ended, this remarkable man was surviving once more, as wildfires licked around the outskirts of his residence in Malibu. He saw off those, as he had the consequences of his stroke. Michael Johnson always had another race to run.

IT'S THE CLIMB

'There's always gonna be another mountain
I'm always gonna wanna make it move
Always gonna be an uphill battle
Sometimes I'm gonna have to lose
Ain't about how fast I get there
Ain't about what's waiting on the other side
It's the climb.'

Words by Miley Cyrus

I HAD recently turned 66 years of age and if I hadn't felt whole for several years, it came as a terrible shock to discover I *was* incontrovertibly a good deal less than I used to be. What was more, I might never be completely restored in this life. That was in the lap of God. It was going to be one heck of a climb.

All those months of inner turmoil had come to a shocking head. It was not as if I could expunge old hurts. They lingered, digging away. What mattered now was concentrating on the recovery process, not knowing how long it would be. Was the worst over? What if I suffered another stroke, a far from uncommon occurrence? Most of my brain cells were still in operation but could they work a healing miracle?

When strokes struck, dignity was stripped away the moment you were assigned a hospital bed. That which you once controlled, almost without thinking about it, had been rendered uncontrollable. In the initial stages in hospital, you peed in your pants for the sake of brevity but as time went on, I became – a trifle smugly – adept at using the shoe-shaped cardboard receptacles next to the bed for urine collection, with remarkably few mishaps.

Remember, I had one working arm and was, for now, for the most part, bodily horizontal. To have a wee required lifting myself up as much as I could, peeling apart the sticky tape that held my nappy in place, manoeuvring it below my knees, uncurling my willy, positioning what there was of it in the receptacle before peeing and – balancing the cardboard between my knees – shaking away the remnants of urine with my right-hand, grabbing for the pee-pod and finding somewhere to place it where the risk of it being knocked over was minimalised.

(It happened just the once, and it wasn't my fault. There was a bit of commotion around Steve's bed, the curtains were drawn, and the nurse couldn't see as she backed out sideways and rammed straight into my right elbow as I was trying to balance the receptacle, causing a minor flood of urine, much subsequent mopping, and a lingering stench.)

Once the pee container was (relatively) steady, I could wrench my nappy back up and try to refasten it before settling back into some position of relaxation. Repeated four times a day and twice at night when there was much straining to reach the light switch. There were Olympic disciplines easier than this.

Doing a No.2 was an altogether more convoluted affair. The board above my bed noted that I required two nurses to help me when it came to posterior ablutions. The curtains around each bed were of an ugly beige and orange hue and if they did the trick in terms of visual privacy, sound proofing was not part of the package.

An audible assembly of grunts, passing of wind and unexpurgated expletives became part and parcel of one's daily tribulations. There was no conceivable way you could keep your bowel movements to yourself.

Fundamentally. I possessed the coordination of a sack of King Edwards, constantly listing to the left, trying to heave myself up, using all the strength in the right arm, to a position near enough vertical to reach out with the good arm and grab the reinforced plastic frame at the bottom of the bed. This took enormous effort while at the same time I was desperately holding my breath to contain poorly timed tummy rumbles.

If you managed a successful grab at the first time of asking you got a bonus point (in your imagination). Usually, it required a good two or three lumbering half-rises and immediate collapses to port before the manoeuvre was successful.

Transference to the commode required assistance but once there it felt as if you had achieved something before you had done anything (if you get my drift). Now came the most important part, passing excreta and not sitting there wishing you had stayed where you were because all you had to offer were a couple of wishful windy blow-outs.

Mind you, a decent food intake was necessary to sustain what was left of your strength. A major issue with the type of stroke I had suffered was its impact on the throat muscles and – as a distressing consequence – my (lack of) ability to swallow.

On day two in the ward, a couple of nurses approached, one with a tub of yoghurt and plastic spoon. 'Okay let's see how you do it,' the senior nurse said to the junior who was being monitored as she undertook my initiation with the swallow test.

A little of the yoghurt was scooped from the tub and gently inserted towards the back of my throat. I was told to gulp while at the same time the junior nurse rubbed my neck in the vicinity of the Adam's apple to make sure I could take it down and didn't choke.

The yoghurt disappeared, so at least it was presumed I could take food that was easily ingested. Harder evidence was required when it came to chewing. The left side of my mouth only partially opened, the lips at that end tended to stick together and the molars ground against each other in a manner bound to induce bouts of toothache *in extremis*.

And my throat was parched all the time, requiring much re-moistening of the lips and the introduction to my repertoire of an awful clacking sound of tongue against the roof my mouth when preparing to eat.

Every mealtime became an assault course, trying to cut the food with one hand into small enough pieces for me to chase around the plate and, once snared, raise to mouth level and digest without convulsing.

That was predicated on the successful operation of half a functioning mouth, a tongue that seemed to have grown to twice its normal size, teeth that crunched against each other and a tendency to dribble when I put too much on the fork with which I often stabbed myself in the left cheek. Hell, this was fun. The food was agreeable – any of which I managed to get into my mouth.

A regular dessert option was cheese and biscuits – a long-time personal favourite – though why anyone would offer these to a stroke patient was sadism of the highest order. Both the crackers and cheese had to be extracted from thin paper wrapping with no locatable edges and worse still the butter was served in those little tubs that were the staple of English hotel breakfasts.

I couldn't pull the bloody top away with my one decent hand and more than once, trying to use my teeth to do the job, small pieces of foil would become lodged between them, causing much coughing, spluttering and expectoration.

The crackers couldn't be swallowed without a wedge of butter on them, and I was determined to persevere because I liked the stuff. This whole charade reminded me of nights of teenage silliness as a trainee journalist studying at Harlow Technical College in the mid-seventies when we Vic Railton* wannabees would enjoy social evenings at the Plume of Feathers pub.

A regular competition was the challenge of one of our number trying to sink five pints of beer while another attempted to devour five plain Jacob's crackers. Bets would be laid as to who would complete the task first. Believe me, if you managed to get to the fifth cracker, your throat was like a dustbowl. Swallowing was nigh-on impossible. Fifty years on and with a mouth reduced to 50 per cent workability I still believed I could polish off a pack. What an idiot.

There was no point attempting to spread the butter evenly, I'd just finger a splodge of oily residue from the bottom of the tub on to what was left of the cracker (most of which had disintegrated and lodged in the folds of my clothes) bite off a bit of cheese and try to make the best of a messy job. 'You all right Neil?' was a particularly superfluous enquiry.

I did try the combo a couple more times without any greater success, was tempted by the sticky toffee pudding before I realised it contained neither toffee nor possessed any adhesive qualities and plumped for the rest of my time in hospital for vanilla ice cream which went down a treat, though largely via the left side of my chin and on to my T-shirts of many coloured stains.

**Vic Railton was a legendary* London Evening News *football reporter of the 1960s and seventies.*

***

The occasional body bag was wheeled past the door of D ward. As I was in an acute unit, this ought not to have come as a shock but to witness someone, anonymous now but recently a living, breathing soul being taken away on a trolley with top-hatted funeral directors fore and aft, brought you closer to the finality of life than you would want.

They were moved with as much dignity as was possible in the circumstances. I made the sign of the cross, closed my eyes and bade them a silent prayer of farewell. Thankfully, all of those who departed our ward during my four weeks there, did so in decent shape as far as these things went.

The first to be moved out was Kenny. He left quite a void. He was the boisterous one, mischievous, noisy and a Tottenham fan. While most of the guys wore some degree of clothing, Kenny spent most days naked save for his nappy. He didn't take kindly to being manhandled and wasn't shy in expressing his dislike of bed-changing routines.

It would often take at least two nurses to contend with him and he was outrageously picky about his food, often not touching a morsel. He was told he needed to eat to get his strength up but was having none of it. 'You can't expect me to eat this rubbish,' he'd shout, 'and don't touch my leg, I don't know who you are. Only my sister can touch my leg!!'

Many times – and this was not to be cruel – Kenny would have the rest of us in hysterics as the curtains billowed around his bed and nurses came and went in several stages of dishevelment. It was as close to a re-run of *Carry on Matron* as you were ever likely to see.

Directly opposite Kenny was a younger chap – I never found out his name – who was a bit upset in the head.

Any woman, be she a nurse or visitor who ventured past his bed was leered at, 'How old are you love? I prefer older women.' Most ignored him, others turned distinctly crimson.

The bloke had kids of his own and would speak to them most evenings with his mobile phone at full volume so everyone in the ward could hear what passed for a conversation on a crackly line (the internet was crap), him shouting, them responding in kind so that it sounded like an episode of *The Clangers*.

He noisily demanded to be wheeled outside for a cigarette at least twice a day. I was astonished that a hospital would allow such an unhealthy extravagance and went along with his demands so willingly.

Probably it meant a quieter life but was it the best for his health and wellbeing? When he wheeled himself to my end of the ward and tried to make small talk I feigned dozing, discomfort or the pressing need for a shit, anything to keep him and his appalling discoloured teeth and smoky breath at a decent distance.

I wasn't the least upset when he was wheeled out for the final time, waving and hollering as he went and obviously expecting a warm farewell. Knowing he couldn't hear because of all the noise he was generating, I shouted, 'bloody good riddance' and felt both ashamed and inwardly satisfied.

***

It was time to concentrate on getting out of here myself, the success of which required a daily commitment to physical activity. My limitations were obvious, I couldn't walk for one thing and so priority number one was to restore some life back into my left leg, which still had the consistency of blancmange.

The first piece of exercise equipment I was shown was a Moto Med, a form of exercise bike which I could use while seated in a wheelchair. My feet would be strapped in, and I'd pedal away for 20 minutes by which time I was exhausted and desperate for water.

There must have been another distinct post-stroke alteration to my internal workings, though: I used to break into a sweat at the mere sniff of exercise equipment, but now I could pedal away like a madman, and my armpits and back remained luxuriantly dry.

The physiotherapists had some more adventurous items with which to challenge me. Sophie, appointed to my care, asked if I'd ever worn a corset and I said I'd never been into cross-dressing.

But before we could advance the conversation further, I was woman-handled into a girdle-like contraption that squeezed my incidentals rather too tightly and then attached to something called the LiteGait from which I was suspended, displaying all the grace of Daddy Woodentop from the *Watch with Mother* 1960s children's series.

Initially dangled in mid-air, I was lowered so my feet touched the floor, and I could simulate making a stride knowing that I couldn't fall. This unlikely adaptation of suspended animation gave me a degree of confidence that I might one day be able to put one foot in front of the other without the need for a genital-squishing harness.

'You play golf don't you Neil?' Sophie asked. 'It's my ambition to get back out there one day,' I replied. She handed me a cane, told me to hold it upside down and pretend I was on the putting green.

From the boxes of stuff located in every cranny of what passed for a gymnasium in the Royal Berks, she extricated a couple of golf balls and as I connected and they moved where I was aiming even with just one arm for guidance (I'd always been a decent putter), it felt for a fleeting moment that I was back in the land of the living.

***

My progress on the LiteGait was such that Sophie asked if I wouldn't mind indulging in a bit of modelling.

One of the group of institutions that supported the Royal Berks, the Castle Royle Golf and Country Club, on the nearby A4, had raised enough funds for the hospital to be able to purchase the machine outright and the members wanted to see what they were getting for their charitable endeavours.

I was wheeled into a room full of amiable folk wearing name badges, manoeuvred on to the plinth from where I was adjusted into my corset, the straps were attached and up I bounded, a human marionette, and did my best Scottie Scheffler impersonation to the click of cameras and much appreciative cooing.

I said all the right things and indeed, this was a magnificent piece of machinery for us legless folk. Those patrons of Castle Royle who had put their hands into their pockets could be assured their generosity would help make those trapped in the land of immobility feel as if they had regained a purpose.

I was sad when they had to leave, after much shaking of hands and sincere well wishes, as they were able to return to the fairways and greens of real life as I was wheeled back to the dispiriting monotony of trying to hack my way out of the rough.

***

Maureen dutifully delivered the *Daily Mail* to my bedside each afternoon (the nursing staff weren't overly impressed by the choice of newspaper) but as I found that the pages were incredibly difficult to turn – agony for a journalist – I inevitably turned to my laptop and scrolled Twitter (now X) for much of my media diet.

This was a mistake. I could become wound up about things over which I had no control while dejected at the sheer hopelessness of life overall when I should have been concentrating on myself.

Social media had long since stopped being a vehicle to enrich our lives and enhance positivity; instead it fuelled the worst instincts of human nature. People fought everywhere: in shops, on pavements, in parks, at the beach. I watched in dismay as the world caught fire, our beautiful land was filled with rubbish and sewage, immigration spiralled out of control and knife crime flourished.

I couldn't help thinking how horrified my parents – both of whose lives had been blighted by world war – would have been to see it. There was so much insanity and so little effort by those in power to stop it. Britain was in danger of falling apart.

Browsing these outlets may have helped to pass the time, but it was important not to become stressed, especially given my problems with blood pressure which, should the readings stay in the red zone, could trigger a relapse if I persisted in letting things get on top of me.

A hospital bed seemed like a decent sanctuary from all this madness but like any other patient, my most pressing focus was to get the hell out of there.

Still, I had three edible meals a day, as much tea as I could take without needing half-a-dozen nappy changes, a button to press if I wanted for anything and the ability to lose myself in my own befuddled world.

I could have been at home, getting stick for being a shirker, not showing any initiative around the house, or trying to drive from one end of Wokingham to the other in less time than it took to reach the Isle of Wight. Confinement had its consolations.

***

Three weeks into convalescence and my mobile lit up. Though I had sent a tweet in the immediate aftermath of the stroke to let my dwindling collection of followers know why they wouldn't be hearing from me for a while, I had kept public announcement to a bare minimum. It was not as if being a freshly minted invalid was something you broadcast too widely.

My daughter Kathleen had taken a snap of me seated in my wheelchair, left arm resting on a pillow and a cannula with two tubes inserted into the top of my hand while offering a rather pathetic wave with my right.

When I looked back at it over a year on, two things came to mind: one, I was smiling (when I was about as miserable as it was possible to be) and two, my regulation hospital top was about three sizes too small.

Anyway, I sent it to a couple of close friends in the tennis world and within a couple of days a reply came from John Morris, someone I'd known for ages first as a coach on the British scene and then, when he entered the field of player representation, for the prodigious work he had done, especially with Nick Kyrgios.

John had spotted a raw and fascinating potential in a chubby kid from Queensland nobody else had positively related to, had helped nurture his talent and watched as Nick developed into someone who might be very special, a potential champion if he hadn't acted like such a bloody idiot most of the time.

They had parted company about a year back, John having stayed loyal for longer than Nick deserved but eventually the toll of sitting in his player box listening to his protégé railing against everybody and everything while failing to live up to his talents, became too exasperating.

When he couldn't be there in person, John's phone would constantly light up with calls or messages from my fellow journalists asking for a comment from him on one or another Kyrgios outburst. He needed a reset for his own wellbeing.

But had he leapt from frying pan into fire? John remained on the circuit but in a new management company – SeventyTwo Sports Group – where he was working, among others, with Andrey Rublev, a mercurial Russian who appeared to be possessed by a curious demon and took to thumping himself with his own racket when points weren't going his way.

In my reporting days, Mikhail Youzhny, another highly-strung Russian, was similarly afflicted. Once, on court in Miami with me sat 20 yards away, he drew blood when he hit himself so hard on the forehead with the graphite frame of his racket, he split his own skin. What the hell did they put in the *solyanka?*

Gael Monfils, the supremely talented Frenchman whose own father had suffered a stroke a few years ago, and Gael's wife Elina Svitolina from Ukraine were also represented by John, so there was some element of contentment to his daily work patterns.

Typical of the man, when he heard of my predicament and hospitalisation, John had spoken to a number of those whose paths I had crossed in the past 25 years and assembled a montage of messages.

I told him that the timing of their arrival and the sincerity of their words had done me a power of good. Just knowing people would stop and take the time to say a few nice things about an old journalist warmed the cockles.

Introducing the messages, John said he knew that the weeks ahead wouldn't be easy, 'especially as you'll have to start doing what you're told for once,' a reflection of those many times in my writing career when I had struck a defiantly obstinate, some might say contrary, path.

He added he hoped we might be talking about future book projects before too long. Boy wouldn't that be nice. Plenty of opportunities there to get my brain recharged with imaginative thoughts.

John wanted me to know I was in people's prayers, I was very highly thought of and that getting back, 'to the Neil we all know and love' was paramount. For the first time, apart from those first appearances of family at my bedside when I choked up inside, I was feeling a touch shaky.

Up popped the face of my old mate Pat Rafter, a former Australian of the Year no less, and one of the unluckiest men never to have won Wimbledon. His momentous five-set final of 2001 against Goran Ivanisevic of Croatia that concluded on the 'People's Monday' remained a distinctive memory.

'G'day Neil, Pat here,' he said, thinking I wouldn't have recognised him. 'I'm very sorry I haven't aged well but at least I do have my hair, mate (he had lost nothing of his puckish humour, thankfully). I hear you've had some rough trot and I'm thinking about you, big fella. I've always been a fan of yours, we both respected each other and had a bit of fun back in our day. I'm thinking about you mate and hope to see you someday soon down here in Australia.'

That was a message echoed by Craig Tiley, the tournament director of the Australian Open, with whom I'd had many a conversation across the years about the direction of tennis and why the championship in Melbourne had transformed the perception of how the sport could be transported to a wider, contemporary audience.

The Aussie Open was far ahead of its time, burgeoning in popularity and success year after year, much of which had to do with the boss's imaginative thinking. The old tennis order bristled indignantly as Craig upset the established applecart which was why I found his approach so welcoming.

'I'm so sorry to hear about the challenges you're having Neil,' he said. 'I wanted to take this opportunity to wish you all the best in your recovery, look forward to seeing you sometime soon and don't forget the promise we made to each other that you will get back down to the Australian Open. We plan on welcoming you whenever you can get here. Take care of yourself my friend and get healthy soon.'

As an up-and-coming tournament director, Chris Kermode had caught my eye in the early 2000s, moving first to run the wonderful Queen's Club tournament held each June and then (with a bit of promotion from yours truly) becoming top dog at the O2 Arena, when the ATP Finals moved there in 2009. Such had been the enduring success of the event, Chris was promoted to CEO of the men's tour itself, a stunning and deserved accolade.

He messaged, 'Nothing can stop "the Harmanator" (a nickname I'd acquired during my days at *The Times*). You're a legend in the sport to all those who know you, so keep the faith, keep strong, you're going to smash this, and hopefully we'll see you back in New York at the microphone singing more of those great standards. God be with you.'

Good people like Greg Rusedski, Jamie Murray and Marcus Willis (remember him from Centre Court,

Wimbledon against Roger Federer a few years back?) also offered their regards, and I did well to keep it together. It seemed to me that I had done something decent in my reporting life after all.

There had not been a single word or message of concern, support (or otherwise) from either the present hierarchy of Wimbledon or the last paper I had served as tennis correspondent, *The Times*.

***

Rod Laver sent a delightfully thoughtful email in response to my request to speak to him about the stroke which had left him clinging to life 26 years earlier. In recent years Rod had agreed to fewer and fewer interviews, preferring a relatively low profile in keeping with his characteristic modesty. His note to me was a positive boost.

He was unwilling to speak face-to-face about something from long ago and instead I was pointed to an article in *World Tennis* in which the great Australian left-hander went into detail about the scrambling of his senses during a television interview in Los Angeles in 1998.

Rod described it as a run-of-the-mill day, with few exceptions – an experience to which many of his fellow sufferers could immediately relate. These stroke shocks tend come out of the blue with no advanced notice or warning signs.

He said his fingers suddenly went numb, he vomited and was on the verge of collapse. A TV producer who was standing to one side as the interview unfolded, had seen his father having a stroke and remembered that immediate first aid was vital.

The interview's location was, portentously, a mere two blocks from the UCLA Medical Center where Michael Johnson was admitted two decades later. Laver was being examined within 15 minutes of the initial semi-collapse.

In the *World Tennis* article, he described in strikingly vivid terms that, 'I had seizures, awfully high blood pressure, a fever they had trouble controlling – 106 degrees for a few days – and brain swelling.'

He was placed on a bed of ice to bring the fever down, and had to be restrained at times – 'I guess I wanted out of there' and ripped out his IVs. His speech was slurred and he lost 30lb in weight.

'I was like a kid again, had to re-learn telling the time, and a lot of other things. My right side was paralysed for a while. I had no use of the right hand. Sometimes I'd be sitting on it without even noticing.'

The bleeding in the brain stopped without surgery and one day, when he was sent for a CAT scan, the technician said, 'Your brain? There's nothing there.'

'I thought he was trying to be funny,' said Laver, 'but he meant it was blood free. That was good news.'

His now late wife Mary said at the time, 'The therapists were exhausted, too. Rod wore them out, he was so determined to recover. They'd never worked with someone like him. His determination as a player was showing itself.'

The only man in history to have won the four Grand Slam singles titles in the same year in both the amateur and professional eras (1962 and 1969) believed the experience gathered from his hours of court work was a significant element in his recovery process. Muscle memory helped get his feet and arms moving, so much so that he was able to resume tennis, golf and public appearance work.

His home was on a golf course and he progressed to being able to play two holes at a time, taking a mobile phone with him in case anything went wrong.

'Well, something did. My ball went into a trap [bunker], and without thinking I took my sand wedge and went after it. Trouble was I wasn't strong enough to walk out, and the phone was in the cart. Nobody was around, and I had a hell of a time crawling up and out.'

He worked hard with his speech therapists. 'I would utter odd words that had no relationship to anything, and my wife would say, "where did that come from?"'

He had this message for stroke patients: 'You're a viable entity. Try. Work at your therapy. I hope it helped them.'

Twenty-six years on from the stroke, 2024 was Rod Laver's 87th year, he still travelled the world attending tennis tournaments, meeting and greeting fans and players, and had a major venue in Melbourne and an international tournament named for him.

The 'Rocket' was perhaps the shiniest example of the belief that if stroke was recognised and treated early and your attitude to the condition was unrelentingly positive, it needed never be a life sentence.

***

On 23 May 2023 – 15 days after my stroke – the day dawned delightfully bright. I was extremely thankful. My younger daughter Kathleen was to be married to James Brady at the quaint old St Nicholas church in Cranleigh, Surrey. They had first met as four-year-olds at St Teresa's Catholic school in Wokingham.

From those innocent days, a love had endured to the extent that they were to make a lifelong commitment. My role, naturally, as father of the bride, entailed walking my daughter down the aisle and making a speech, hopefully one that would bring a few smiles and not be too decadent.

My last trip abroad, three weeks pre-stroke, had been a boys-only long weekend with the groom and his friends in a remote field outside Amsterdam, where I'd proved to be the worst go-kart driver of all time and not been able to last the social pace as I had when I was their age. I thought I'd given up sleeping on the floor when I'd left the scouts.

I had been excited to get to see the lads again but now, unable to move much of my body and spending most of the day in horizontal semi-repose, I reconciled to taking no part in the wedding celebration, which I knew would make it an emotionally strained day.

However, a cunning plan had been hatched whereby Lisa the wedding photographer would have a camera attached across her shoulders so I could tune in 'live' to the service and feel as if I was right there. But who would do the fatherly honours? Up stepped Mrs H, not for the first time.

As the church doors opened, the sun burst in and my little girl (no more) stood there in all her glory with Maureen radiant at her side, I simply dissolved. I put it down to my advanced state of emotional turmoil but the onrush of tears was such that Derek, my next-door neighbour in the ward, buzzed the staff for extra tissues.

When the Rev. Tim asked who gave this woman to this man, he then announced to the congregation that he knew I was watching on-line and that I should speak the words. It had to have been the loudest 'I do' in the ward since the nurses demanded of the assembled bed dwellers which of us wanted a laxative.

The rest of the celebration went by in something of a blur, but I was roused on hearing the 'Prince of Denmark's March', a coruscating finale to the service I'd specifically chosen, and watched as the congregation departed the church before I drifted back off to sleep.

I would catch up with my wife's speech in my place at the reception – which became an absolute crowd pleaser – once my faculties had stabilised.

***

Retaining a sense of humour, finding something funny even in your direst predicament, was an absolute imperative in stroke recovery. To laugh out loud was a mercy. Indulging in mischief (as much as was possible lying flat in a hospital bed) and tossing a sarcastic comment into the mix of ward noises was mandatory in my case.

I watched Tommy Cooper and Dick ('Ooh you are awful') Emery re-runs on *YouTube* until the tears streamed down my face and I had to gasp for breath, which was made tougher by my difficulty swallowing properly. At least those moments of silliness and joy got me through many an otherwise numbingly barren day. But, sadly, bouts of sadness were inescapable.

Having endured a near-death experience – another hour on the floor after the initial bleed and I would have been knocking hopefully on the door to one of the many rooms in God's house – the departure of those you cherished became especially trying.

And they began to occur with what felt like devastating frequency, even though it was probably not as often as I had imagined in my semi-unbalanced state.

I am not using his example first because he was more deserving than others who had passed these past 24 months or so, but the loss that hit me hardest was the death of Mike Dickson in January 2024.

It happened ten days before Mike would have turned 60 and only a few weeks after we had sat on a hospital sun terrace taking tea and biscuits. And Dicko was not really a 'sun' person.

He had been honest enough to say he hadn't visited earlier because he was concerned what sort of 'me' might await him. I well understood. Form an image of a stroke victim before you saw one for yourself, and it was inevitably a bit squeamish: bed-ridden, incontinent, blabbering, dribbling and generally away with the fairies.

When this person was a mate you had witnessed for years in complete engagement with his work, dashing around, sociable and free, it must have been that much harder to imagine them as somehow a partial person trapped in a very different place in their life.

I assured Mike I had come out on the other side of any frighteningly palsied vision (more or less) of me he may have pictured, though my hill-climbing days were probably long gone.

Dicko had been my successor as tennis correspondent of the *Daily Mail* in 1990, when liquid lunches were a staple of journalistic tradition. The *Mail* sports department powers-that-be returned from the pub one day that summer having decided they wanted me to become the paper's chief football writer (they appeared sober). And we all went back to the pub to celebrate before I was offered the role officially, which I duly accepted. I recommended Dicko to replace me.

Some 20 years further on – from tennis to cricket and back again on the *Mail* in Mike's case and now tennis correspondent of *The Times* in mine – we found ourselves together reporting on a Masters tournament in Indian Wells, California. It was a venue of quite breathtaking beauty, both scenically and meteorologically.

In contrast, our billet was a rather cheap and cheerful highway Holiday Inn Express. Directly across from the hotel and behind a mini-mall of shops rose a cluster of steep hills, maybe to 1,500ft high and on which, we discovered, was a local hotspot called the 'Bump and Grind Trail' – the christening of which would become increasingly apparent as the morning unfolded.

It must have been a Saturday because neither of us had Sunday commitments and no break-of-dawn composition was required (the time difference with the US west coast demanded a regular laptop opening at 5am with coffee on permanent reheat). We decided to tackle the 4km hike in our sneakers, without appropriate protective headgear or enough sunscreen and not sure what we were doing.

Onwards and upwards we ploughed, in temperatures of 80F by eight in the morning. Dicko, pale of skin, ginger of hair and sometimes stiff of movement, was nonetheless dogged in his determination that we should at least reach the first rest station before deciding whether to keep climbing or call the whole thing off.

Passing on the narrow ledges should have been *verboten* but young bucks in athletic vests and the occasional wacky Californian cyclist would risk snorting derision by brushing past us, often on the inside, thus sending us perilously close to the edge.

Dicko looked like a fielder at the Gabba, zinc smeared on his face, hat pulled down, sunglasses attached by a band around his neck but bless him, he was indefatigable as we carefully picked our route up the rock face. I was eight years his elder – not exactly decrepit – but had begun to puff and pant.

Suffice to say we eventually made it to a base-camp plateau that took in the sprawling flatlands of Indian Wells, Palm Desert, Bermuda Dunes and beyond looking east. Below us lay Porcupine Creek, the property of Oracle founder and mega-billionaire Larry Ellison (who also owned the tennis tournament) and which was clearly the private members' golf club to end all private members' golf clubs.

There was not a single human playing on a Saturday morning – access was strictly by invitation only – but there were ground staff on every hole, pampering and pruning flower beds of radiant beauty, mowing the two-toned verdant fairways and raking bunkers that might never see a wayward ball disturb their symmetrical precision. Mike was a member of Royal Liverpool GC, but he'd never witnessed anything quite like this Elysian Field.

Retreating down the trail was just as difficult as the struggle upwards, for the pathways would crumble and absolute vigilance was required in placing one's feet. Ever more ridiculous cyclists flashed past. At the end Mike and I bear-hugged until we realised we were stuck together by the other's sweat and gently prised ourselves apart.

We had been bumped and grinded and yet here we still were. Just.

***

I mentioned climbing as means of a reference to the eulogy delivered by Mike's son Sam at the service in April to mark his untimely death. I didn't know how I was going to react to the occasion and how those there would respond to me given my condition that, I discovered, not that many knew about.

The former BBC tennis correspondent Jonathan Overend – a long-time travelling companion and first-class commentator – volunteered a lift and offered his arm by means of moral and physical support as we neared the venue.

I had also sensibly packed my new super-duper walker to help navigate difficult tracts and perform as a battering ram or deterrent for anyone coming too close and unaware of my indiscriminate losses of balance and consequent frantic arm gestures.

We made it to the entrance of St Mary's church in Wimbledon and I shuffled into the very last pew. It was to be a highly charged service in an over-crowded church – those who couldn't claim a seat had to make do with a tent outside where the service was streamed – and became especially powerful when young Sam rose to speak.

On tour, writers would get so immersed in the event we were covering, so intense as deadlines approached, so caught up in our own words and worlds that when it was time to relax, family life rarely made it into conversation. We discussed the day's play, pontificated, argued about silly things, debated newspaper politics and then it was time for last orders or, in my case, a last song if there was a pianist in residence.

Mike had obviously been a wonderful father to his three children, but he would never have admitted to it to us, as perhaps it might be seen as a sign of, dare one say, over sentimentality.

It was strange that we were a good deal more comfortable discussing the merits or otherwise of those with whom we had a relatively distant relationship – or presumed we knew – rather than close family and friends. We should have talked about our kids more.

As Sam spoke, I could feel myself reaching for the tissues and trying, with my one workable hand, to pull the packet open and extract one. I attempted to dab my eyes as surreptitiously as possible because had I unloaded and been unable to completely control myself, it might have turned heads away from the importance of the celebration.

Nearing the end of his eulogy, Sam said, 'We've lost a great man and I loved it that he was his own person through and through as well as being a guiding light, role model and inspiration for my life.' When he spoke of the mountains Mike had climbed and that there were so many peaks he had left to aspire to, I pictured that day in the desert when we ploughed ever upwards and stood proudly as desert California spread its wealth beneath us.

How bloody unfair it was Mike was denied more opportunities like that in the years ahead. I couldn't help but reflect, too, on the day he drove to the neuro rehab centre where I was to spend the months of July and August 2023, and discussed whatever life had in store in the real world.

We had sat on the terrace reminiscing on the days of work and nights of social pleasure spent at the sportswriting coalface. Dicko had just completed an uninterrupted 33-year spell on the *Mail* and begun to wonder how many more he could endure. He presented me with a copy of what would be his last book, his account of the British starlet Emma Raducanu, who had come from the qualifying competition to win the 2021 US Open women's singles title in outrageous style.

I was a touch envious not to have been able to report on such an achievement myself, but delighted Mike had been chosen to translate the most uplifting British tennis story of the past decade into hardback form.

Reflecting that he had filed six separate pieces for the Mail Online on that one final – momentous as it was – the last was an attempt to 'distil the sense of the immediate past and the future'. Mike wrote, 'Emma's values will be tested at times in the coming years, tennis does that to young people. But that can wait. Better now to reflect on two weeks that were spontaneous, innocent and utterly glorious.'

It was a lovely summation, but my mind was numbed by the revelation that it required *six* different articles to pick the bones from one tennis match. Well yes, when Andy Murray won his first Wimbledon in 2013, *The Times* produced at 12-page special for Tuesday's edition (largely my work) but at least I'd had a night's sleep, albeit fitful, so my brain was decently recharged.

My sportswriting career was terminated before the internet wound its tentacles so securely around a journalist's neck. We were able to get a bit of rest back in the day but now the demands were intolerable and compassionate rest non-existent. Deadlines were for relics. Everything was open-ended.

Three of the four Grand Slam tennis tournaments now incorporated night play while Wimbledon often didn't finish until gone ten in the evening and the workload there had become increasingly immense and mentally taxing. It was difficult to unwind, and most of Mike's social chums had retired or, like me, simply departed the scene. 'Sad that one by one a lot of my old reference points are fading away,' he texted from a 'frighteningly expensive' New York in September.

When there was an opportunity to pop out for a drink at the end of play, the younger fraternity preferred to head to their rooms to devour the latest blandishments on Netflix or TikTok. We would polish off a couple of bottles of NYC's finest at Bill's (our resident pitstop on E 54th St). And Dicko would always disappear for ten minutes for a crafty fag.

'I can't see myself lasting [in the job] more than a couple more years,' he confided. 'It's not the way it used to be.'

Our final text exchange was heartbreaking in its poignancy. I told him I'd become a grandfather and that in my most recent conversation with the stroke specialist, I was told I was doing fine. Mike said he'd swing by the house for a coffee once I had been discharged and that, 'I always knew you'd be equal to this.'

He said there were several platforms he had to serve for the *Mail* these days and that, 'they get you going on so many different things. 2023 wasn't a great tennis year tbh [to be honest], but I think '24 will be better'.

The next I heard about (rather than from) Dicko was a call around 8am on 17 January from Oliver Holt, the *Mail*'s chief sportswriter, asking if the bad tidings had reached me. I said I didn't know what he was on about and he delivered the crushing news.

Mike had collapsed and died in his Melbourne apartment a short walk from Rod Laver Arena, and we would never climb another mountain together. I wasn't sure the loss of such a fine man before reaching 60 would ever truly seem real.

Trying to explain to people that tennis was often a hellish sport to cover would draw much eyebrow raising. But consider it. A football match lasts 90 minutes (well, 100 now with so much ridiculous time added on), a round of golf is four hours give or take and though a cricket Test can last five full days, once the light fades or the rain falls, the day is done.

The escalation of night tennis to just about everywhere may have enhanced the sport's entertainment profile but it has become a never-ending challenge to the staying power of players, fans, tournament staff and those sent to report on it.

The day normally begins at 11am and a night schedule might start at 7.30pm but matches often last for hours on end and there is never a definitive stop or start time for those scheduled after the first one on the order of play.

What an unmitigated chore it has become to cover one of the world's loveliest sports. Of course, I'd have leapt at the chance to still be in the thick of it, but my memory remained sharp and myriad images from the past were indelible.

***

There were others recently departed who had climbed their personal writing peaks and encountered me – for better or worse – along the way. David Irvine, known to all as Noddy, was the *Guardian* tennis correspondent for a decade or more, a character who derived his nickname through a habit of nodding off during dinner and often when he himself was in mid oration.

Noddy wrote with an understated authority and possessed an ability no longer necessary in the modern media, that of dictating his report down a phone line to a copy taker, words that flowed from the pages of his notebook like the red wine he cherished. He had a quarrelsome streak – dinner table conversation would often become overheated – but you could not have stayed angry with him for long.

Ronald Atkin – who never shied away from a good argument – was another legendary figure of our industry, a one-time *Observer* sports editor who worked across the broadsheet titles and made any match report or feature read beautifully. Ron was waspish and sociable in equal measure.

If the deaths of these journalistic titans were not unexpected given their many years, their loss was immense.

I supposed I was a fossil from an era where we played hard, drank hard and worked bloody hard. I cherished those times and toasted old friends who would always have a prized place in my memory, one which, thank the Lord, had been left pretty much unspoiled by the damage to my brain.

***

One journey I couldn't make in 2023 was a return to Manchester for the *Daily Mail* Christmas sports desk reunion that had been held, almost uninterrupted, since the late 1980s when the city's production headquarters that had been the northern soul of British national newspapers was deemed surplus to requirements.

When I moved north in 1981, it was as a novice of seven years as a sports reporter and here I was on a national daily in a teeming city. I fell in love with the place and had been sentimentally attached ever since. Walking proudly into the *Mail*'s office on Deansgate – now demolished – was invigorating and forbidding in equal measure.

The floorboards creaked and the wooden passageways were polished to a shine you could pretty much see your reflection in. This was a newspaper idyll where outrageous characters stalked, foremost of whom was Ian Ogden, a man of Burnley who tolerated my southern upbringing to the extent that we became firm friends.

Oggie was a senior sub-editor on the sports desk and wrote with passion on rugby league – 'a proper game', he'd frequently remind the union writer, Derek Marshall. He had struggled in the recent past with bouts of breathlessness and it was felt best for the lunch organiser (the indefatigable Peter Ferguson) to find a restaurant as near to a tram stop as possible for the sake of his lungs.

My problem was that I hadn't been on public transport since my stroke and the thought of getting to Manchester from Reading and back via the cramped, four-carriage, one toilet with a door that didn't lock properly world of

Cross-Country trains was too much to contemplate. I had to bail out.

Then I heard Oggie hadn't been able to make it either, fearing he would be exhausted before the socials got going. Worse than that, barely a few weeks later came news that he had passed away.

I could see him in my mind's eye and hear his voice when I closed my eyes and concentrated, so it felt as if he was still here, chiding me for a grammatical bollock-drop one minute and dragging me across Deansgate to the pub for a pint and pep-talk the next.

***

On departing the north, my first report as tennis correspondent of the *Daily Mail* in the autumn of 1986 was from the Brighton Centre, on the sea front there, and focused on Jo Durie, the British No.1 at the time.

Jo was coached by Alan Jones, someone who would become pivotal to my life and writing across the next 25-plus years. I don't think I met anyone more committed to expanding the horizons of the British game than Jonesy.

He worked with experienced players and more especially juniors making their way, all hours of the day and night, extolling in them the virtues of hard toil, technique and the sheer enjoyment that playing tennis offered. Jo reached the semi-finals of two Grand Slams, became ranked No.5 in the world and drew every ounce from her talent.

Jonesy didn't waste a single second of his coaching time, and I doubted there was a player in the country who fell under his spell who wouldn't freely confess that without his drive and determination, they wouldn't have achieved all they did.

He became a constant source of inspiration for me as my career unfolded and was always there if I needed him. If Alan wanted to unload a particular thought or consideration on the state of British tennis – usually stressing he should remain anonymous – he invariably rang me. Conversation was typically one-sided, him talking and me grateful I had mastered 100 wpm shorthand so I could keep up.

He was badly shaken when I lost my job in 2014, inviting me to visit his camps around London as often as I wanted. These opportunities to remain in touch with tennis in the raw provided a massive fillip in bad times, and I wasn't the least surprised when his was one of the first names to light up on my phone in the immediate aftermath of my hospitalisation.

In the early spring of 2024, he called again, 'Come on Harman, get yourself up and come and see the new batch of juniors I'm working with. Got a few with half a chance.' I said that as soon as I could drive again, I'd be there. Within days of that call, I was told Alan had fallen seriously ill and I could hardly believe it when he passed away with devastating suddenness.

I didn't have the physical strength to attend his funeral which was greatly upsetting. His last message to me had, like all the others across the many moons, been relentlessly upbeat.

And so, with too many supportive voices sadly stilled, it was back to the climb.

NOEL BLAKE

NOEL BLAKE walked through Trentham Gardens on the outskirts of Stoke-on-Trent staring up at the trees and making a mental note of those with the sturdiest branches. What he was trying to get clear in his head in those fleeting moments only he could really know.

There comes a time in most stroke healing – or the lack of hope for it – when the victim reflects on the dark side. It is a passing tribulation for the most part, but it is in there, nonetheless, and there is little you can do about it, bar shake your head and tell yourself not to be so stupid.

For professional athletes to be robbed of that they cherished most – their athleticism – must be the hardest cut of all.

It was 1980 or thereabouts that I first encountered Noel, a Jamaican-born, Brummie-raised kid who was a committed fan of Birmingham City in his early teens. He had been swiped from under City's nose by the 'hated enemy' Aston Villa, for whom he was a prodigious youth-team performer, but – in 1982 – he switched sides again and joined the Blues.

I was a reporter for the *Birmingham Evening Mail* in his early days, eager to buddy up to the young talent in the West Midlands who might become something special. There was no doubting Noel's promise, for he was a tough-as-old-boots kid with a prodigious physique and an innate understanding of football's art.

He had been a centre-forward in his formative years, once chosen as the outstanding player of a local parks tournament in the city and handed the trophy by none other than 'Gentleman' Joe Bradford, Birmingham's leading all-time goal scorer, who kept a beady eye open for talent on the urban green fields.

In his teens, Noel would bustle defenders off their game only to be switched to central defence to see if he might do even better there. He did. He was a 'thou shalt not pass' last line, committed and (largely) disciplined.

I said largely because in 1983, in the Villa-Birmingham derby on a rain-sodden pitch at Villa Park, he notably missed a penalty that would have earned Birmingham a point and at the final whistle met Villa's Steve McMahon – who had somehow escaped a sending off for a shocking tackle on Kevan Broadhurst – forehead to forehead right in front of the referee who took no action. VAR would have blown every fuse if it had been in operation back then.

This was a small, if memorably notorious cameo in a professional playing career of just over 20 years, most productively for the Blues, Portsmouth, Leeds United and Stoke City, ending with almost 150 appearances for Exeter City, before he was appointed the club's manager in 2000.

Gareth Ainsworth, who became a great friend during a year I spent writing about Wycombe Wanderers, recalled his first goal playing for Blackburn reserves against Leeds' second string way back when. It wasn't so much the thrill of such a moment in a fledgling footballer's career that made it so special, but that he won his chance in a tackle against Noel Blake and from there was able to score. 'Not many people could say they'd done that,' Gareth purred.

At the completion of his playing days Noel embarked on a varied coaching career, which embraced five years with the Football Association as coach to the England under-19 team. The stressful nature of his departure from that post was, in his estimation – as there could be no definitive proof – the root cause of his stroke in 2015 at the age of 52.

'There was inevitable trauma every time a new regime came into any football club or association and made changes,' he said. 'Many people in the game could relate to that. I didn't regard it as a problem initially but the way I was spoken to [by those inside the FA] resonated then and still does to this day.

'It was an emotional trigger. Because of legalities, I can't go into it any more deeply. One day I may be able to tell the world how I really felt about it.

'Dan Ashworth had come in [to the FA] as the technical director and he had every right to make changes. I went and Kenny Swain [the former Chelsea and Aston Villa defender] left as well. It all really affected me, more than I realised at the time.'

Having tried to deal with the debilitating FA experience, Noel joined Blackpool but almost immediately became centre-stage in another upheaval. 'The Belgian Jose Riga was the manager, I discovered through a third party that he needed a coach, and we spoke,' he said. 'There were a lot of financial difficulties at that time, but we got on well and I had no issues with him.

'The club wasn't in a healthy position, there was disquiet between him and the owner, Jose left [after four months, the second shortest appointment in the club's history] and Lee Clark was appointed after he had left Birmingham.

'I asked what he wanted from me and how long he wanted me to stay as I'd had an offer from the Professional Footballers' Association [the players' union]. Lee said he wanted me, so I put the other thing aside and within two weeks he brought his best friend, a lad called Paul

Stephenson, on to the coaching staff, which wasn't a problem even though it blindsided me a bit.

'I had a feeling it wouldn't work, and I left soon afterwards. I'd lost my job at the FA, then Blackpool, the PFA position had gone and all of that took a toll. I was looking out for work and there was nothing available, people wouldn't return your calls, it was the brick wall.'

Within six weeks of departing Bloomfield Road, Noel's life altered irrevocably. 'A couple of friends had come over to see me, we were chatting, and suddenly they said they couldn't understand what I was saying. My speech was slurring.

'I had walked from Wolverhampton to my home in Newcastle-under-Lyme that morning and felt wobbly, just very lethargic. I was sapped of any energy and a couple of times I felt as though I might stumble but I didn't.' Then came the mumbling episode.

'I rang my wife at the Royal Stoke Hospital where she worked as a personal assistant and described what had happened. She gave my symptoms to one of the consultants who told her to collect me straight away and take me to triage. Within minutes of being assessed, they said I'd probably had a stroke and I was admitted there and then.

'After a couple of hours which seemed more like an eternity I was on a ward and when they confirmed a stroke I kind of broke down. A nurse said, "You see that gentleman over there, he's had a severe stroke, he can't walk, he can't speak and though yours is bad it's not nearly as bad as that."

'That gave me a small sense of relief, but it was when I telephoned my mum to tell her, that's when I lost it emotionally. I was 51 years old and in decent physical shape if obviously not quite like the old days.

'My knees were pretty shattered from all the years of football, but I'd never been a big drinker, maybe a beer with my meal and that was it. I never smoked, never took a drug, my diet had always been that of an athlete. I wasn't doing anything that would suggest the potential for a stroke. The only thing I could point to was related to stress, which went back to when I left the FA.'

As his doctors completed rounds of intensive medical tests, they discovered that on top of the debilitating effect of the stroke, Blake had a hole in his big heart. It was another frightening discovery – he had played so many years unaware of a weakness that could have had catastrophic consequences. Surgeons repaired the hole, inserting mesh to plug the gap and it was another warning to take life a little bit easier.

'I'm glad I didn't realise I had the condition when I was playing but I remembered how I used to struggle when it came to the long distances in training and had to take quite a bit of time to recover,' he said. 'When I reflected on players who had collapsed and, in some cases, died on the field of play it did make me wonder that if I had found out about it earlier, would I have been able to enjoy a full career?'

But he did complete it manfully, and now required similar fortitude in another more punishing challenge. 'I came to terms with following the process and the acceptance that it [the stroke] was not my doing. I couldn't move any faster physically or mentally and I couldn't absorb information any quicker.

'It was a bit like going back to when I played where others were technically better in my position, but I relied on my own strengths in terms of what I could offer. I applied that same logic now. There was no point trying to do more than you could just because you got frustrated.'

***

As he watched the unfolding of the 2024 European Championship in Germany – trying not to get carried away – Noel's memory sharpened about those days he was in his element, coaching many of the best young players in the country, who were now on full, unvarnished display.

'I'd spent 47 years in the game as that tournament started – you were there in my infancy, Neil,' he said. 'When England reached the semi-final of the 2018 World Cup in Russia there were 18 players in that squad I'd had some involvement with, either with the under-16s, 19s, or 21s.

'By the 2020 Euros [delayed by the pandemic until summer 2021, in which England lost to Italy in the final on penalties at Wembley] I'd worked with 15 lads in the squad through the development groups, great talents, from the captain, Harry Kane, to Eric Dier, Conor Coady, Marcus Rashford and Alex Oxlade-Chamberlain.'

If you fast forwarded to the expectant summer of '24, Jordan Pickford, Kyle Walker, John Stones, Kieran Trippier, Joe Gomez and Trent Alexander-Arnold [imagine their cumulative worth] were added to Noel's honourable roll-call. 'My greatest pleasure was helping these lads along the way, being part of their journey,' he said.

'I had never wanted to be a manager, even though I did a short stint at Exeter. I always knew I could coach and make a difference that way. I wanted to make people better. When I was a young player growing up in the Midlands you wouldn't believe the number of people who told me I'd never be good enough.'

Everybody needs a ray of positive sunshine as they grow into their relative professions. My career turning point arrived in 1981 when I was employed by the *Daily Mail* in Manchester, where the late Bryan Webster was a sports editor of meticulous craftsmanship with a genius for mentoring he may not have known he possessed. I had never felt more inspired at work, before or since.

In Blake's case, after all the teenage knockbacks, he was spotted playing in the Birmingham Sunday leagues by Larry Canning, a wily ex-professional player from Scotland who had reinvented himself as a radio journalist in the West Midlands, where he became the resident football commentator for what was then BBC Radio 2 Sport.

'Larry's son Andy and I were in the same school team, playing up front together,' Noel said. 'Then Larry took over our Sunday team and I learned so much from him, he always believed in me, and I wanted to transfer the kind of enthusiasm and positivity Larry had shown into my coaching.'

Not only did Noel encourage and inspire young players, but he worked with the League Managers' Association, alongside such stalwarts as Frank Clark, David Pleat and Keith Burkinshaw to mentor would-be managers, the likes of Sammy Lee and Brian Laws.

As for the present day, when the 2024/25 season got underway, he was continuing his work as a match delegate in the Premier League, a role which took in a raft of responsibilities, the most important and potentially delicate of which involved communication between clubs and the match officials.

These conversations could begin the night before a match with a meeting with the referee and his assistants, followed by talking with the appointed referee's assessor and building bridges with club managers, before compiling a report for the refereeing authorities on how each of the officials handled their role.

'We looked at how the referee managed a game and if there were any discrepancies with official protocol.

I reported back to the PGMOL [Professional Game Match Officials Limited] about his performance, casting a critical but objective eye over how he handled the entire occasion, both on and off the pitch.'

Blake was in a group consisting of bright-as-a-button ex-pros with Micky Adams, Martin Allen, and Chris Woods, who stayed involved in the game in a constructive capacity to pass down their years of experience – while in his case especially, it helped to take his mind off an element in his life that might have otherwise used up all his energy.

The healing process after a stroke is forever ongoing. 'I had mine ten years ago and only three years back there were times when I wouldn't have been able to face a room full of people, I'd just turn away,' Noel said. 'I tried to deal with what was in front of me, not something somebody else might have expected from me.

'I'm not fully there yet but I'm getting better over time. Everybody has a different story to tell, and no two individual cases are identical. It depends on how the stroke affected you; mine was more emotional than physical and that could take its toll, it was damn awful. There were times when I literally wanted it all to end.' The walk in Trentham Gardens was the darkest of those moments.

Noel continued: 'Self-pity came into it as I was a proud man, and I became reliant on others to help me especially if I was having one of my mood swings. I was an efficient person and it hurt when I couldn't do what I knew I could do.

'If I could spin a coin tomorrow, I'd be back into coaching because I loved it, but I couldn't do it [now] because I may have been able to last one day but the next, I'd be absolutely shattered.

'Honestly Neil if you saw me, you wouldn't have thought I'd had a stroke. I can walk, I can jog, I can lift weights. I can do the cooking, the ironing, and the cleaning but if I do more than three things in a day, I have no energy. I would be burned out. It's the mental side of it that bothers me.'

In his time on the touchline, Noel Blake was full on, committed, urgent. He said watching Jürgen Klopp managing Liverpool brought his own career back to him and he wasn't the least surprised when the German decided to step away from Anfield in 2024 having exhausted himself to the point of emotional collapse.

'I understood that completely,' Noel said. 'When I looked at Klopp on the side of the pitch, he reminded me of how I was, a passionate coach who drove himself and his players. It struck me that when foreign coaches behaved like that it was accepted but if it was a British coach, we were accused of being too animated. As a coach I just worked how I was, no point changing who you were.'

***

Noel played in a charity match for his old mate Brendan Ormsby with a group of ex-Leeds United players against non-League Farsley Celtic in 2015. 'Brendan had had a stroke and about three weeks after playing this game for him, I had mine,' he said.

'I reflected often on the irony of that. Brendan and I played together in the youth team at Aston Villa, and at Leeds as well. We were good friends. Brendan was the worst stroke victim I had ever seen, he had a second stroke soon after the first and couldn't speak. He's been in a nursing home for a few years now.

'I sometimes reflect that it could have been me. I'd known his wife, Wendy from our early teenage years when she was first going out with Brendan. She started to lose her hair with the stress of looking after him, so when I look at what happened to me compared with Brendan's situation, I count myself very lucky.

'I say my prayers for Wendy and Brendan every day; a lovely person like him. It was tragic.'

***

As the journey of writing this book continued, I endeavoured to keep in touch with Noel as often as possible, without being a burden.

I appreciated that he still suffered from occasional bouts of depression to the extent that I insisted he should pick up the phone and call me if ever life seemed impossibly bleak.

On the face of it all might have appeared well, but it was behind the façade, when life closed in and the means of acquiring full freedom faded, that anyone was vulnerable. A conversation, short or long, could have a profound effect.

He was an uplift to me in so many ways during this odyssey. 'I don't want to be condescending Neil, but keep telling yourself that you will get there,' he said more than once. 'Keep the faith. You will get better up to a point but where it takes you from there no one can tell. Trust the process.'

A SINGLE TO BEACHY HEAD

I SUPPOSE you wouldn't be human if you didn't ask – probably a few times more than is good for your state of mind – why me? And, in addition, why now? In my case there had been no warning signs, no incendiary spark that could have led me to suspect a personal Armageddon in the offing.

I did discover – a little too late as it happened – that my blood pressure was off the charts and no doubt had been for some little time. So that had to be it then. Probably. Maybe.

All victims of stroke search for reasons, question what they could have done differently and as you are more likely to have a second life-ending stroke if you don't mend your ways, it felt particularly important to have a hint about the root cause of the original malfunction.

A psychologist was on call both in the hospital and again on my release if I wanted to disgorge myself of lingering fears. Once I suggested to a visiting physiotherapist that if I was going to stay in this physical state for the next five years, I'd be purchasing a one-way ticket to Beachy Head. I was probably just being flippant, but she had a psychologist appointment booked quicker than you could say spasticity.

Initially, I was reluctant to engage with a stranger on personal issues and declined approaches to talk, but after deciding to relent, I found these conversations a useful means of working my way through the complexities of an invalid's mindset and engagement with the process, even if I didn't feel I was ever completely relaxed or convincing.

I did confess in one session that after the trauma of my sacking from *The Times* – I was 57 years old with a decent track record of 40 years of unbroken journalistic service (33 on the nationals) and plenty of petrol left in the tank – my self-worth and confidence plummeted.

If I had been caught fiddling expenses on a weekly basis or lied on my CV, I'd have had a better chance of staying in a job than being condemned as a plagiarist (using excerpts in the Wimbledon yearbook from different papers without the usual acknowledgement) which effectively rendered me unemployable in the only profession I'd known.

In my opinion these were minor infractions, upsetting fragile, envious egos, but they cost me both a career and reputation. It was easy to say now but had my own copy appeared in an annual without first being asked, I'd have brushed it off with a 'ho hum, so what?' A lot of confected fuss about bugger all.

The circumstances of my departure from an organisation not blessed with a reputation for admirable ethics ate away for years. *The Times* could easily have chastised and demoted me. Yet they had chosen to show me the door without so much as a chance to say goodbye to my colleagues or raise a glass. I had run through brick walls for them, worked all hours of the day and night, and this was my thanks.

Could this treatment have been a factor in any susceptibility to a health crisis further down the line? I believed absolutely it was and the psychologist didn't disabuse me of such feelings. From being the life and soul of many trips, newspaper offices and press boxes to being shunned and sidelined slowly wore me down.

I found I couldn't watch more than a few points of tennis, a sport for which I had been glued to my seat for hours on end for the best part of 25 years. To have it on in the house reinforced grim memories and I got angry with myself and others for no good reason. I either requested a change of channels or simply walked out.

The psychologist said that when we keep things bottled up and have no release valve, it will eat away over time and suddenly things can go 'pop'. I suppose it could have been prevented.

Each year at *The Times* I had undergone a BUPA physical as part of the company's private health scheme. A check on one's blood pressure, cholesterol levels, dietary habits and prostate function (an annual finger up the backside wasn't too much of an inconvenience), was a heartening means of keeping tabs on an employee's condition in a job which demanded the daily challenge of deadlines and continuous travelling stresses.

Once these protections were removed, I should have taken my own blood pressure on a regular basis and asked my GP to monitor the other functions, but hardly ever got round to it. Typical male.

Here was a salutary message for all those who might have thought they were fit and well never to take anything for granted. Nothing should have been too inconvenient. Regrets, we could have many.

***

I unfolded my copy of the *Daily Mail* one morning to be greeted with the banner front-page headline, 'Nurses drugged stroke patients for an easy life'. I formed an image of the ASU staff at the Royal Berks fighting over a paper they despised (no, not for hints).

The story revealed that two nurses at a hospital in Blackpool had 'allegedly' prescribed sedatives to two patients, most notably zopiclone, an insomnia drug I was offered every now and again in hospital if sleep was proving hard to come by. One of the nurses, Catherine

Hudson, wrote in a text, 'I sedated one of them to within an inch of her life *lol* (laugh out loud). Bet she's flat out for a week ha-ha.'

Hudson texted her colleague, Charlotte Wilmot, saying, 'I'm going to kill bed five xx,' and later that day added, 'if bed five starts again he will be getting sedated to hell.'

At their trial later in 2023 it was revealed that a student nurse had witnessed these events while on work placement on the stroke unit. She informed senior management who called the police. The student – whose identity was protected for her own safety – told officers she was especially concerned over the use of zopiclone 'which could be life threatening if given inappropriately'.

In their defence, both Hudson and Wilmot denied all the allegations and said the messages were 'banter' and not supposed to be taken seriously. They said the 'gallows humour' was the venting of their frustrations at working in a chronically understaffed unit.

Hudson was found guilty of giving unprescribed sedatives to two patients, conspiring with Wilmot to sedate a third and was jailed for seven years and two months. Wilmot was sentenced to three years.

I was the first to admit that stroke patients could be unbearably demanding at times. For most, it was not our fault. This egregious condition could have frighteningly far-reaching consequences and most of us were simply shit scared and all we wanted was a little love, understanding and help to pull our nappies up or down.

There were those whose behaviour was frustrating, not only to the nursing staff but their fellow patients. Many were the times I tested the patience of nurses, I was sure of it, but the thought that one of them might have slipped something nasty into my last cup of tea of the day never entered my head.

I read the story of these Blackpool wretches with nothing but shock and contempt. Most wards were probably understaffed. Most doctors and nurses were seriously underpaid and – in certain circumstances – grossly undervalued. Would you have liked to spend several hours a day wiping the arses of a group of strangers? I knew I wouldn't.

But that didn't give anyone the right to think it might be fun (even jokingly) to prolong any patient's suffering. I hoped these two were going to be spending a very miserable time at His Majesty's pleasure.

***

The *Mail* was providing all sorts of feature articles on health that, rather than buck me up, were a regular depressant. Maureen left a copy on the bed-table open at a spread by the *Mail*'s resident 'NHS psychiatrist' Max Pemberton who informed me I should, 'let go of that stroke-inducing grudge'.

Pemberton said that it had been known for years that from a psychological perspective, bearing a grudge wasn't healthy and that, 'holding on to anger clouded people's judgement and impacted on their long-term mood'.

He doubled down by revealing that a new study suggested that even brief bouts of anger, triggered by recalling past experiences, impaired blood vessels and raised the risk of a stroke or heart attack.

'Feeling constantly resentful is upsetting for you and other people in your life,' he wrote. 'It comes across as making you bitter and entrenched. But letting go of a grudge isn't necessarily about forgiveness but about no longer holding on to the anger.'

Had the good doctor ever been on a stroke ward and seen for himself the utter helplessness of the place? Did he have the first clue about any of us? We did anger and resentment because stroke did that to people. And as for that grudge, the woman executive who – in our first and only meeting in *The Times* offices – had told me my career meant nothing and pointed me to the door, was now employed in some highfalutin position on the *Wall Street Journal* and lived in an apartment on Manhattan's trendy Upper West Side.

I tore the page from the paper, screwed it up and took imprecise, cack-handed aim at the ward's rubbish bin.

***

If you did your job properly as a sporting correspondent, it meant dedicating life and soul to it, often at the expense of things that ought to have mattered more.

In the seven years I was the *Mail*'s chief football writer both my daughters were born and thus my contribution to their formative years could best be described as fleeting. I rarely took a day off to which I was entitled, I was always going somewhere, an interview, a press conference, a training session, a match, a tournament or into the office.

The role of tennis correspondent first with the *Mail*, then *Sunday Telegraph* and finally *The Times* was less intense on a day-to-day basis but nonetheless all-consuming at specific times of the year. If I had a pound for every time I explained to Maureen, 'but I *have* to go to this tournament honey, it's vital', I wouldn't have needed to waste money on a lottery ticket.

Working for *The Times* was immensely fulfilling, not least because in my time there the paper was consistently recognised as the best for sport, collecting awards on a near annual basis. We were the tops both individually and as a team across the sporting range.

A couple of personal accolades were acutely humbling and at no time did I ever take my foot off the gas. I went into every event heart and soul, often the first to arrive and the last to leave.

But the spark that had burned brightly for so many years had been extinguished and anything that reminded me of the glory days was largely intolerable. Maureen said I should snap out of it, get a new job, use my talents (such as they were) to do something else but nothing could possibly replicate the reporter's fix.

I don't think I'd ever felt as low in my life as having to attend a Job Centre on a weekly basis to make certain I received my unemployment entitlement. I had a distinct feeling that those faceless folk who sat behind the desks to which I was pointed, thought of me as a skiver. Nothing I was offered ever suited. I would need time alone in my car after each session to try to compose myself.

There would be the occasional message of concern from those for whom I had a deal of respect, but these were few and far between. I expected certain people to have offered more moral support but as Maureen repeatedly said, 'out of sight is out of mind'.

And that was how it remained.

***

Over the tennis years I had developed a strong working relationship with Boris Becker. It wasn't an exaggeration to say I liked him, and he trusted me. I was on Centre Court when he won Wimbledon at the age of 17, one of those 'pinch me' moments when a boy became a man before your eyes.

There were more titles there, those at the US Open, various indoor venues (nights at Madison Square Garden with John McEnroe in full New York flow were the best of all), and the Wimbledon circle was completed for Boris and me in 1999 when he drank in the applause, including my own, on his final appearance in SW19.

Boris moved into the media world as did so many former players before he dipped his toe into coaching. He had afforded me an excellent one-off interview – seated in the snug at the Dog and Fox on Wimbledon High Street – when he was recruited by Novak Djokovic, an association that was never less than an intriguing collusion of gigantic egos.

I don't remember how it happened, but soon after they'd sacked me, I agreed to arrange an interview with Boris for *The Times*' magazine, even directing the interviewer to the old champion's home just off Wimbledon Common, letting them get on with their conversation in private as I sat chatting with his then wife Lily, and two of his lawyers, at the kitchen table.

At the conclusion of the interview, I noticed the writer had left her tape recorder in the living room, I collected it and went off in pursuit. The way the paper had treated me, I should have left it where it was (or stamped on it) but that wasn't my style.

There were suggestions that night, opaque admittedly, that I might help Boris with his public relations going forward. On the face of it he needed somebody. I paid my way to Melbourne in 2018, running around after him at his hotel and on site at the Australian Open, but when it came to a straightforward conversation about working with him, there was always something more important he had to do.

That said, I put him in contact with a world-renowned documentary producer in London – joining the pair to start the negotiations to tell his story. I was paid an introductory fee which was very nice, but contact was soon lost again, not to be restored.

The next time I saw Boris was in a different TV situation altogether, heading to court in Wandsworth and then on to jail, over his financial affairs. I don't know if I could have helped him over the years – been there, offered a shoulder or a bit of old-school wisdom – but I couldn't have done anything then.

***

Another sportsman with whom I was reacquainted in my empty years was Stan Collymore, a footballer I'd first come across when he played with such fervour and natural enthusiasm for my home-town club Southend United.

I reported on his productive spells at both Nottingham Forest and Liverpool – most remarkably his stoppage-time winner in Liverpool's 4-3 victory at Anfield against title-chasing Newcastle United in 1996, a match that remained one of the highlights of my writing career and certainly the one with the record number of intros (opening paragraphs) that I ripped up and threw away.

The match ebbed deliriously and not until Collymore's late flourish in front of the Kop was it decided in a manner that all but crushed Kevin Keegan's hopes of managing the Geordies to the Premier League championship. Nights rarely came more spectacular.

I was there for Stan's international breakthrough when Terry Venables brought him into the England squad for a tournament in 1995. We had kept in sporadic touch when my football writing days came to an end, and he had moved from playing the game to commentating on it.

After losing his job with TalkSport, he was seeking to regenerate his career and a suggestion was made that I might be able to lend him a hand with his media and PR profile. I was happy to help, indeed inspired to believe I could have made a difference.

After a couple of meetings which I thought went well, my calls and texts went unanswered, and I couldn't understand why. I wrote to his lawyer who had attended one of the meetings but still nothing.

I have chosen to relate these examples by way of explaining how much my personality changed from sociable optimist to an introvert plagued by insecurities. Maureen regularly called me 'Victor' as in Meldrew. My daughter Kathleen reflected that, 'you were never this way when you were working, Dad. You've really changed'.

When a psychologist came to see me in the early throes of my rehabilitation, I took her into my confidence (against my sceptical nature). 'The whole of my married life I was the breadwinner, and it was accepted, sometimes reluctantly, that I needed to concentrate on my work to stay at the top of my game,' I said.

'Imagine having that taken from you and no one would give you the chance to redeem yourself. I thus gained weight and drank a little more than was beneficial and lost so much of my sense of worth.'

The psychologist was as certain as she could be that this inner despair – I kept it all locked inside – rendered me increasingly vulnerable to both physical and mental decline.

***

There was an ocean of empty space into which the mind could dive during the hours of stroke ward isolation when the remoteness of your fellow patients wasn't the only barrier to your attempt to retain a positive mindset.

It would hardly be human not to reflect upon your own mortality (and in my case shout 'bollocks' and 'shit' a little too loudly and for no reason in particular) but all the same it was counterproductive to waste precious time dwelling on the miseries of infirmity.

They say don't look back in anger and for most of my life I had nothing to be angry about, so I tried focusing for mental refreshment on those occasions when I'd been privy to sporting treasures.

As evidence, the Wimbledon final of 2013 when Andy Murray turned the pages of British tennis history with such a spectacular flourish – I saw that live and pumped my fists at him as he had done to the Brits in the press seats as his instinctive gesture of victory.

I had reported on every Grand Slam final Roger Federer and Rafael Nadal contested at the indulgent height of their brilliance. The extraordinary 2012 Australian Open final where Novak Djokovic beat Nadal, necessitated sitting through six compelling hours (though I twice went for Melbourne Park's finest fish and chips and a glass or three of local plonk for fortification and probably needed to dash out for a pee at least half-a-dozen times).

I picked old Aussie pal Pat Cash (not then in the top ten) to win Wimbledon in 1987 – my greatest piece of crystal-ball gazing, given front-page projection in the *Mail* – and was seated ten yards from his historic climb to the players' box, beginning a trend that everyone copies these days.

A friendly US tennis fan had kindly pointed me in the direction of two sisters named Williams with beads in their hair practising on the back courts of Crandon Park in Key Biscayne, Florida, before they would lay waste to the women's game.

I was dispatched to report on Jennifer Capriati's breakthrough tournament as a 14-year-old phenomenon in 1990. I ghosted John McEnroe's columns for a couple of years including one in the week of 9/11 which was his finest work. I sang with Gladys Knight in a tennis commentary box in Indian Wells and she declared me an honorary Pip.

In my No.1 football days, I reported on each one of the matches when Graham Taylor and Terry Venables managed the England team – the rough and smooth of international football, you could say. I was hair-dried by Sir Alex Ferguson more than once and lived to tell the tale and had a front-row seat as unquestionably the finest seasons of the Premier League era, between 1992 and '98, were played out.

I'd been a lucky bugger, no doubt about it and reflecting on these moments of magic from my hospital bed would momentarily raise my spirits. But this was almost certainly the end of my live sport experience since I had been a terribly long time redundant and was still unable to move half of my fingers, toes, face, or anything else that might extend a tolerable lease of life.

***

I knew I wouldn't get anywhere unless I tried to stand up. Good luck with that when only one leg worked properly and the other was a weird cross between jelly one minute and a ball and chain the next.

This was one of the very peculiar juxtapositions of losing a third of your muscle mass. The bits of your body you would like to go stiff had all but given up the ghost and those from which you needed a degree of flexibility were now rigid and excruciating to the touch. As for moving around, without a wheelchair I was nothing. I had never imagined myself in one of these contraptions, the getting into and hauling out of which took every measure of my strength. I required the assistance of someone (or two) to help heave me up, turn me around and plop me into the chair. As time went on and my courage grew, I would attempt to master this manoeuvre on my own which meant a lot of thrashing around, trying to grab the furthest right armrest with my good hand as the left bounced uncontrollably, which required all manner of ducking moves by those who had ventured closer to discover the cause of all the expletives.

However, with only one arm that functioned, I was unable to take myself off on my own. Any attempt to guide the wheelchair would have ended up with me heading in a vicious circle – round and round endlessly, to finish precisely where I had started.

It had become something of a running sideshow in the ward when I was pressed into physical activity. I became indignant for any failure that wasn't my fault and I simply couldn't control my albeit shortened temper. How was it that everyone else accepted their predicament with such stoicism? I had to let it all go, there was no other way.

Getting dressed – now that was a saga. I was still wearing a nappy throughout the day in case of emergencies (days of dashing to the loo were long gone). I was never incontinent, thank the Lord, but the urge would suddenly arrive and there was nothing you could do about it if the nurse's call button was out of reach, which seemed to be 95 per cent of the bloody time.

Maureen kept me well stocked in clean clothes, all neatly ironed and laid out perfectly in the cupboard next to my bed – though at just the wrong height for me to reach by myself when the time came to wash and dress.

The bed bath came first, not the romantic, mollycoddling experience it sounded like. In the (unreal) world of 75 per cent incapacity, it was a crude, exceedingly messy affair. A nurse would approach with a cardboard container of tepid water into which a couple of wipes would be dipped in a vain attempt to form a lather.

You were delegated to wash your naughty bits while the nurse ran the wipes across your chest and face and down your legs so that most parts received a decent wetting. You helped towel yourself dry, probably exaggerating the bits around your genitals in the hope they might respond by showing a bit of life – not that anyone would have been remotely interested if they had (which they didn't).

Once you were reasonably dry came the arduous task of attempting a wet shave with your only functioning hand. The first bit was tough, positioning the can of shaving cream as close as possible to your left hand which inevitably chose that moment to convulse and thus necessitated taking aim at a moving target.

I ended up with foam between my fingers and up my nose – often because I had pointed the nozzle the wrong way round – just about anywhere but the palm of my redundant hand from where I could scoop it up and spread across the face and neck.

For that you needed to find a space on your cluttered bedtable for a mirror, without knocking the spittoon over and covering yourself in cold water, bits of whisker and remnants of watery foam. I suffered numerable nicks and cuts, more reasons to outwardly curse my inadequacies.

The time for dressing had arrived. One of the many difficulties I endured was that I had lost the ability to bend and if I crouched a little the danger was I would either fall flat on my face or topple backwards if there was nothing nearby to cling to. I had to dress while seated but my left hip had next to no flexibility so drawing my left leg over and across the right thigh was searingly painful.

Once I had found a bearable spot, I attempted to pull my shorts over my left foot (the toes that had forfeited all movement bar an inward curl had a dastardly habit of getting trapped in the lining, causing a backward lilt), and far enough up my leg that they could be hauled over my buttocks and secured into place.

After countless attempts and failures, one of the nurses took pity and gave me a hint about putting on a T-shirt. First and most importantly was to make sure the left sleeve was above your elbow *before* you tried to pull your head and other arm through their appointed slots. Then it was, supposedly, a piece of cake.

Socks were a real SOB. Most pairs had a springy rim and the minute your fingers forfeited a grip, the socks would fly off into the middle distance, well out of your reach, necessitating more cries for help.

Maureen then showed me how to put on a sock with one hand, which was to extend the right hand as deep as I could into the sock, stretch and manoeuvre it over my toes and far enough above the ankle bone that I could pull the heel and toe sections into place.

If I thought I had cracked it feet wise, there was no way I could tie my trainers because I had no movement or strength in the fingers of my left hand and could not grip anything as delicate as shoelaces. It thus required a nurse or a physio to help with the basic daily routine of putting on my footwear.

The nurses could change your bedclothes with you still lying on top of them, something I had presumed was impossible, not that I'd given it a great deal of thought. The patient played a part, albeit a small one, in putting up no resistance when being rolled first on to your left side so the old bedding could be whipped from beneath you then spun back the other way for the process to be completed.

It all happened so quickly; your head was in a bit of a mess. But this was your home for the foreseeable future, and you were grateful that it was tended so expertly and that, consequently, your surroundings smelled perennially fresh – until you next had a touch of the basement rumbles.

***

I regularly tried to place myself into the mindset of a nurse on a stroke ward. Effectively, there was next to nothing most patients could do for themselves, we were like children again but with a grown-up's needs and wants.

The loss of dignity was so abrupt that by the time you spent a couple of days in the ward, you let the nurses get on with it, no point trying to put up any resistance and pretending to be all macho.

There was nothing to gain by being embarrassed, either. Everyone was in the same leaky boat and my attitude was to be as helpful and well-mannered as possible. I knew where I was and what I was doing (nearly) which was an advantage over some of my more mentally stricken companions.

For some reason, the staff took a shine to me. I was the one that the junior nurses looking to make their way in the profession invariably came to with the forms to fill in registering patient satisfaction. They soon worked out that I was an old softie and never gave less than four stars in any category.

My bed also became the No.1 go-to location for medical students who, as part of their education process, needed to test their abilities on a patient least likely to refuse to cooperate. They made an immediate beeline for me, and it couldn't have been just for my looks.

They would set a stopwatch and time each other as they variously prodded and probed, asked me questions about my illness and sought to determine the extent of the reflexes I possessed. In the end, my bedclothes were all over the shop. They clubbed my knee, tickled my toes, tried to instil some life into my fingers, while all the time I looked on and feigned contentment.

An animated gabble ensued as they exchanged notes – quite often in a foreign tongue – so I didn't have a clue what they were saying about me though they always went about their work with a smile on their faces, so I presumed I'd passed the test.

This was serious stuff though; they marked each other scrupulously (I supposed) and it was important for their future careers that they knew their stuff, especially where neuro recuperation was concerned. I made a point at the end of each session of wishing them well for the future, before one-handedly readjusting my surroundings to a semblance of respectable tidiness.

MICHAEL LYNAGH

MY MUCH-MISSED tennis comrade, David Irvine, had a second, far deeper sporting passion – rugby union. He communicated with loving authority about the oval ball game for many years and along the way I'm sure he had perfectly articulated the talents of Michael Lynagh, the gifted Australian fly-half who became the Wallabies' captain.

David may not have known, though, that Lynagh also possessed the nickname Noddy, and for the same reason – falling asleep at the drop of a hat. In Michael's case it was a one-off at junior school; David's pet name came later in life, as dinner tables in Paris and New York reverberated to the rhythm of his snorting semi-consciousness.

Michael Lynagh had a stroke at the age of 48. In his book *Blindsided*, he spared no emotional punches and wanted no over-elaborate sympathy. I asked those rugby experts I knew about what they considered his guiding force and before they reflected on his immense sporting ability, all commented what a smashing human being he was.

'I bet you haven't found a negative, Michael's the nicest bloke in the world,' Owen Slot, chief sportswriter of *The Times*, said; 'Just exceptional,' Peter Jackson, former rugby correspondent of the *Daily Mail* added. These two old colleagues knew their rugby union onions. 'I first interviewed him post-match at Llanelli, on the Wallabies' tour of 1981,' Jacko said. 'He was always approachable and amenable.'

Lynagh did have reservations about putting his stroke story to text, sensitive to getting the tone just right, cutting through the schmaltz as best he could. He said,

'I didn't know if I wanted to write another book because I'd done one before which was rugby centric, I knew what went into it and I didn't want people just thinking, "poor soul me".

'The author [Scottish writer Mark Eglinton] asked me to tell him what happened, and he'd write a chapter, let me read it and see if we wanted to continue. He wrote it so well. I showed it to my wife, and she said "he's nailed you perfectly" so we ended up working together. I really enjoyed the process – it was good for me just to talk about it. But I didn't know if anyone would care after all this time.'

Michael admitted in the book that there was more than one moment in his post-stroke trauma 'when it seemed too hard to fight' to the extent that he gave his father his bank account passwords and various other bits of business so that his wife Isabella could have access in the event of his death.

'It occurred to me that almost every facet of life, much like a game of rugby, boils down to decisions made at critical moments, the obvious difference being that a wrong call on the field might lose you a game, whereas in life's case, choices can have much more far-reaching effects' he wrote. 'Given my awful predicament, the calmness with which I was able to evaluate the situation shocks me a little when I consider it now.'

That calm evaluation brought to a head the survivor's instinct, and 13 years later Michael was able to reflect that the transformative effects of stroke should never be seen in a relentlessly negative context.

He had accepted the end of his glittering professional career with the same equanimity as he did all the rewards from playing the sport. 'It [retirement] wasn't hard for me because I was ready,' he said when we spoke. 'I had other things I wanted to go and do. I never put on a boot again after I stopped.'

I did wonder if so many years of being kicked in the head on the rugby field may have had a contributory effect to his stroke, even if it had come many moons after hanging up those boots. As he took me step-by-step through the immediate build-up to the fateful day, it was clear he wouldn't hold his former profession to blame for anything that later befell him.

Instead, he put it all down to, 'my perfect storm'.

The story opened with what – on the face of it – should have been a straightforward trip from his London home to Singapore to attend a charity dinner, which instead became an exasperating, exhausting tale of over 24 hours spent spinning in circles. 'I missed my connection in Dubai and had to stay 12 hours at the airport which was terribly stressful in itself,' Michael said.

'I eventually arrived in Singapore and went straight to play golf in 100 per cent humidity and barely had time to prepare for the evening's event. There were about 800 people there, so I was stressed again having to make a speech.

'I'd had no sleep, got to my room about midnight and went to check-in to my flights to Australia the next morning because I'd decided to use the trip to go home and see family and friends for a while.

'I found all my flights had been cancelled because as soon as you missed one flight the booking cancelled itself, so I spent most of the night trying to find new flights and re-book. I finally got on the plane to Brisbane, slept fitfully on the flight and again played golf straight away when I landed, this time with my father.

'That evening I went to see some old school friends at a local pub. I had a couple of light beers and something to eat, not much, somebody told a joke, I laughed, a sip of beer went down the wrong way and bang, that was it.'

A stroke was 'it'.

Lynagh recalled, 'a searing pain in my head and I lost sight for a minute'. He placed his hands over his eyes because so much that was happening frightened him and he wanted to try to focus. 'I didn't know what was going on,' he said. 'I couldn't see properly but just thought I was a bit dizzy from the fatigue and if I took a few deep breaths, I'd be all right. Obviously, I wasn't.

'The guy sitting on my right who was a mate from school, a prop forward, was a physiotherapist. I was shaking my head trying to make sense of what was happening, and he kept saying, "are you okay mate?"

'I asked him to give me a moment because I didn't know. He wondered if I thought he should call an ambulance and I said yes please. I was sitting there with my old mates, mostly rugby forwards and they were probably thinking, "come on toughen up mate what's the matter with you? Have another beer."'

Very soon the ambulance arrived, transferred him from the party table to a brain scanner at the Royal Brisbane hospital and this superstar of world rugby union was being told what to him was alarming and unbelievable news. And like all of us when the word 'stroke' was first uttered, he had questions that could not be answered to his satisfaction.

Given the fact he had spent so many years being chased down by massive men almost twice his size and regularly poleaxed by them, it crossed his mind that the stroke was a result of hundreds of thumps to the head. The cumulative effect of these attacks – how could it otherwise be described within reason? – must have played a part.

And it just so happened that Michael should suffer his stroke at the very moment discussion and debate was roaring about the effects of repeated head contact in his sport. 'The first thing I asked the medics was about any long-standing rugby weakness and from all I learned, it was unlikely that something from my career suddenly came to the fore,' he said.

'An old injury could stay hidden for years and though the doctors couldn't rule it out, I hadn't played for so long and they said they were sure I would have displayed symptoms before then.

'I was approached a number of times to be a part of legal actions in rugby union about brain injury given my situation, but I didn't want to get involved. I did feel for the guys who were suffering, but I thought it would be very difficult to prove beyond doubt that a rugby incident or a combination of rugby incidents led to this. The debate shone a light for the better though.'

Lynagh's lingering problem was a difficulty in focus. Whatever the cause of his stroke, it affected his vision to the extent that peripheral images that had been so important in his reading of opposing players' intent or when to shift the ball quickly from his hands in his days lauding it on the field, were now blurred beyond any sharp distinction.

He said, 'Neil, if you close your left eye, I assume you still have peripheral vision in your right [I had]. I didn't. When my brain took a picture of something, developed it, and sent it back to me, I couldn't see it properly.

'What the doctors couldn't understand was why that was all that was wrong with me. The very minimum that should have happened was that I struggled to walk or speak and yet all I lost was a certain amount of vision. They couldn't figure that out.

'How they explained it was that when you had a stroke, all the wires in your brain took a hit. It depended what wires were most affected as to what befell you. They did say I was lucky to be alive, so I had a lot to be grateful for.

'If all the wires were hit, it would be devastating. It wasn't so much that I dodged a bullet, more a bloody great cannonball. The doctors said to me once, "we can't understand why you're still here." That was a bit of a head-shaker.

'I supposed that everything that had to go right, did. And for so many people things didn't go right at all. It could have happened to me on the plane, while I was in Singapore or Dubai, but I was with people I knew and who reacted quickly. I was in my hometown of Brisbane where my parents lived, and I had many friends.

'I was in hospital pretty quickly but those first three or four days were really tough. I was bad.' Slowly, though, Michael began to mend. Rather than indulge in self-defeatist woe, his competitive instincts kicked back in, and he girded his loins for the challenges ahead.

'I did suffer a bit from survivor's guilt because I didn't have to do a lot of recovery work,' he said. 'My balance had gone but I recovered it quickly. There were those who said I was blessed because I was a former rugby player, but I said it was simply because I was lucky.

'I didn't know what I could and couldn't do because of any past experiences but I drove myself to have the best recovery I could. It was hard at first because I bumped into a lot of things, I'd run into stuff. My emotional state would lurch between euphoric to terribly depressed very quickly.

'When I was at my parents' place in Brisbane, I was aware that I was talking a lot and almost hyper. I'd repeat over and again to them that I was just happy to be here. I couldn't contain all this emotion and then I'd be sleeping for five hours in the afternoon. I found that became very important.

'When you injured an arm, you worked it, then rested it. The same was true of the brain. You could exercise a little but then it [the brain] needed time to recover. I was very aware of that, because I didn't just nap, it was proper jet-lag sleep. Sometimes I woke up not knowing where I was, had some dinner and then went back into a deep sleep for another ten hours.'

***

Apart from the black-rimmed spectacles, and his hair having gone a little greyer than his sandy-blond playing days, the Michael Lynagh of my mind's eye hadn't changed much at all when we spoke in 2024. He was about to go and watch his son Louis play on the wing for Italy – the nation of his birth – in the Six Nations Championship. A very proud father indeed.

His vision remained partial, and he recounted his nervousness in supermarkets as he was unable to see far enough around corners at the end of a shopping aisle to prepare to avoid what might have been embarrassing collisions with fellow customers or surreptitiously stacked tins of Quality Street.

'If I was at Waterloo station and my mind was wandering, I'd find myself walking into people. There were a lot of apologies,' he said.

'Every now and then I still got the odd tingling sensation on my left-hand side, heat down my leg. But my movement hadn't been affected at all, it was just my sight hadn't fully come back. There were certain lines of vision which remained affected.' (Michael would peer at the screen on which we were having our Zoom conversation and say he couldn't really see me distinctly.)

'There wasn't much I could do,' he said. 'I was seeing an eye specialist who said that unless it happened quickly it was unlikely that I'd get any better than I was now. I still struggled. If I was playing golf, I couldn't read deviations on the green. I almost gave it up. I didn't play for three years, and I'd really loved it.

'I was off about six [handicap], but when I came back, I was playing to 19 or 20 which didn't feel right. I wasn't playing well, I wasn't enjoying it and one afternoon, I came home and said to my wife, "that's it, I'm finished with golf, it's too frustrating".

'She looked at me and said, "You should be grateful that you're out there and able to walk around with your friends, it doesn't matter how you play. You should be playing more." What wife would ever tell her husband to go out and play *more* golf? I got myself back down to ten and some days I'd go out and it would just be a disaster, but so what?

'My putting from about ten feet in wasn't good because I kept blocking them to the right which was obviously because of my eyes. If I had a short putt, none of my mates would offer a gimme. I used to say, "You bastards, I can't see." They said, "That's why we're not giving it to you."'

THE GIFT OF GRACE

'Blessed is the crisis that made you grow, the fall that made you gaze up to Heaven, the problem that made you look for God.'

St Pio of Pietrelcina

I PONDERED my faith daily, not for as long as I should have, probably. Most days I prayed, sometimes my head was clouded by irrational thoughts, and I couldn't clear it. Finding the right words could be too difficult. I knew God was there to help me deal with the emptiness – especially the acute emptiness of stroke survival – but what to say to bring Him to the fore? Even a practised journalist didn't necessarily have all the vocabulary.

My presumption was that for most people, faith was an intensely private matter and that writing about it could make those who knew you feel a little queasy and those who didn't, prefer to flip the page and move on to something more knockabout. Putting your faith to paper required, well, faith.

I had returned first to the congregation at Wokingham's Corpus Christi RC church and after a few weeks plucked up the courage to climb to the choir loft – going up 15 concrete stairs took a while to get my head around and coming down backwards carrying my stick while clinging to a handrail, was obviously hazardous.

At one Mass early on in proceedings, I was listening earnestly to a homily delivered by our Deacon, Ben Ndubuisi, who said something that gave me reason to ponder deeply. Ben declared that we should rejoice in illness or infirmity and praise God for the opportunities it presented us. This was an earthly summons and no mistake.

I hadn't thought of personal predicament in such a way and drew Ben back to it when we met in the porch after Mass. He said he had used similar words preaching in Ireland and was verbally accosted by a woman parishioner affronted by the suggestion that disability was worthy of glorifying.

I could appreciate both sides of the coin but, after consideration, knew that God was to be lauded regardless of one's own situation, however awful, and we shouldn't be deterred from offering our prayers and petitions to Him just because we'd endured a nasty blow-out in the head.

What was any burden when measured against His son's suffering on the cross for us? Life wasn't meant to be an eternal bed of roses, not if you lived it conscientiously. Somewhere along the way, we sinners were bound to be tested and here was another of mine, very full on.

Maybe stroke and the challenge it presented was meant as a personal test to accept Christ's call to us to be more forgiving, more holy, more loving, more prayerful, to live in a greater state of grace (that wasn't easy when your boxers repeatedly tumbled around your ankles, and you couldn't squat deeply enough to reach them).

The Catholic family certainly rallied round. Of the visitations during my initial recovery and convalescence, those not from relations or old journalistic mates were either fellow choristers, members of the Corpus Christi congregation or clergy from local churches, who ministered to the spiritual needs of their sickly flock.

Dozing one late afternoon in D ward, I had a sense of someone at the foot of my bed and stirred to see a red New York Yankee baseball cap atop a wide black face, gap-toothed grin, dog collar slightly moth-eaten and a warm-hearted introduction. 'Mr Neil, I'm Father Daniel and I've been sent to come and see you.' He didn't say by whom and I forgot to ask.

Father shook my hand warmly, read a gospel passage, we recited the Gloria, the Lord's Prayer and he gave me the oils of Anointing of the Sick before I received Holy Communion. With a cheery wave, he bounded out as silently as he had come in and everywhere around mouths were agape. I didn't see him again.

Parishioners from Corpus Christi were welcome well-wishers. One, Richard, presented me with an oversize carton of black grapes, real whoppers. Normally I would have polished them off gleefully but in my condition, swallowing was risky at the best of times and the skin on grapes best avoided.

The poor fellow. As I explained my predicament, a look of sheer terror crossed his face. Imagine if had he watched me turn blue and choke on his gift when he had come all this way to do me a good Christian turn.

The same was true of Rose, a fellow chorister who arrived armed with a massive box of popcorn, enough for a double feature. I smiled even though I loathed the stuff but if they'd been my favourite thing on earth, trying to swallow this mixture of salty kernels, oil and butter with my arid throat was a nightmare prospect. Rose, like Richard, departed with the present she'd come with.

Not everyone's hospitality threatened a seizure. I was kept in abundant supply of local fruit produce, strawberries, raspberries and blackberries (all perfect for swallowing) by Maureen who also sneaked in my favourite blueberry muffins and the odd can of Guinness – zero per cent alcohol of course – to be taken when she'd wheeled me to the patio garden which acted as a sanctuary from the ennui of ward existence.

I could sense a degree of envy from fellow inmates who didn't appear to receive any of this nice wholesome stuff.

***

I was spending an awful lot of time cheering up my visitors, when that was what they were there to do for me. It was clearly the familiarity of the surroundings, the faint whiff of melancholy and antiseptic wipes that brought out the 'did I tell you about the time I was in such-and-such hospital?' in most of them.

The bedside arrivals just about got around to asking me how I was faring before I was escorted through their medical history, having to say 'there, there', while nodding sympathetically at past plights. My knowledge of the agonies of suffering a slipped disc, enlarged thyroid and the intimate details of an endoscopy improved immeasurably during these times.

On Saturday mornings, the Reading hospital radio presenters would bustle in, all smiley faces, sugary charm, and clipboards, asking if you'd like a piece of music played in your honour on the station's weekend request show.

Once I'd eagerly engaged with them on their first visit, they rarely left me alone and their entirely well-meaning joviality became ever-so slightly exhausting. At least I smiled back (not easy through gritted teeth and a mouth that was only semi operational).

A lot of my fellow inmates sneered or feigned sleep to escape the visitors which I considered to be extremely ill-mannered. If the radio folk were offended by what they must have recognised was deliberate non-cooperation, they never showed it.

If someone was going to be nice to you, why be miserable back even if they often timed their arrival on the ward just as you were prepping for a bowel movement?

They were only trying to help. And there was something strangely uplifting to hear later, 'Hey, it's Gerard here on Reading hospital radio, I've been on the stroke ward where Neil has asked to hear "Confusion" by the Electric Light Orchestra.' (I liked to think the title perfectly summarised my state of mind.)

And the radio was free of charge. If you wanted to watch television after midday – when there was some bloody awful stuff on – it cost a veritable arm and a leg – perhaps not the best use of an analogy in my state. My son-in-law James paid for me to watch a couple of football matches, but the screen was tiny, the picture indistinct and I tended to doze off (especially if Manchester United were playing), so I told him not to waste any more money.

And whoever had decided that these TV contraptions should be hung from the ceiling and had to be manoeuvred one-handed to just in front of your face, had clearly never had a stroke. There was much flailing, ducking and cursing. Smack yourself on the head with one of these and your recovery was right back to square one.

Entertainment was therefore restricted to playing music either through a laptop – which required all sorts of bodily callisthenics to move it into position – or your iPhone, which had a habit of falling out of your grasp and getting trapped in the mechanism of the bed.

The nurse's call button was a boon no patient could live without. The only trouble was its lead often became entangled with the laptop cable, so you were constantly yanking one or the other from the socket on the wall behind you and had to shout for a nurse because the summoning apparatus had been disconnected from its power source.

Being a considerate chap, I preferred sparse use of the button and tried to solve my (often self-made) problems as best I could. Others would be demanding nurses every minute of the day when the staff had so much to do besides retrieving things you had dropped, spilled, or mislaid. I'd rather they were left alone to concentrate on making sure they were giving me the right pills and some half-decent food.

The staff at the Royal Berks were splendid in the business-like way that limited saccharine and promoted self-help. None of the gathered infirm had full control of our faculties where bodily function was concerned. We needed attention, reassurance, help, guidance, a firm hand, a gentle touch, a word of encouragement, a word of authority and, when it came to the messier elements of life, someone to clean up that mess.

Going to the toilet was an ordeal of its own. When you have a stroke, incapability is profound. What nobility you possessed is best parked at the door, alongside your pride, such as it was. Those in my state – which wasn't everyone – needed two people to help us have a poo, one to take down and pull up your pants and the other to wipe your backside.

The only consolation was that the nurses would close the curtains around the bed, but everyone knew you were having a shit because a commode had been rolled across the ward and something called the rotunda was also parked bedside. This piece of equipment was akin to a porter's trolley at Billingsgate market, used to stack and transport boxes of fish.

Rising from my bed to be positioned to climb on to the rotunda was a tiresome, ham-fisted effort. My left side remained the consistency of rice pudding, so I had to shuffle along and down the bed, hook my right leg over the left-hand side of the mattress, swing around and attempt to grab the plastic base, hoping I didn't flail at thin air and collapse back on to my useless left-hand side.

The nurses could assist but it became important mentally to master this technique on my own and after many swings, attempted grips, and Hail Mary misses, the first time I pulled myself up without assistance I couldn't remember when last I'd puffed out my chest – what was left of it – so prominently.

There was no time to pat myself on the back (I'd have collapsed into a heap on my painful shoulder again) because I had to quickly grab the top bar on the rotunda with my right hand and haul myself to an upright stance.

I was told to stand tall and not look down so the nurse could swing the contraption around and position it in front of the commode on to which I lowered myself as gently as a useless lump of human flesh would permit.

All the time of course I desperately hoped my bowels wouldn't open in anticipation of the joys ahead before I could nestle on to the plastic seat and relax for the first time in what felt like hours.

The nurses departed which allowed me to complete the task in relative privacy after which I pressed the call button attached to the rotunda's frame, to summon them back (which could often take a while as I wasn't the only bum who needed putting in its place).

They yanked me up, placed a discreet cover over the faeces, wiped my backside while I concentrated on an invisible mark on the ceiling, spun me back around and returned me to the bed so I could shuffle back under the sheet. Big job done.

I supposed the staff had to do this probably 20 times a day for those who were working both the male and female wards. These people were two steps towards sainthood in my book.

Yes, I'd catch them rolling their eyes and attempting to camouflage the sense of despair that must have entered even the softest nursing heart. When I told my wife about this pooping process she said, 'If you think I'm going to be wiping your arse when you get home, you've got another think coming. You'll have to learn to do it yourself.' Right enough.

At this stage any (non-bowel) movement of mine away from the bed was either by wheelchair or commode. Walking hadn't yet entered the equation. Getting on a sock or a sneaker was still a distressingly painful and laborious task.

Challenges were everywhere and how I dealt with them both physically and spiritually would go a long way to establishing the fulfilment of the rest of my life.

***

Not long into my transfer to a neuro rehab unit (of which more later), I was paid a weekly visit by the local clergy in the eternally sunny form of the Rev. Simon who held a Sunday afternoon service in the hospital's ground floor library.

A corner section of the room was set aside and the staff were able to manoeuvre those of us wheelchair-bound into a semicircle around the place where Simon had assembled a small altar with enough space for a screen on to which he projected the order of service and the words to the hymns.

The first occasion I attended was remarkable in that a gentleman in his 60s had been wheeled to the far end of the line by his son who, at the end of the service, announced that he wanted to be baptised, a request that shook everyone bar the reverend who immediately started to rummage through his satchel.

From it came various religious artefacts: Simon reached for a small container of holy water, blessed it, and poured it across the young man's head, reciting a prayer the rest of us repeated. Those who were able to applaud, did so, while the likes of me gestured in appreciation of a new convert with the one arm it was possible to raise above elbow height.

Every week, the Rev. would deliver a tender homily, sang the hymns with gusto and left us spiritually replenished. One Sunday when I missed the service because I had drifted into the netherworld, he came bustling into the ward, whisked me away to the terrace and set up an altar all to myself where we prayed quietly together and took communion.

He really was the epitome of a shepherd gathering and tending to his wayward sheep, though in my condition I couldn't have wandered far.

***

Ursula Skrakowski, a fellow chorister at Corpus Christi, pointed me in the direction of an iPhone app called Hallow with its daily prayers and stimulating gospel passages. The acclaimed American actor Mark Wahlberg was a committed disciple of Hallow and it became a real godsend.

An 8am ritual – in between slurps of tea and small bites of toast and marmalade – helped soothe a bed-ridden patient before the day's trials took too much of a toll. One of my favourite readings was that from the second letter of St Paul to Timothy, a call to remain steadfast, both in faith and physical effort, to try to see this through until these tribulations had been banished.

'The Lord stood by me and gave me power, so that through me the whole message might be proclaimed for all the pagans

to hear; and so, I was rescued from the lion's mouth. The Lord will rescue me from all evil attempts on me and bring me safely to his heavenly Kingdom. To him be glory forever and ever. Amen.'

In this pit of physical weakness, this passage gave me so much of the internal strength I needed.

The reassurance of touch, one human to another, was also vital. One Sunday in July 2024, Father Danny McAvoy arrived from Bracknell (via Paisley) to celebrate Mass at Corpus Christi. I had not heard him preach before and his profound message of 'love without shadow' reached deep.

I sought him out after the service to thank him for his words. Noticing the stick, he asked what I'd done to myself, and I told him the story in short form. He rested his right hand on my left shoulder and said quietly, 'strength to strength'.

For a second, I became both moist-eyed and deeply moved, and wandered out into the summer rain feeling as if something very special had happened.

Fr Danny reminded me much of Fr James McLaughlin, his fellow Scot, who had for several years been the pastor at St Francis of Assisi Catholic Church in La Quinta, California, a five-minute drive from the site of the Indian Wells tennis tournament. I used to attend Mass each Sunday during the event and had now become a regular online follower of the services there.

Maybe it was Fr James's gentle accent, more likely it was the unwavering message of God's love for us, but he became a source of empowerment when I most needed it.

***

I had never been a reader of music, but loved to sing, a fact any of my old travelling companions in the sportswriting world would confirm. At the end of a demanding stretch at the US Open in New York City, my release in the early hours was to plonk myself on a bar stool next to the piano and gaze longingly at the microphone until the resident player handed it over (some more reluctantly than others).

Billy Joel's iconic 'Piano Man' and 'Bring Him Home' from *Les Miserables* were my go-to regulars as was 'I'm Getting Married in the Morning' from *My Fair Lady* in my best Stanley Holloway, which normally required three US measures of gin (plus ice, tonic, and a segment of lime) for Dutch courage.

It was a natural progression, then, that I should join the choir at Corpus Christi, becoming the second bass alongside the irrepressible John Robins. From there, I graduated to become one of four cantors who took it in turns to sing the psalm at the 9am Mass on Sunday.

I regretted never having had music-reading lessons and had to record the choir's Wednesday evening practice sessions, spending the next three days walking the dog – singing the psalms as I went. What the neighbours must have thought I didn't bother asking.

The Easter Vigil on Holy Saturday was the longest, most solemn, and yet most supremely uplifting Mass of the year. The service began with the church in darkness, a single flame on the Easter candle was carried forward from which a taper held by each member of the congregation was lit. It had a startling effect.

The service was special in that there were four readings and four psalms to be performed. For the first time in 2022, I was entrusted with a psalm, following a reading from the book of *Exodus* where the armies of Pharaoh, in pursuit of the Israelites, were drowned in the Red Sea when Moses called upon God to save his people.

Uniquely in the liturgical year, in this instance there was no pause between the end of the reading and the start of the psalm. *'I will sing to the Lord, glorious His triumph!'* had to be delivered the instant the reader completed his or her duty.

High in the choir loft there was much hustle and bustle, the microphone had to be handed from the first cantor to the second (me), I needed to press a little button on the bottom to turn it back on, then place it on its stand and take a deep breath.

In the semi-dark and trying to remember the tune, I fumbled the microphone and, already switched to 'on' status, it fell to the ground with a noise that sounded like a cross between a car backfiring and a pistol shot. There was an audible gasp from the congregation, jolted from the solemnity of the moment.

I managed to complete the psalm without further mishap and on reflection recalled that I had recently begun to fumble many things inadvertently, dropping cutlery, tubes of toothpaste, pieces of fruit and wondered, albeit a trifle belatedly, if it had been an advance warning of more significant problems ahead.

All was forgiven after my haemorrhage and in 2024, Susan Vosser, our choir leader, asked if I'd consider re-joining the cantors. I said I would. My first outing would be the Vigil, with the same psalm as I remembered the tune, though my vocal cords had been damaged in the mess of the stroke, precipitating a loss of range and the need for the organ to be played in a lower tone.

It being an evening service, I had all day to fret and after a shower and preparing to get dressed, my left arm from the elbow to the tips of my fingers began to shudder in a manner I had no control over. It took half a minute for the tremor to die away but I had an awful vision that it would return once I was in the loft, sending all manner of music sheets, hymn books and candles flying. Then came a merciful calm.

A chair was placed for me next to the music stand aside the organ, someone else turned on the microphone and put it in its place, so all I had to do was heave myself up, stand tall and sing. Looking down across the church, I saw members of the congregation nudge each other as I began. It felt like an outpouring of unspoken support.

The psalm contained four verses, required plenty of deep breaths (I soon realised I couldn't hold them for as long as I had pre-stroke) but I made it through to the extent that Susan asked if I might sing again the following morning, Easter Day, the slightly less complex, '*This day was made by the Lord; we rejoice and are glad*'. I didn't have time to get nervous and it seemed to go off without a hitch.

One particularly frustrating element of my impacted function was that just as I prepared to sing, the muscles across the bridge of my nose would tighten, my mouth would start to drool from one corner, and breaths shortened. After a couple of months of recurring affliction, brought on I was sure by nervous reaction to bursts of spasticity I couldn't control, I asked to step away from cantor duties for the foreseeable.

Psalm 100 read, '*Make a joyful noise to the Lord all the earth! Serve the Lord with gladness! Come into his presence with singing!*' but I'm sure He would rather I might do so without consistently needing to gasp for a decent breath.

JACK GREALISH'S CALVES

IN BRAIN-BLEED survival, the torment is coping with the daily grind of physical distress and the sheer terror that this could be your life for who knew how long. Beckett's words, 'I'll go on; I can't go on,' rang true. I couldn't quit even if there were times when I wondered if there was any other way.

Watching those more elderly being able to get up and walk around, one grew increasingly frustrated. Not everyone who had a stroke lost aspects of physical control, for some the marbles were seriously impacted.

My cognitive powers had remained intact which meant I knew precisely how scared I felt and aware of what it might take to get me back on my feet, confidently place one foot ahead of the other and hold something in my left hand without fumbling it.

The initial concern on D ward was to stabilise the patient, make sure he was medically sound and then determine a programme of physiotherapy and occupational therapy to build strength and confidence.

I must confess to having found OT a chore but followed the rules without open complaint. I had to make a cup of tea: boil a kettle, reach for the milk, open a sugar sachet without spilling it all over the kitchen counter, stir the contents, sample my good works, and then wash and dry the dishes trying to use my bad hand as much as possible.

Once I inadvertently touched the kettle post-boil with a flapping finger and a welt appeared with alarming speed. My language was appropriately colourful.

***

As 50 per cent of the bottom half of my body was effectively lifeless, the doctors needed to make sure that blood clots didn't form in my legs with potentially disastrous consequences.

For a while, my left calf swelled to such a size you could have compared it to Jack Grealish, which drew admiring glances from the female staff but gave rise to chin-rubbing exchanges within the specialist ranks. And so, before I sought a good night's rest – vital but a rarity – the nurses were told to wrap both my legs in what were ostensibly blood pressure gauges plugged into a machine on the end of the bed.

It was purgatory trying to drop off when your legs were being squeezed, momentarily relaxed, and then squeezed again during the hours of darkness. I was told that until I was able to walk to the toilet unaided this would be the nightly norm to prevent potentially fatal clots forming.

It wouldn't have been so bad, but the bloody machine would turn itself off in the middle of the night and emit a beeping noise that woke everybody on the ward. All you could do was attempt a sheepish apology, though I had lost the ability to shrug my left shoulder, so looked a bigger prat than I felt.

I asked as kindly as I could to have these lumpy things removed but there was to be no relenting and given the alternative, a clot making its way to my already sozzled brain, I supposed it was an inconvenience I could just about tolerate. About a month into this dastardly regimen, I was told that rather than have my legs mummified, I could plump for a nightly injection into my stomach which did the same trick.

It was the choice between momentary discomfort and a night-time of agony though the relish with which the nursing staff approached with the needle, saying 'sharp scratch' (as if that comforted the patient) before plunging it into my one-pack did make me wonder how else they got their thrills.

There was exercise to be done in bed as well – no not that, sadly. The slickness of the plastic mattress cover meant you'd often end up with your head where your arse should have been, and you had to haul yourself up, so your toes didn't slide through the spaces at the bottom of the surrounds and become trapped, resulting in much opportunity for unfriendly outbursts.

I concluded that this work-out three times a day would at least help me develop a decent right bicep but in terms of a real keep-fit session, it hardly cut the mustard. No, I needed to make a stand in every sense of the phrase.

That meant the day was coming when I would leave the relative comfort of the wheelchair for a more precarious posture. Sophie, the lovely physio, pushed me into a corridor probably 30 yards long in which there was a handrail on either side and she and her assistant, Gwyneth, helped me out of the chair and to my feet.

I held the rail with my right hand, Gwyneth grasped my left and Sophie, seated on a stool on casters in front of me pushed her left arm through my crotch area to move my knee and raise my foot so that I might take a simple stride. What a blooming kerfuffle, as we inched our way along with me desperately trying to focus on the end of the corridor and not look down. Life, one painstaking stumble at a time.

This was to become my daily rigour, an attempt to manipulate my leg and remind it what it was there for. As messages to the brain had become seriously disrupted, the plan was to nudge it back into full operation. This would take a tremendous amount of time, but it was not as if I was going anywhere fast.

In concert with a dead leg, I also had a useless, unresponsive arm, at the end of which was a hand and fingers that just lay there, limp, curved inwards. In a strange respect, the loss of a working arm was more devastating than anything. A left-hander without a functioning left hand was a waste. I had lost the ability to hold a pen much less write with one.

Would I ever be able to use a laptop again? Would I be able to do a crossword, a Sudoku? These things mattered, especially to a writer. I would need to train my right hand to take over the responsibility but any time I'd tried that in the past it came out like a passable stab at ancient Greek.

Sarah, a Spanish occupational therapist known as the 'hand lady' would take me by my left hand, gently try to rub some life into it, flex it backwards from the wrist (something it absolutely refused to do) and see if she could persuade my fingers into any other motion than curling into a rather pathetic fist. We had to try to get the digits to extend, the space between them to widen, and, if possible, for each in turn to react individually and tap the table in front of me.

Various devices were used to try to coax my hands back into action. Saebo, a Scandinavian firm, specialised in gadgets designed to stimulate joints and muscles and thus reconnect bits of your body with the mass in your head that once operated them.

I was given a glove that looked like something Peter Bonetti used to wear, though this came with various elastic attachments that would force your fingers to extend while at the same time persuading your wrist that it could bend back beyond the horizontal.

It was frustrating enough trying to get the blasted thing on let alone hoping that with a bit of encouragement, it might achieve what was written on the instructions. Tiny, wetted patches attached to a hand-held voltage pack were stuck on my forearm, triceps and calves which had the effect of jolting redundant muscles into a kind of life. My fingers would ping upwards and outwards, and my leg go into a kind of spasm.

These were minor encouragements, but so long as you felt something worthwhile was being achieved it vastly improved your state of mind and as time dragged by, any step forward, however small, was to be cherished.

On Wednesday afternoons we were invited (told) to participate in 'a stroke odyssey'. Anything for a change of scenery, I supposed. From various wards in the ASU, around a dozen of us were delivered into the hands of a couple of ladies of a theatrical bent. Nice, but a bit eccentric, with twig-thin frames and RADA accents.

The group would engage in special breathing exercises, learning how to enhance the use of our abdomen to inhale and exhale properly while stretching our redundant limbs as far as they could reach within the bounds of comfort. Sarah had to sit on my left-hand side and raise my arm to near shoulder height so that I could properly indulge.

We were asked to pretend we were branches on a tree, as if caught in a middling breeze. God only knew how it looked to passers-by to see crippled bodies strapped into wheelchairs flailing around in demented unison while our teachers urged us on with smiley earnestness.

We should, they told us, gently tap the areas of the body that weren't functioning, to remind the brain of where it should concentrate its healing powers. This provoked much skin-slapping and forced merriment.

We would sing too, up and down the scales, or at least make noises that sounded a bit like singing. I tried to be the life and soul of the party as was my wont though a couple of the more elderly ladies found the enthusiasm of our leaders a little too overbearing and usually nodded off.

The next 'try to take your mind off being a stroke victim' hoot was something called the Grasp Group. I knew everyone had good intentions but trying to make people who couldn't form their hands into any kind of discernible shape pick up tiny blocks of wood and attempt to place one on top of another seemed to me the height of cruelty.

My left arm was still prone to either bouts of uncontrollable shaking or becoming rigidly stiff. When it came to fumbling, I was top of the form. Wooden blocks were scattered everywhere. My problem was with the scapula, the shoulder blade to give it its more common name. All the power in the arm was generated by the strength of the scapula – essentially a bony pivot – and mine had been both displaced and detached from the various muscles on which it depended for stability.

Only by someone forcibly pushing the blade back into its place was I able to have a form of decent mobility but that could only be a temporary measure. I was suffering too from what was described as a muscle 'impingement' in that any backward jolt of my arm was so horrendously painful I had to let out an exclamation, usually a naughty one.

So, a full-throated *'aaaaaargh'* would fill the room in response to any attempt to straighten my spasticity-affected left arm from its go-to 45-degree position. Bollocks and bugger were never far behind.

The physios took it all in good heart, smiled, and bent me a little more gingerly. If only one of these days it might just begin to act like a real arm again, that was all I asked. I didn't want for much.

***

Had it not been for music, I doubt I'd have made any kind of recovery at all, decent or otherwise.

During the night, when often consumed by anxiety, I would reach – right arm fumbling over left, naturally – for my set of headphones and mobile phone and attempt to connect the two. I needed soothing reassurance and here it was in the form of a new kid on the wireless block, Boom Radio, the station 'built by baby boomers for baby boomers'.

Where else across the airwaves would you find in pleasing sequence, 'Truly Scrumptious' from *Chitty Chitty Bang Bang*, 'Ventura Highway' by America, the Tony Hatch theme to *The Champions* TV series, and 'Good Timin'' by The Beach Boys?

I accept what you might be thinking (I'd lost it), but this was musical heaven for me, where I'd often drift back into a warm, comfortable sleep and wake mentally replenished, exactly how you needed to start another recovery day.

The station was also the perfect accompaniment for an evening's wind-down when you had survived more cracking joints, stiff arms and leaden legs with no alcohol to look forward to. I would heartily recommend Boom for any stroke patient – those more stricken in years anyway – who want some short-term escape from the drudgery of debilitating concern.

Some disc jockeys were preferable – it was a matter of individual taste – and my spirits were lifted when I heard a familiar voice. Les Ross had been my morning pick-me-up on *BRMB* back in the *Birmingham Evening Mail* days of the late seventies, and here he was on Sunday morning (then shifted to the afternoon), as effervescent as he had been the best part of 50 years earlier. Andy Marriott at 6am on weekdays and Dave Jamieson at the same time on Sunday had the fizz of an Alka Seltzer.

The only pity was the advertisements – on which its future depended, of course – which spoiled the musical flow. It was vintage this or vintage that (we knew we were old, leave us alone), cashing in old jewellery or worse still those interminable demands to leave some of our will to needy folk, to guide dogs, the RNLI, donkeys, Plaid Cymru. Never The Stroke Association I noted.

At least the commercial radio – where all newsreaders suffered from diction diarrhoea – hadn't (yet) given time to advertisements dwelling on death that bedevilled afternoons on the television.

If it wasn't Sue Cook promoting 'Distinct Cremations' while visiting an Oxfam shop, there was a smirking bloke and his scatty neighbour who could think of nothing else to prattle on about but the late lamented while he buttered the bread for his sandwiches.

Worst of all was the chubby guy laying back in the bath when his wife popped her head round the door to discuss the cremation they'd just attended. The name of the deceased was Millie, who had taken the decision to pay for her farewell up front thanks to a company called Pure Cremation.

The man in the bath said, 'Smart cookie Millie.' Did anyone who put this tosh together not consider using a derivative of the word 'cook' in reference to cremation was a trifle insensitive? And was no consideration given to us pensioners forced to have to watch television in a hospital ward who weren't particularly keen to be constantly reminded of death and how we might afford to pay for it? Just bugger off the lot of you.

There were many ways to lure the elderly and vulnerable out of our savings, Labour governments notwithstanding. Aside from cremation companies vying for your signature, there were the lotteries, thousands of the bloody things – poppy lotteries, puppy lotteries, cat lotteries, donkey lotteries, Age UK lotteries – how much expendable cash do these coinbox rattlers think we have?

I was becoming more and more enraged at constant attempts to part me from the rewards of my life's work which was doing little for my already damagingly high blood pressure.

My personal prize for the stupidest commercial was the one for Assistive Bathing, a constant interruption to favoured episodes of *Inspector Morse* or *Midsomer Murders*. I could inform the idiots who dreamt this nonsense up that no one in need of such bathing aids got into a shower with a towel neatly folded round their chest, wreathed in smiles and could gently lower themselves into soft, sudsy water.

I'd tell them what it was like for those in my condition – towels were all over the place, you constantly dropped the bottle of shampoo you were trying to squirt on to your head (not in your eyes preferably) with your one good arm, the water was too hot or too cold and as you tried to step out on a slippery surface, your bad leg gave way, leaving you clinging to a bar while attempting to retrieve the towel and to cover your inadequacies. All single-handed. Now if they had showed that, perhaps I'd have taken a bit more notice.

Frankly they could stick their assistive bathing where the sun didn't shine. And take that bloody self-satisfied couple on the airplane in the 'All Clear' travel insurance commercials – especially him with his sodding medical conditions – with them.

DECEPTIVE APPEARANCES

'YOU DON'T look as if you've had a stroke,' was a kindly reassurance from visitors and the recipient accepted it – certainly in my case – as a comment born of sincerity and well-meaning. As stroke was in every respect a seismic breakdown in the brain, mental scars took a long time to heal and were not always outwardly apparent.

It was nice to know that on the face of it you were the same person when the reality was you were something completely different. Of course, people wanted to be upbeat, to smile at you, to offer words of optimism and support for which you were genuinely grateful.

Inside our head the wheels were still turning, but the chain had come loose. Concentration became extremely taxing, you could drift away into a space only you comprehended, those looking at you might think they had your full attention, but you were deep in a world of personal disarray they knew nothing about.

Strangely – and I presumed I wasn't alone in this – when I dreamed at night, I was still able-bodied and apparently in better shape than ever. In my case, I was often on a golf course but playing shots from all sorts of weird locations, under a rock face, by a waterfall, across a street and, remarkably, usually with Jack Nicklaus for company.

If I was being chased, I could escape. I didn't drop things. My left arm didn't wave around in the air of its own volition. I didn't yawn and, because my bad hand responded by springing to uncontrolled life, poke myself in the left eye.

I was often seated on an airplane (though in my dreams it never took off). One night I sang 'Any Dream Will

Do' from the musical *Joseph and the Amazing Technicolor Dreamcoat* to a standing ovation from a group of ASU nurses. I was often back in a newspaper office or at a sporting event with colleagues from the depths of my past. I sat next to her late Majesty Queen Elizabeth II discussing how important football clubs were to their towns and Grimsby was mentioned – I had had fish for both lunch and dinner that day which must have triggered something.

But waking to reality, attempting to heave myself off the pillow, extricate myself from the sheets and pull myself to a sitting position, I realised these were simply the remnants of my still vivid imagination. And as the days passed, the aggravation and misery didn't get easier to bear.

Seeing life through the prism of a stroke victim (Maureen constantly chided me for using a description that I didn't like anyway), was an alarming thing. When I drew back the curtain (Tim Rice's lyrics once more), using the cane rather than my left arm which would have upset the occupational therapist, people were strolling along the lane at tranquil ease with the world.

It wasn't their fault that they could walk without thinking about it, but I would suddenly be consumed with envy and shout 'lucky bastards' at them – immediately being grateful for double-glazed windows.

There were a lot of joggers too because of the sparsity of traffic. These were even harder to watch and though I wasn't a regular runner, I had refereed football matches into my mid-60s (trial matches for places in Wycombe FC's academy were no stroll in the park) and prided myself on an ability to match much younger men over both short and extended bursts.

I really shouldn't have been so hard on myself. This was an endurance race, well not so much a race as a plod.

All the experts predicted that after an initial six months of decent progress (if you were willing to put the work in), it was likely your recovery would stall. Rather than measure your own rate of improvement, you came to rely on the evidence of others, 'ooh, you're walking a lot better than the last time I saw you' or 'you've got a nice colour, you must be feeling better', to lift your flagging spirits.

Then again, I sensed people were nervous around me, not unexpectedly as the word 'stroke' conjured fatalistic images. I still walked with a pronounced limp and had a slightly lop-sided mouth. Most of those approaching would veer far enough to the side to avoid eye contact, obviously scrambling their mind for what to say especially if, heaven forfend, I might speak first.

After a while I got fed up with offering a hearty 'good morning' to those who were mute in response, so made do with a simple nod instead. I understood that facing someone clinging to a stroller while trying to act all casual, could make people skittish. I knew what they were thinking: 'What if he's lost a few marbles, and says something completely outlandish or stupid? Best keep out of his way.'

At Mike Dickson's funeral wake at Royal Wimbledon Golf Club, I provoked looks of horror when unexpectedly and without warning I'd throw my right arm across a shoulder, especially if it belonged to someone with whom I hadn't been that familiar before.

I'd say, 'You don't mind, do you?' if they looked to shrug me off. 'I need to use you for balance.' That tended to relax them, though when it came to one former chairman of the All England Club, lovely chap that he was, this closeness was hardly the etiquette of the Royal Box, though he managed a wan expression of solidarity through evident discomfiture.

That afternoon, I defied stroke specialist Dr Flossmann's 'one large glass of expensive wine' edict – just as Dicko would have expected – and at around six o'clock felt an onrushing urge to pee. The clubhouse was crowded, and I was told the gents was in the furthest corner, as if you wouldn't have known it.

I chose to walk around the outside in the spitting rain, using my stick to alert several unmoving groups of my impending presence until a kindly waitress asked how I was doing and as I smiled weakly, she offered me her arm.

There was not a disabled toilet and the gents was down a couple of tricky stairs, thankfully with a handrail for assistance. Walking in, I realised the urinals were of the old-fashioned stand up and beg variety like those in one of my favourite bars of the world, P.J. Clarke's on 3rd Ave in New York City.

I could hardly ask my fellow occupants – including an old football writing colleague who had since moved into higher circles and could barely bring himself to acknowledge my existence – to assist me with my pants.

I had to place my stick to one side, rest my forehead on the ceramic backdrop, fiddle the zip down, locate my willy with my right hand and, now that I was fit to burst, pray I didn't empty the contents down the front of my trousers before I could aim it loosely at its target.

Out of the corner of my dicky eye (my peripheral vision was still operational) I could see others watching, half admiringly at my one-handed dexterity and half fearing I might topple headfirst into my own urine. But no one said anything (or laughed).

I washed my hands, rested my back against a wall so I could zip myself back up, clambered out and the waitress was there waiting to escort me back to my pals on the veranda. I wish I'd remembered to ask for her name for a more personal thank you.

I hated pity, and it abounded. I knew people were sorry for me, I just wished they wouldn't have kept saying it. They had nothing to be sorry for. Neither did I. I imagine it was hard to know what to say to someone who'd had a stroke without it coming across as unnecessarily condescending. And as miserable as I might have been feeling, it was important to retain an outward sheen of positivity.

The emotional side of recovery was often difficult to disguise. I constantly fumed at empty spaces. Getting a piece of clothing impaled on a door handle was bloody infuriating, knocking over a picture frame or a glass of water brought an explosion of expletives.

Spilling my pills was bad enough, but trying to pick them back up, was tiresome and finicky. I had to get them before Arlo reacted and I always managed it though this involved much anguished stick swinging and potential losses of balance.

I don't know how many times I kicked the bottom of a door frame in the house when my left foot would splay outwards, but it must have been in the hundreds.

The dog, bless him, never wandered far from my side if we were home alone but my uncontrollable leg urges were such that I trod on his paw and inadvertently caught him flush on his nose with a flailing limb more than I ever meant. He would give me the odd sideways glance but always forgave me my inadequacies.

***

If I couldn't persuade anyone of my ability to work when I was in full control of my faculties, how might I make myself employable with only partial function? It had to be worth a go.

I saw an advertisement for tennis editor at *The Athletic* the new-fangled online entity that celebrated intelligent writing and sharp-edged news gathering. It was a subscription-only service, launched in the United States in 2017 which had cut a swathe through some of the best sportswriting in British newspapers by luring some great talents.

Initially in Britain it concentrated exclusively on football but was now branching out into other sports. There was some good tennis writing there and the thought of having the chance to excel again was what I needed.

Just affording me an opportunity to talk would have been lovely. In all my 40 years of employment, I had only failed once to land a job after an interview – and then joined the same paper in another position six months later.

I duly applied for the tennis editor's role and heard nothing. A nice note explaining why I had failed to get past first base would have been the least expected for someone with my wealth of experience but there was zero response. The boss of the sports department at the time would go on to become director of sport at the BBC. I hope they found him to be more gracious than he had been to me.

Mind you, that's how I feel about all those who didn't have the common decency to respond to any request to re-join the work force, to which I make an honourable exception of the Lawn Tennis Association.

In truth, across my 12 years leading on tennis for *The Times* I'd had quite a few run-ins with the LTA, an organisation that never seemed to have a clear understanding of what it should do and employed all kinds of odds and sods who clung to their positions with remarkable, and obviously well remunerated, devotion.

It would be wrong to have tarred everyone with the same brush; there were many dedicated folks inside who performed and defended their roles dutifully but as a rule I rather formed the impression the LTA management would have had trouble running a shellfish stall, about which I'd learned a bit during my teenage years.

Not that long after my sacking (at which I'm sure many of those inside the association were delighted), I was astonished to be invited by the then chief executive, Michael Downey, to his office at Roehampton to discuss the organisation's PR prowess.

I was offered coffee and sandwiches, expressed my opinions, and listened to his before departing on what I felt were amiable terms. I did find his habit of resting his feet on a glass-topped table as we talked rather disconcerting (he was Canadian), but I formed the impression it had been an interview of sorts.

That I never heard from the man again, no thanks, no text, no email, no call, summed up either the crassness of the organisation or simply his lack of manners. What had been the motive in his asking me to drive to meet him in the first place? It made no sense.

Perhaps it was a way of dissing me for my past crusading for David Lloyd to become the chief executive, firstly because I knew he would do a brilliant job and secondly, he would turn the place on its axis, which was what was needed.

David would have been a transformational figure and a divisive one – too much for LTA panjandrums with comfortable positions to protect. He was promised a level playing field in the recruitment process, but in my estimation, the hierarchy had little intention of appointing someone who'd quickly make them look less than competent.

It was ironic therefore that his son, Scott – seen as a much more malleable personality – should take the reins and I doubted he would want someone on the premises (me) who he felt may be inclined to keep Dad informed of any misgivings I might have had about the organisation.

Nonetheless, I joined the LTA's mailing list in case a job became available that I thought I could do. That meant understanding what the role entailed, despite their vague and wordy advertising. What was a recruitment and onboarding partner when it was at home?

I was quite happy to find out when I was invited to the interview but that never happened. At least the rejection was polite. I didn't match up to whatever the requirements were, even though the advertisement indicated that they particularly welcomed applications from disabled people.

***

During my 20-odd years delving into the wacky world of British tennis, I made what I considered to be decent friends with several players. Dan Evans was one such, a maverick character blessed with a beautiful game, superb technique and from a journalist's perspective, a way with words which made him distinctly relatable.

It occurred to me in 2022 that a year spent alongside him on the ATP Tour might produce a revelatory book. He was prone to the odd bout of controversy, played colourful tennis, and was – I hope he doesn't mind me saying – something of a character. He took to the book suggestion avidly but financing it presented a challenge. Even if I had travelled to only half of his year's tournaments, it would add up to a significant expense.

I put my idea to someone in the tennis world who had not quite made it to professional level but was earning a good living for himself in finance. Might he be interested in investing in my idea?

He suggested a round of golf at Queenwood – a particularly exclusive club in Surrey – to introduce me to some well-heeled sport-loving acquaintances who might be persuaded there was something to be made from supporting such a venture.

I tried my best – conceding four-foot putts, raking the bunkers for them, that kind of thing – but like other promising opportunities raised in recent years, they were unimpressed, and so the idea was ditched.

Dan went on to have the kind of year that would have made a terrific story, so my unhappiness was magnified.

Then imagine the profound surprise and frustration a couple of years later when I heard that the company where my initial contact worked had joined the group of Evans's financial backers. I ought to have started to check my blood pressure levels there and then.

***

In a crazy sort of way, stroke could have a liberating effect. Instead of keeping things bottled up, you could howl at the moon, though any such behaviour was best practised when you were in a room without human company. I screamed 'bollocks' and worse at many an unresponsive wall.

If you happened to be among people and their reaction to your outbursts was one of concern or dismay, the accepted response was that you'd had a stroke and your character had undergone a less than subtle transformation. You weren't your old self; your brain was all over the shop and therefore you couldn't be deemed responsible for bouts of outrageousness.

Maureen described it – with her disdain for pussyfooting around any subject – as me playing the victim card. If I didn't get what I wanted, I would moan that I was an invalid and people should treat me as such. But call me an invalid and I took great umbrage. It was almost a win-win.

The day my DVLA blue badge came through the post was the cause for an extra-large glass of expensive wine. Here was establishment's proof of my infirmity. I placed it with pride on top of the dashboard. I wasn't one of those who would park in a disabled bay at Tesco, then hop and skip to the front entrance as if in the first flush of youth. I was kosher disabled.

I suggested to Maureen that she should brandish it whenever she used the car – I was still unable to drive at this time – but she wouldn't hear of it. It would only be used if I was in the passenger seat and needed to get out of the vehicle for any reason. Otherwise, it remained in the glove compartment.

***

To stay home or take in the odd communal occasion – that was the question long before I was struck down. My public life had not been exactly full to overflowing once unemployment was forced upon me.

Journalists were by their very nature sociable animals but when you weren't on the tour, not in the business and not around many people, opportunities fell off a cliff. By and large my drinking mates had been my travelling buddies, and they spent their time with different folk now.

Since 2014 I had been out and about completing a trio of books, on gambling, football and sportswriting, there was the odd invitation for a round of golf, but Maureen was working full time, the kids had their own lives and who wanted to spend time with someone who had become unnaturally introverted and didn't really want to talk about the one thing others were always keen to know about? I wouldn't have enjoyed me for company.

For an uplifting and challenging change, I played two rounds of golf in the week immediately preceding my stroke. David Lloyd invited me to Harleyford golf club near Marlow where he teamed with his brother-in-law and a fellow journalist of mine Bob Hammond against me and Colin Pearce, who I christened the David Niven of the links, for his debonair demeanour and impeccable manners.

A see-saw match was halved on the 18th and a couple of days later Colin called to ask if I'd like to play at his club, Gerrards Cross, on a glorious May morning, my first experience of a challenging track with its fair share of undulating fairways and tough greens where, to my surprise and satisfaction, I hit some of my finest shots for quite a while.

How was I to know that it might end up being the last round I ever played? Four days later, I was in another world.

It did seem so bloody unfair. The golf course had been one of the few places of refuge where I could lay personal dispiritedness to one side, enjoy the fresh air, and relish the best of company. Whenever he was back in the country from his home in Florida, David was always on the phone telling me to get to this course or that for some vigorous competition.

Now laying in a hospital bed unable to grasp anything with my left hand, the thought of swinging a club seemed rather remote. Colin was one of the first to arrive at my bedside at the Royal Berks, unfailingly cheerful and insistent that I'd be on the course again one day with my old swing back.

‘Bollocks to that,’ I said. I wouldn’t have wished anybody to be lumbered with my travesty of a golf swing, though to complete half a shoulder turn without falling flat on my face would at that moment have been rated a minor miracle.

Being able to stand up at all remained a foggy hope. My left leg had no strength whatsoever. That would need to be built back over a long period of rehabilitation and only after I was able to take the first step. Of itself, this was one of the most terrifying challenges of my life.

The wheelchair had become a sanctuary, a safe place I had learned to get into and more importantly, out of with as little fuss as possible. To my surprise, I quickly mastered the ‘banana’ means of transfer.

One end of a piece of sturdy, curved, bright blue (should have been yellow I know) plastic was placed on the edge of the bed and the other on the seat of the wheelchair. It was important that the end from which the manoeuvre started was slightly above the destination, so I wasn’t trying to slide uphill.

Once I had shuffled my backside on to the banana I had to semi-glide and otherwise edge my buttocks from one end to the other without falling through the open space in the middle.

To be fair, Maureen did congratulate me on the success of the mission, admitting she had horrible visions of me crash-landing on the floor. The nurses were impressed at my dexterity and consistently amiable disposition, saying no patient had mastered the banana as quickly.

Once I had been loaded into the chair, being pushed around the ward and occasionally into the garden which doubled as a place of respite and conviviality, carried a certain integrity.

***

My first visitor from the sportswriting world was Peter Dixon, a former assistant sports editor on *The Times*, who had become the paper's golf correspondent, a role which was to be made redundant in one of the more stupid moves by the hierarchy. *The Times was* golf to those who followed the sport and wanted their reading of it to reflect authority and integrity.

On a couple of occasions in the early 2000s, I was a small cog in the team covering the Open Championship and had been allowed to strike out solo and cover the Solheim Cup in Sweden in 2004. Peter, who had by then earned his first major writing role on the paper, replacing the inimitable and now retired John Hopkins, was a terrific colleague and gifted scribe.

When he visited me, he looked at me with some surprise when I asked him to navigate his way into the garden pushing me in a wheelchair, not a task he had probably anticipated. What gave me great encouragement from our conversation was when he noted my memory was so sharp, he was taken aback at my recall of times, dates, and places from my career. He insisted on coming back a second time to keep me company.

Oliver Holt was next in – not just any old hack but the chief sportswriter of the *Daily Mail*. Given his extended commitments to the paper across a range of sports, for Ollie to take the time to visit was a huge fillip. He probably hadn't expected to be pushing me around either but hadn't flinched when I asked.

We chatted about contemporary developments in football, especially, the latest gossip on the street (how I missed that being away for so long) and gloried in his upcoming assignments. He had been there for me at my lowest professional ebb, always supportive – one of the good guys.

Ollie had brought a gift, *The Survivor*, a book written by another long-time chum, Michael Calvin, a former sportswriter of the year, and journalist par excellence who had turned his talents to the world of books with enormous success.

In a place far removed from the inconsequence of sport, Mike worked in conjunction with Josef Lewkowicz*, a man who had survived being a prisoner in six concentration camps during the Second World War – during which over 100 of his family members perished – to become a dogged pursuer of Nazi war criminals.

I had once been a quick reader, but the process now exhausted me. Turning the pages with one hand was a constant frustration, because the book would slip from my grasp, and I'd have to retrace the pages to remember where I was. And the content of this particular book was so disturbing I couldn't take in more than a couple of chapters at a time before needing a pause to contain my emotions.

The degradation that people are capable of inflicting on their fellow human beings was enough to break your heart. What was the point complaining that your food was a little curled up at the sides or not particularly flavourful when put into the context of the conditions inflicted upon these poor souls?

The penultimate chapter of Michael's book, called Choose Life, resonated deeply. The words came, remember, from a man who had been tortured day after day, night after night in appalling conditions, yet there was nothing but kindness in his heart.

'Choose life,' Josef said, 'and choose goodness. That's what I tell anyone who asks. I confess to saying unkind words to people who were already unhappy, making things worse for them. I unnecessarily added to their bitterness and lack of self-esteem. That happened to me, in return: occasionally I would go to someone for advice and be treated harshly.

'The only consolation is that even the most righteous among us is not good all the time. We all have human faults and failings, but we have an opportunity to help others. If you have a positive spirit and a charitable nature you have a better account in the world to come.'

It was a remarkable book, one of the best I've read, and I cannot recommend it more, especially to those seeking a greater perspective in their own lives, of which I counted myself as one.

**Josef, a hero to the last, passed away peacefully in the final week of 2024 at the age of 98.*

***

The extraordinary Roger Federer gave the commencement address to a group of students at Dartmouth College in New Hampshire in June 2024, about his approach to life and its many contradictions. I was engrossed.

Roger was as eloquent behind the microphone as he was on the tennis court and his incredibly moving words – delivered without recourse to notes it appeared – profoundly impacted on the graduates.

Ostensibly his message centred on how to deal with the adversities that were part and parcel of living. He said, 'Perfection is impossible. In the 1,526 singles matches I played, how many points do you think I won? The answer is only 54 per cent, in other words even top-ranked tennis players won barely more than half of the points they played.

'When you lose every second point on average you learn not to dwell on every shot, instead teach yourself to think, "Okay I double faulted, it's only a point. I got passed but it's only a point. When an overhead backhand smash of mine ended up on the top ten playlist on ESPN, it was just a point."

'Here's why I'm telling you this – when you are playing a point it has to be the most important thing in the world but when it's behind you, you move on to the next point, then to the next point after that with intensity, clarity and focus.

'The truth is whatever game you play in life sometimes you will lose a point, a match, a season, a job, with many ups and downs and it's natural to doubt yourself, to feel sorry for yourself, and by the way your opponents have self-doubt too, don't ever forget that.

'Negative energy is wasted energy. To become a master at overcoming hard moments, that to me is the sign of a champion. I learned how to deal with these losses, to accept them and move on, adapting, growing, working harder, and working smarter. Always remember to work smarter.'

Roger was right of course. His words echoed around my study. Where my case differed in context was that I'd never been granted the opportunity to lose again and again.

My first loss was my last, not because that was the way I wanted it to be but because second chances weren't offered. If, therefore, I reflected with a degree of bitterness, it may have been both a costly and unfulfilling emotion, but was anyone in my situation supposed simply to shrug and accept?

I hadn't seen Roger lose that many matches and when he did, he was not the easiest person to deal with. I recalled vividly the occasions after a defeat when his imminent arrival in a press conference room filled with faces unfamiliar to him would send a chill down the back of the media operatives in men's tennis.

I received several taps on the shoulder from anxious PR staff pleading with me to go to the interview room and ask the first question so that at least Roger would answer to someone he knew rather than sit there stony faced. If this was in America and his expectation was of dumb comments (generally spot on), he was liable to be more het up than usual.

That wasn't the case in New England as Roger set out his *modus operandi* for positive living. While I could get hugely frustrated at a perceived lack of improvement in my own physical function, those who hadn't seen me for a while would point out that I was walking better, my alertness had improved, I looked stronger in my legs and my fingers had better dexterity.

It took me back to an offering on the Stroke Association community discussion that resounded as I attempted to come to terms with any perceived obstruction in the recovery process. This message was so imperative.

'I felt I was deteriorating many times,' the contributor wrote. 'The more progress I made, the more I was dissatisfied with my condition. Finally, I understood my body was doing the best it could, and I felt I could let go a bit, and just try to stay out of trouble until better days arrived.

'I'm more stable now, though anything unfamiliar upsets me. I boast that I'm not touched by fatigue, but I can only do a fraction of what I could before stroke. In time I will notice the bigger picture. Hopefully.'

A cheerful stroke survivor would make swifter progress than a miserable one. So, my fellow sufferers, sound advice was to not be too hard on yourself, accentuate the good days and as Roger Federer said, place past disappointments where they belonged, as best you could. And work smarter moving forward.

***

On Monday, 27 May 2024, there was one sporting appointment I had to keep. In my years as a tennis correspondent, if there was one player whom I had a special affinity with and appreciation for, it was Rafael Nadal*, the incredible Spaniard.

I was old enough to be his father but somehow a bond developed between us as the years passed. I couldn't explain precisely why. I had never come across anyone like him, and there was something about the brutality of his game which was an alluring contrast to his off-court decency and diffidence.

We engaged in many press briefings, interviews, quiet chats in player lounges, an invitation to Majorca one pre-Christmas and once playing a spectacular golf course in Indian Wells. After insisting I should drive the buggy, Rafa would suddenly throw his left leg across mine and slam it on the accelerator when he wanted to take a quicker route to his ball. Nothing he did was ever at a sedate Englishman's pace.

To see him return to the upper echelons of the game with as much panache and power as he could muster, was inspirational for me. He even had my hairline now.

Nadal arrived in the first round of the French Open in 2024 as a non-seed, his ranking having dropped by virtue of a distinct lack of match play in the preceding months. This stunning champion of clay was now what we in the business called a 'dangerous floater'.

There was no pandering to his previous historic achievements and Rafa drew the number four seed, Germany's Alexander Zverev who came into the tournament on the back of a stunning success in Rome. Was it plausible for Nadal, his body not what it was and carrying so many impossible dreams, to summon the strength to beat a player 12 years his junior and in sparkling form?

In flashes the old boy was there, alive and himself. The lion would roar but had lost too much of its bite. When it was done and dusted – Rafa lost in straight sets and Zverev quite properly handed him the microphone rather than make a speech himself – I suspected this was the last time he'd grace what was his and my favourite tournament.

Sadness, sudden and immense, got the better of me and I was glad to have just myself for company in a quiet room at home.

I put my emotions down to the fact that in stroke recovery nothing was ever quite right. My left eye played up anyway. Thanks to the neuro breakdown the muscles around it had weakened to the extent that, at times, it felt as though there was a wind tunnel behind the retina and the skin around it was delicate to the touch.

This affliction caused me to blink more than I used to, though it had not affected my vision, which was a blessing.

As Rafa spoke and the cameras focused on crumpled French faces in the crowd, my left eye filled to the brim. I told myself that this was silly and then felt one tear after another running down that side of my nose.

**Rafael Nadal duly retired at the end of the year, after a final appearance for Spain in the Davis Cup finals in Malaga. He said he would like to be remembered simply as 'a good person from a small village in Majorca'. For the record, he won 22 Grand Slam singles titles, (14 at the French Open), 92 titles* *on the ATP tour (11 in Monte Carlo), 5 Davis Cups and the Olympic gold medal in both singles and doubles. He spent 209 weeks ranked as the world No.1. And never stopped being a good person.*

ALI TURPIE

THE APRAXIA Man was having to re-learn the art of making sounds that made sense. Like a baby, the first were a little like 'Ma-ma' and 'Da-da' and then, catching everyone by surprise – not least himself – he said, 'Basic bitch.' Well, it was a start, if a somewhat alarming one.

Just prior to Christmas 2020 at the age of 28, Ali Turpie had been told by a stroke specialist that – based on the available evidence – it was doubtful that he would ever speak again. That didn't seem believable to one so young, and at any age, most people would have crawled back under the sheets and sobbed themselves to silent sleep.

Ali saw such a devastating conclusion as a call to action: if not to be reciting the Gettysburg Address within a couple of months, at least to string a couple of decipherable sentences together. Four years down the line as we pondered strokes in their many destructive forms, his diction was infinitely clearer than mine (and no, I'd only had a small glass of non-alcoholic beer).

His story, like many, began with a bolt from the blue but the fact that he was written off and might have spent the rest of his days struck dumb, his renaissance warranted a spot in my stroke recovery Hall of Fame. To be frank, the more he told me of it – and every word was crystal clear – the more astonishing it became.

At 16, he had pictured himself a footballer, maybe good enough to turn professional one day, having played in the Crystal Palace academy side and then signing for non-league Woking, a goalkeeper with a passion for perfecting his art. During the intense period of his GCSE examinations, young Ali was completely sideswiped by the death of his father Max, who took his own life.

Naturally, much of his youthful bravado ebbed away. 'My confidence was badly shaken,' he said. 'I was wondering why I didn't play that well after Dad died. I came to goalkeeping quite late, but I was told I was a natural and if I had progressed between 16 and 18 as I had from 14 to 16, I'd have been a good academy goalkeeper. Losing my dad was heartbreaking.

'I completed my time at Woking but fell completely out of love with playing football, though I still enjoyed watching it. I applied for work experience at Sky Sports and said to myself, "this is what I want to do". I could be close to football, without playing it. Sky offered me a job as a runner, making teas and coffees and I absolutely loved it.

'I spent three years there and when I was 21 was offered a job as an assistant producer at BeIN Sports in Doha. I relocated for two years and loved that too but was conscious of being a prisoner to the money out there, decent wage, tax free, and came back at 24 to do the same job for BT Sport.

'I was promoted to senior assistant producer and then became a junior director, working on all things Champions League, Premier League, National League – everything that came under the umbrella of BT Sport's football coverage I had a hand in.'

It was Match Day 6 of the 2020/21 Champions League, Wednesday 11 December, and the usual fayre of defining contests: a 3-0 victory for Manchester City over Marseille; and Liverpool taking a first-minute lead through Mohamed Salah against Midtjylland, before the Danish side recovered to draw 1-1. Ali finished his studio shift as a presentation director late into the evening and was preparing for a period off over the Christmas holiday.

'I had worked something ridiculous like 30 of the previous 48 hours,' he said. 'On the Tuesday evening I'd been in the Telegenic studios in High Wycombe doing match replay reviews and was back at the BT HQ in Stratford the following night.'

A presentation director was responsible for all the preview and post-match coverage while the match director took charge of the game itself. 'I didn't do match directing on the Champions League because that was the pinnacle; BT Sport were host providers for all the English teams so UEFA would appoint a match director working for them, and we on the presentation side would take the feed from the match truck.

'But it was super high-pressure, super high-stress intensity and I used to love it. I thought of myself as a big-game player, because I felt it was easy to do a job in TV to a mediocre standard, and that was never me. I loved times when the running order had to be changed five minutes before a match, all the plans went out of the window and you had to make it up on the hoof. That was when I came alive – when my mettle was truly tested. I lived for those moments. (In that, he reminded me of me on big writing nights.)

'On the night of the stroke, if I'm honest, I think I'd been overworked. I had written an email to my boss saying I was doing too much two months earlier, and it plays a lot in me now, thinking why I hadn't put my foot down and instead just carried on working so hard.'

As he travelled home in the back of an Uber from east London to his apartment in mid-Surrey, a journey that took over an hour, he was on his phone overseeing production procedures as well as making small talk to the driver, though that was somewhat restricted as mask-wearing was still obligatory under Covid rules.

The cab arrived, and Ali asked the driver to wait while he went upstairs to collect some clothes before dropping him off at his girlfriend Olivia's family home a further quarter of an hour away. The following morning, he was due to run with his friend Ian, part of an initiative in honour of his late father, running 10K a day during the second lockdown. He had invited people to follow his progress on Instagram, where they could discuss and debate any mental health problems of their own and share in his progress.

'I had the stroke in my spare room,' he said. 'It was like I'd drunk 12 pints of beer one after the other. There was no pain. No sign of anything at all. I kind of steadied myself and got the rest of my stuff. I wasn't physically disabled in any way and though I felt mentally lucid, I'd forgotten my trainers for the next day's run, so I clearly wasn't 100 per cent with it.

'I went back downstairs and couldn't say a word. Anytime I'd try to say to the driver where I needed to go, nothing came out except this odd noise that sounded like "uuuurgh". (Ali was still wearing a mask and was conscious that his mouth had drooped, which didn't make things any easier.) I wanted to tell him to take me to my girlfriend's mum's house but of course he didn't have a clue where that was.

'I was dreadfully tired and thought if I just went upstairs and slept it off, everything would be fine.'

By this time the Uber driver had flagged down a passing AA man and was overheard suggesting that his passenger had gone upstairs and must have taken drugs, which was a nonsense but perhaps understandable as the circumstances unfolded.

Ali recalled the AA driver going on to his own phone and bringing up Google Maps and between frustrated grunts and much gesticulation, Ali managed to show them where he wanted to go.

***

Olivia, Ali's girlfriend, was in a deep sleep and didn't take too kindly to being roused from it. She was confused to be confronted by Ali, unable to say anything but gesturing her to come downstairs and speak to a now thoroughly perplexed Uber driver, who tried to explain to her the events of the previous two hours.

Once he had departed, Olivia sat Ali down on the sofa and realised he was freezing cold, wrapped him in blankets and tried to make some sense of what he couldn't say. She had the presence of mind to Google 'face trauma, can't speak' and the word 'stroke' appeared.

'She phoned for an ambulance and – directed by the operator – started asking me loads of questions, but I couldn't make out what she was saying,' Ali said. 'She asked me if I could move my arms, I didn't totally understand, but managed to indicate "No".

'I think it was a sliding doors moment when I didn't hear her, I didn't wave my arms around, and was still unable to speak, prompting the paramedics to realise something serious was happening.'

Now came the tricky bit, attempting to discover the precise nature of what had suddenly afflicted an otherwise totally rational young man. He was taken to St Peter's hospital in Woking where initial consideration of a brain tumour was ruled out, as was a haemorrhage and it was decided Ali had suffered an ischaemic stroke. He recalled later that a haemorrhage was far more likely in a person of his age and that had he been treated for such, there could have been fatal consequences. And it had now been just over four hours since the stroke – regarded as the 'golden' period in which to ascertain the classification of the illness and begin to treat it. He had a thrombolytic procedure to break up the clot on his brain and rested for what little was left of that morning.

***

For an overwhelming majority of stroke victims, I would have thought that the very idea of filming one's predicament would be furthest from what remained of your mind.

I was forever wanting to pull the bed sheets up and over my head to keep the world out, whereas Ali – well versed in the contemporary need for Insta gratification – was happy to produce live content from his new resting place.

As it happened, it turned out to be a masterstroke (and I use the term advisedly). First and foremost, because of Covid, FaceTime was the only means he had of communicating with his mother and girlfriend. It began with the basics: thumbs up for yes, thumbs down for no from him, to comforting messages from them. But when they first came to the hospital for a meeting with the doctors, the message was about as dispiriting as it could be, Ali had had a severe stroke and it was thought he wouldn't be able to talk again.

It took them a couple of days to pluck up the courage to tell him the news – 'and that was the best thing they could have done because it made me so fiercely determined and motivated to do everything I could to get my speech back,' he said. 'The nurses came to my bed and asked if I could lick my lips, and even that was a real struggle.

'I was able to move my mouth in a way that resembled syllables, "errrr", "arrrrr", things like that. The consultant came back a day or so later and said I'd made significant progress, but still doubted I'd ever be able to form a sentence.

'A week later I could say "m-err, k-err, a-rrr, p-urr", and a week after that, I was multi-syllabic. I don't know why but I relished being in that bubble going through this. On 15 December I was discharged to the Bradley stroke unit in Woking for specialist speech therapy, usually twice a day. They worked me particularly hard because of my age. I was allowed home on Christmas Eve, much to my Mum's delight.'

On Boxing Day, he would begin a second series of speech therapy sessions, his morale boosted by an extraordinary response to his '10K Turpie' series of runs for mental health charities.

'I was a bit of a hot topic locally and when I had the stroke, people couldn't believe it,' he said. 'There was a run of donations on my page, and I managed to raise £60,000 which all went to speech therapy.'

Yet there was a double whammy in Ali's case: he was suffering from both apraxia and aphasia, meaning he could neither formulate words nor construct sentences, as the part of his brain that controlled language expression and comprehension had been mangled.

Because he couldn't find another example of anyone afflicted by these conditions simultaneously, that was the final compulsion for him to record the stages of his recovery. 'I had no idea where it would all end up,' he said, 'but at least I could offer some encouragement if anyone else ever found themselves in the same situation.'

***

Thus, the Apraxia Man was born. Ali's Instagram following grew significantly as people were lured to his extraordinary fighting spirit. It was there that the words 'basic' and 'bitch' were first heard, soon to be followed by 'Mum', a little to his embarrassment. 'Basic was two syllables, bay followed by sic, and bitch was one. I don't know where they came from,' he said.

His progress, especially in years two to four since that frightening first night, has been remarkable. 'I sadly had to leave the TV world as it was too high pressure and I wanted to work to my own time scale but the level I forced myself to reach there served me well and I think it was the main reason I progressed so much in the past two years,' he said.

Inspired by the desire to build a level of physical fitness to help offset his oral disabilities, Ali persuaded his future in-laws that he could use their garage as a functioning gymnasium. By becoming a personal trainer, he could combine the desire to help others with their fitness levels with his own need to stay strong for the very different challenges ahead.

'I'd always been into fitness and as much as it was important to stay physically fit, it did so much for me mentally to be able to show up for the sessions the best way I could,' he said. 'It was mad because I could snatch 100 kilos and couldn't say a fucking word.

'I very much paired my speech recovery and training together. I was doing everything I could possibly do to make my brain heal more quickly.'

He called his fledgling business Calm and Chaos, two words that exemplified his approach to dealing with his stroke recovery. 'You needed to stay calm, so the gym would have cold water therapy, breathing stimulus and such like, while the chaos element was the physical training side,' Ali said.

His target for the future was running a wellness studio with ice baths, sauna *et al.* 'I was building a good client list as word got out and I presumed more people had discovered my story on my Instagram feed.

'When I graduated from my speech therapist and she said she couldn't help me anymore, she advised me to take up a presenting role where people could ask questions and I was forced to respond. It was a real turning point: I got a job at my local gym as a coach working with members who peppered me with questions. I did that for two years, left there and took up on my own with a lot of clients who wanted to build up their strength and endurance.

'My advice to you [me] would be the same as I gave to them: to move as much as you could. And to sleep as much as possible because the brain only healed when you were asleep. I got overwhelmingly tired in the first year. If I was invited to a pub with a bunch of mates, they would have a conversation and just keeping up with them would be exhausting.

'I still suffer even now from cognitive fatigue. I will coach for three hours maximum and then need a 20-minute nap. Sleep is undoubtedly your best friend.'

On Ali's Instagram account (The Apraxia Man) he articulates – with the slightest hesitation but otherwise brilliantly – *Invictus* by famed British poet William Ernest Henley, written in 1875 and which was said to have been recited often by Nelson Mandela during the former South African president's 27-year incarceration for treason against the old oppressive apartheid regimes.

'Out of the night that covers me, Black as the Pit from pole to pole, I thank whatever gods may be, For my unconquerable soul.

In the fell clutch of circumstance, I have not winced nor cried aloud. Under the bludgeonings of chance, My head is bloodied but unbowed.

Beyond this place of wrath and tears, Looms but the horrors of the shade. And yet the menace of the years, Finds and shall find me unafraid.

It matters not how strait the gate, How charged with punishments the scroll. I am master of my fate, I am the captain of my soul.'

THATCHAM

AT THE regular bedside visits from one of the Royal Berks's senior stroke specialists – followed by a whispered gaggle of junior doctors tapping your notes into their laptops – there were suggestions I was showing the potential required to be released to a new 'home'.

This mecca for bewildered brains was the neuro rehabilitation centre in Thatcham, just across the way from Newbury racecourse.

From all the inside information I could gather, the expertise on offer there was superb, and were you to be nominated among the chosen few for a coveted spot, expectations grew of more favourable hopes for recovery. This was doing my spirits no end of good.

But as the days went by and I kept being told I was almost there, it was like trying to get through to a GP receptionist: a piped voice said, 'you're at position No.1 in the queue', another 15 minutes of life passed by, and you were then told to call back the next day (not before 11).

I had begun to lose a degree of hope when, in the middle of a lunchtime game of dominoes in the 'Grasp Group' and with a potentially winning hand (except that I kept knocking the bloody things over), Sophie sprang up behind me, released the handbrake on my wheelchair and whispered, 'you're going to Thatcham'.

With that, and barely time to acknowledge my fellow competitors, I was reversed out of the room and taken back to the ward. As the beds in Thatcham were the equivalent of gold dust, I was told I had to be out of the Royal Berks and shifted across county by four that afternoon or I would lose my place. No ifs, no buts.

Maureen had to down tools at work and race across to Reading to pack my bags so I would have something clean to change into at my new digs. I was shunted into the back of an ambulance which careered down the A4 in a flash and drew up outside a homely looking location from where I was taken to the Highclere Ward and allocated once more the bed nearest the window, left-hand side.

From the clamour of a town centre, this venue was sparse and eerily quiet. There were only five beds in the ward, and wouldn't you know it, in the first on the right lay Kenny, the noisiest occupant of D ward, who had lost little of his spark. I remembered his name – who could forget it? – but I had to remind him of mine. He seemed genuinely delighted to see me.

Next to Kenny was a resplendent Indian gentleman who introduced himself as Ravi; in the bed on my immediate right was Ronald, who looked as if he may have been a retired civil servant, and in the far corner, Bijay who I discovered was a former Gurkha from Nepal. We made for a reasonably happy group, given our combined physical frailty and mental conflict.

There was a new nursing staff to meet, endlessly attentive people for whom nothing was at first sight too much trouble. My attention was immediately drawn to the first three characters I met wearing white tops, as opposed to the traditional nursing blue.

Keith was in his late 50s I'd guess, with a full head of grey hair and a ruddy demeanour and he reminded me of Charlie Fairhead of *Casualty* fame. When I discovered that he lived on a houseboat somewhere in deepest Northamptonshire and set off at some unearthly hour to be there to take our blood pressure at six in the morning, I was in awe of his devotion to his patients. Nothing ever fazed or was too trivial a request for Keith, which I found especially reassuring.

The same was true also of Tegan and Shannon, who could easily have been cast as front-line characters in a hospital soap. Neither went in for excessive fussiness, and I liked that. We would laugh at daft stuff together, even the messier elements of stroke ward life, especially me making a dreadful splatter of a full-to-the-rim bowl of porridge or trying to pull on a pair of springy socks.

Some patients may have been disconcerted by their ear and nose piercings and extravagant tattoos but for some reason it all felt very normal – though I doubted matron from the hospitals of yesteryear would have seen it that way.

Since my medical condition had been stabilised at the Royal Berks – the blood pressure had regulated and the bloods themselves provided acceptable readings – the emphasis was now fairly and squarely on physical recuperation and occupational therapy.

A daily timetable was handed out each evening, so you knew precisely when you had to be ready for work the following day. There were at least two and often three hour-long sessions, designed to build up your stamina and exercise routine. It was going to be tough, but I wanted to walk out of this place, not be pushed.

In the far corner of the ward was a single toilet with a shower nearby and I still required the aid of a wheelchair to get me to and from it. If I felt overly brave, I could request a pair of socks with semi-adhesive soles, and shuffle with the aid of a walking stick and a nurse's arm for my ablutions.

Once accomplished, there was a call button to summon assistance, and a sign in big red letters on the wall extolling you to avoid the risk of falls

AT ALL COST, which was a little like stating the bleedin' obvious.

I was still wearing protective nappies in case of accident but another of the nursing assistants, a no-nonsense Pole named Isabella, said that she wouldn't give me any more to wear and I had to get used to my boxer shorts in bed and start to act like a grown up. Was she being serious? You'd better believe it.

A need for self-sufficiency was vital in the healing process – you couldn't always rely on someone else to clean up your shit. As days and nights went on, I became increasingly confident in my ability to see the hours through without embarrassing incident.

Isabella had made me wake up to the fact that normality was not that far away, and that getting there required me – literally and metaphorically – to stand on my own two feet.

***

Kenny was a reluctant participator in any physical exercise, preferring the sanctuary of his bed and often refusing all pleas that he needed to get up and live a little if he was to make a substantive recovery.

Ravi had lost the power in both of his legs and shuffled with the aid of a walker, though in a dignified manner which demanded constant respect. He also independently showered, got himself dressed, never had a hair out of place, didn't complain, and seemed to spend all his spare time squatting cross-legged on his bed while on the phone doing business deals – more admirable qualities.

My neighbour Ronald spent the hours when he was not in bed wheeling himself painstakingly around: a man given to few words. I sensed he was extremely bright if a mite fussy, constantly making and remaking his bed from his wheelchair when the nurses had already made it for him.

He was stubborn, too, often trying to get to his feet when he couldn't properly stand. More than once, I rang my call button and pointed at him as a nurse came towards my bed, to let them know that he was in danger of falling and doing himself a considerable mischief. He had bloody guts though, I gave him that.

Bijay often had his nose buried in a puzzle book: a man of cheerful disposition but whose lack of communication skills meant he could only make himself understood half the time, so we largely conversed through nods and other gestures. He had not lost his competitive instincts, however, as sports day would prove.

Yes, we had sports day for stroke victims. It was a July afternoon, the air was thick but at least we were outside, contestants from both male and female wards were wheeled down to a few square yards of grass near the car park to be presented with a scene straight out of infant school.

There were bean bags, building blocks, traffic cones, tin cans and various other paraphernalia for us to launch, heave, be wheeled around, aim at, or otherwise try to lift and earn plaudits for our accuracy and determination.

Bijay was in his element, especially where a target was involved though I was proud of my own contribution, not least as I was having to chuck things around with my right hand, which had never been used for such things before.

I was glad that no one who might recognise me was passing and could see the rather pathetic state into which I had descended but, hey, we invalids had to get our kicks in some fashion. If it meant scoring 50 points for hitting a bullseye with a beanbag from five yards' range while seated in a wheelchair and cheering like I had drained a six-footer downhill, left to right on the 18th at St Andrews, who the bloody hell cared?

All triumphs, if apparently insignificant, had to be cherished. For a fleeting moment you forgot the state you were in and enjoyed a tiny sense of achievement. There was even a trophy presentation, greeted by much clapping and whooping, and I was frankly miffed not to have won the prize for the most enthusiastic competitor. I was the loudest without question.

And if there had been a medal for the noisiest dresser, it would have been no contest. Once more, everyone seemed to be able to pull on the day's wardrobe with barely so much as a squeak. Over in my corner, all hell was breaking loose. It got to the stage where I would ask for two paracetamols *before* getting dressed rather than wait for a headache the experience was bound to induce.

The pain in my left hip was still such that trying to raise my leg up and lay it across my right knee caused all kinds of agony and requisite curses.

I discovered a new word, 'buggeration', and often tossed in the odd 'bollocks' for good measure. There was much rolling of the eyes from my fellow occupants but what was a man to do when every movement caused a jabbing pain, or a piece of clothing either turned in on itself, slid below my knees or in the case of socks, sprang into the distance just far enough away that I couldn't reach them?

Heaven knows how much time and energy I wasted attempting to perform what had been simple tasks for 60 years.

Once I had managed to become fully clothed, I was so knackered it would take five minutes to compose myself, which required a series of deep breaths and copious gulps of water, watching the nurses in the far corner having a right good chuckle at my expense.

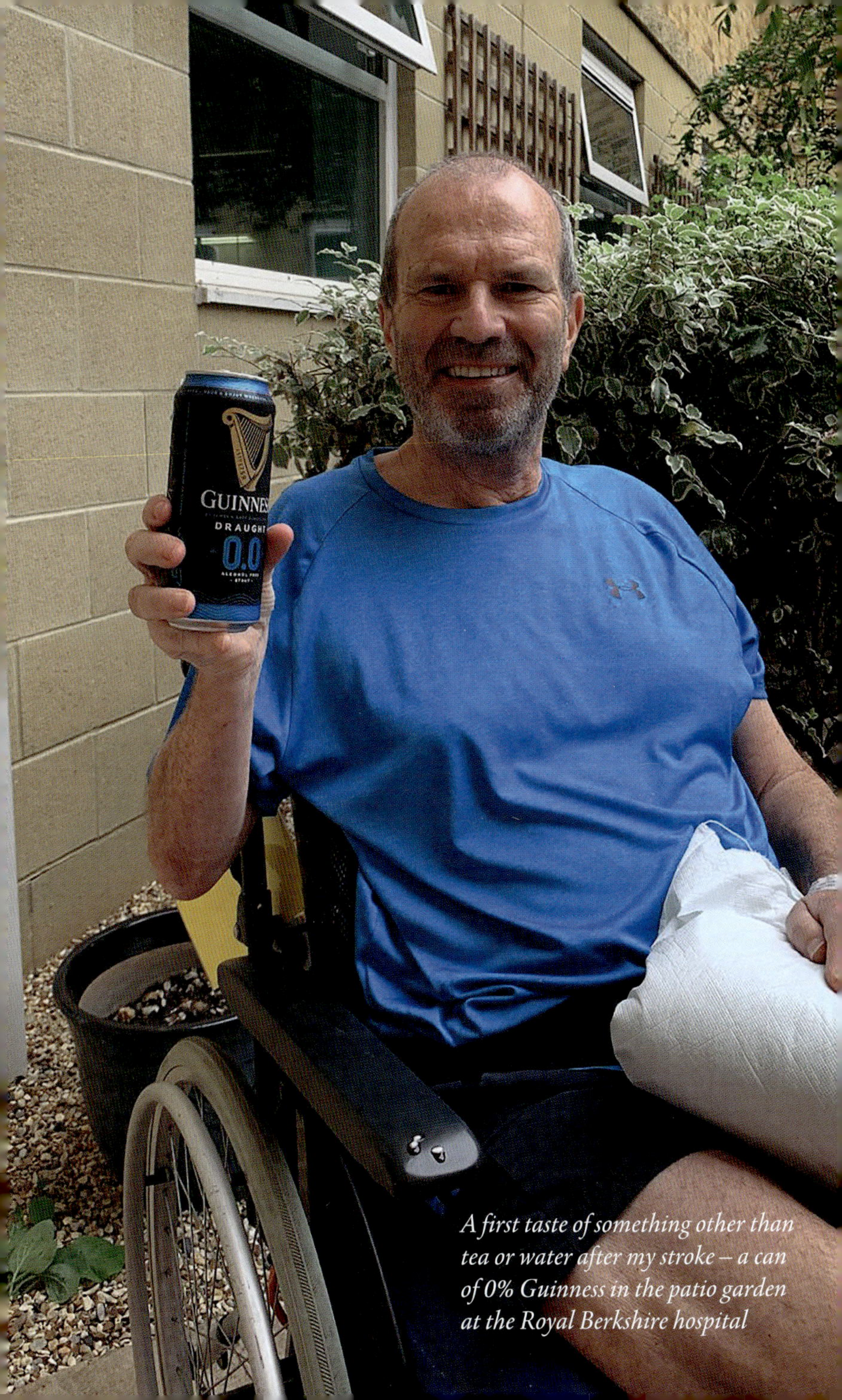

A first taste of something other than tea or water after my stroke – a can of 0% Guinness in the patio garden at the Royal Berkshire hospital

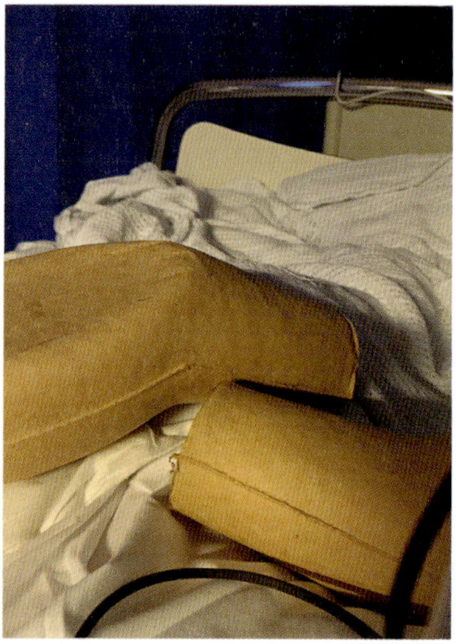

Urine receptacles lined up for emergency use if the nurses couldn't get to you quickly enough.

A curry, Royal Berks style, which was usually followed by a rapid summons for the commode.

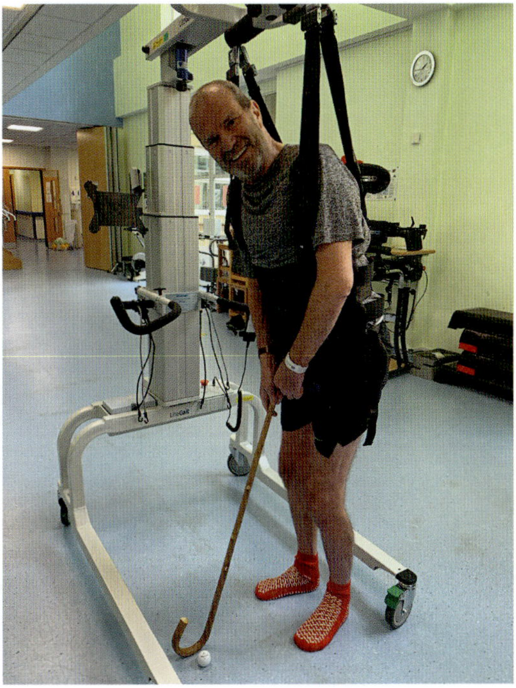

Showing off my golfing skills on the LiteGait*, the contraption from which I was dangled to be able to walk without falling flat on my face.*

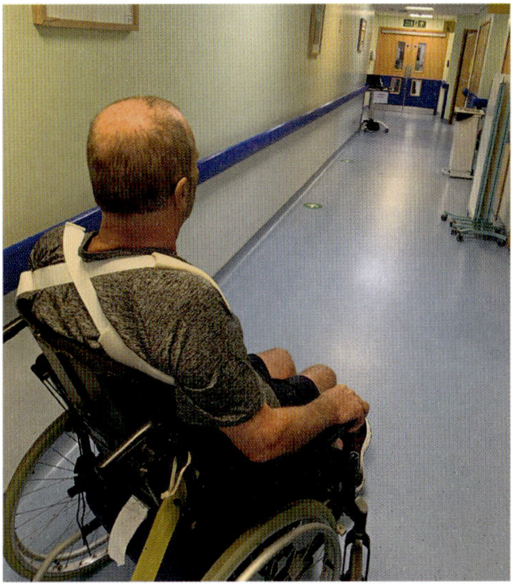

Summoning the courage to be lifted out of my wheelchair and attempt to take my first strides as an invalid.

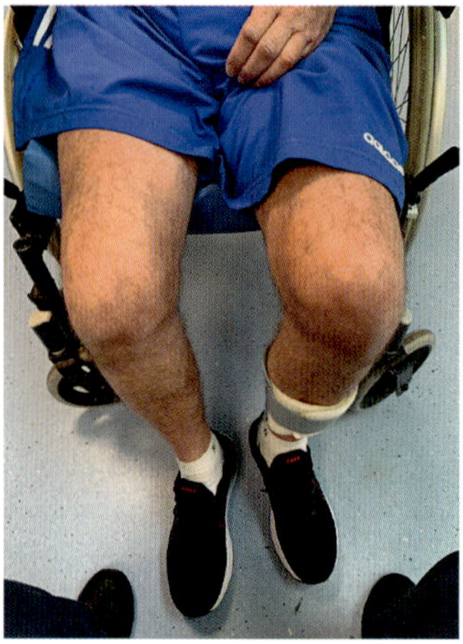

A swollen left knee and calf which required nightly blood pressure treatment to stop clots forming.

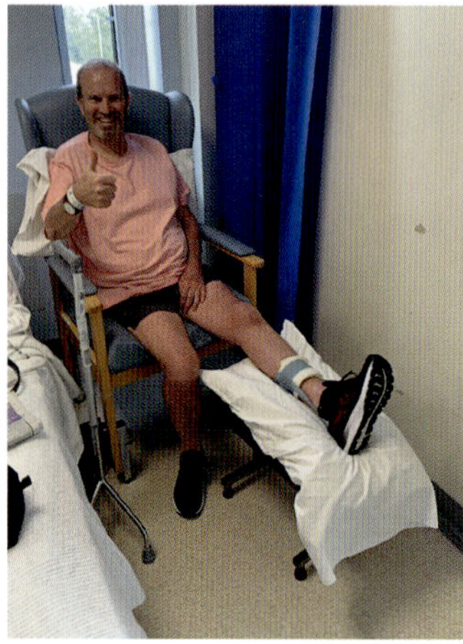

Putting on a brave face at Thatcham before the agony of hamstring stretches for my bad leg.

Noel Blake, as drawn by John Gorman.

Shaun Slater, the PT man in neuro rehabilitation, helps me back to the ward after a particularly vigorous exercise session.

Not a particularly reassuring front page headline from the Daily Mail *during my period in stroke rehab.*

Meeting up with the captain of Wycombe Wanderers, Jack Grimmer, on my return to Adams Park in August 2024.

Lunch at Motcombs, on the first trip to London since my stroke with football-writing mates, (l to r) Alex Montgomery, Patrick Barclay, Patrick Collins and Bob Harris.

Michael Johnson sets a world record time winning gold in the 1996 Olympic 200 metres in Atlanta, the greatest athlete of his generation

The famous Johnson golden shoes, a promotion by his clothing company Nike, that he loved to wear

Michael Lynagh in his pomp, kicking for goal for Australia.

John Gorman, (left) when assistant manager at Tottenham, sits with manager Glenn Hoddle and coach Chris Hughton at Elland Road, Leeds

***

As was the case in Reading, conversation between inmates was limited but joy of joys, there was a decent-sized television to which I was closest and thus the remote was often placed on my bed and sometimes even within reach. Ownership of the remote meant control of the room. I could wreak a bit of havoc now.

The TV was automatically tuned to the BBC which, on the face of it, seemed a smart move. That was until you tried to concentrate on the programmes and discovered that your recently acquired limited attention span came in very useful.

You were too busy focusing on how to place a heaped spoonful of porridge into your partially closed mouth to waste too much time engaging with *BBC Breakfast*, save for its irrepressibly jolly weather forecaster Carol Kirkwood with whom I had once had my picture taken at Wimbledon (a minor claim to fame). I found concentration on food hard to maintain when the meteorological discussion turned to the imminent arrival of Carol's warm fronts.

Once she had told us to expect a few close nights – not in here sadly – there were few audible complaints if I'd switch to *Good Morning Britain* on ITV (Piers Morgan had long gone by this time) though this was usually followed by an immediate summons to the nursing staff requesting sedatives all round.

Bijay opened his puzzle books, Ravi turned up his Indian music, Ronald rolled over, Kenny had a spat with one of the nurses about the quality of his breakfast, and I put my headphones on and tuned to Boom Radio. The TV became background colour.

Once our daily exercise routines were completed, there wasn't much more to do than seek some means of relaxation. I'd have preferred to spend less time inactive, but the physio sessions knocked all the stuffing out of you, and recuperation was essential. A high-backed chair had been wheeled next to my bed, a great alternative to horizontal living and much better for one's posture.

From mid-afternoon, the television was turned back on and the timing of my arrival in Thatcham happened to coincide with the second week of Wimbledon, which silenced any internal debate over programme choice.

The constant switching of coverage from BBC One to BBC Two when matches were in mid flow was aggravating enough with control of the remote, but now the nurses were leaving it by the set and those most interested couldn't get out of bed without assistance. The nurses were in constant demand, flicking from one match to another and back again before a consensus was reached.

A week of tennis did at least spare us from the horrors of incessant, mind-numbing programmes about antiques, especially the appalling one where two teams dressed in red and blue ran around trying to find bargains, egged on by 'experts' and hosts who were altogether too ludicrous for words. Was this what was meant by assisted dying?

And I'd prefer it if you didn't get me started on the early evening's aptly named *Pointless*. What in heaven's name was that all about? The host was Alexander 'you've fought off all the competition and won an ugly paperweight' Armstrong, who was far too energetic for we in varying degrees of turmoil.

He and his smug assistants (I exonerated Gyles Brandreth, who brings gravitas to any show) looked down their noses as the hapless contestants tried to recall presidents of Brazil since 1960 or countries with the most native populations of mute swans that 100 unidentified people had been asked to name (the country, not the swans).

Those who guessed the *least* number selected by these random miscreants, were deemed the winners. The studio audience – if there was one for real – persisted in applauding at the most inappropriate moments. I demanded to know from my utterly disinterested fellow patients who was responsible for getting this daily dose of tosh past the BBC programme censors.

Ronald, not given to outbursts of any kind, harrumphed loudly when it was time for *Pointless*, insistent that I called for a nurse to draw the curtains around my bed and so block his view of the set. I was one metaphorical step ahead of him.

***

Kenny wasn't interested in the TV at all and suddenly one day, without warning, he was rolled out of the ward, not to be seen again. He could barely raise a palsied right arm to gesture to us as he departed, and I genuinely worried for him.

His voice had grown weaker over the days and though I may have been in a minority, I missed him. You needed a distraction or two in a stroke ward, laugh-out-loud moments were hardly the norm and Kenny had certainly provided his fair share of comedic gold.

Into his swiftly refreshed bed came Colin, another former occupant of D ward at the Royal Berks, an altogether quieter chap whose stroke had, I recognised, affected his speech as much as his mobility.

There was nothing wrong with his appetite, though, and whereas Kenny had been a fussy eater, Colin devoured everything put in front of him and never refused seconds. Three rounds of toast to kick off the day was not a burden.

And he had certainly lost none of his sense of hearing, for though he seemed to spend every waking moment asleep (if that made sense), as soon as the distant rattle of the tea trolley was audible, with the expectation of two packets of biscuits, he was as alert as any Buckingham Palace sentry.

I found amusement in the silliest things, a long-time penchant for the absurd exacerbated by being stranded in a room full of people who weren't quite with it – a bit like being back on the *Daily Mail*.

Twice a day, the refreshment trolley was pushed into the ward, and the considerable thump of its wheels had a warmly neutralising effect. After a while the staff would get to know your order (tea, dash of milk, no sugar, no biscuits thank you, in my case) and pour without asking first.

Poor Colin could never quite make his desires known, largely because he burbled rather than spoke. After a while, the nurses placed a sign above his bed reading 'tea no sugar' at which he would point feebly when the trolley arrived at his bedside and the attendant shouted, 'Tea? Coffee?'

I don't know why I found this so constantly laugh-out-loud amusing, I guess I'd never lost the juvenile sense of humour even my family had never quite been able to adjust to. My God, if you couldn't laugh in a neuro-rehab ward, you might as well have given up the ghost.

Meanwhile back at the tennis, as there was no alternative this year, I had to force myself to watch Wimbledon and attempt to enjoy being on the outside of a tournament that had dominated so much of my latter working years.

I often described the role of a British tennis correspondent as five months building up to Wimbledon and another five coming down from the high of it. Then you might sneak in a holiday.

Wherever you were in the world, in the back of your mind, Wimbledon either faded or loomed. Other tournaments indulged the Brit writing pack because they knew that the biggest event of them all had our back. That changed for me in 2014 when I came to grief over the contents of the club's yearbook, for which I had been responsible for a decade.

Even now, I could find no rhyme or reason for why I copied extracts from others' work and reprinted them in the annual without taking the trouble to note the origin. It was entirely unprofessional but done with no thought of personal gain, other than completing the job as quickly as I could.

The horror at discovering my errors was exacerbated by the severity of the attacks on me from so many sides. A swarm descended, led by those who ran Wimbledon, egged on by journalists, both those I knew and many I'd never met, especially one particularly obnoxious US writer with whom I'd had at most one conversation in my life. The sheer nastiness of it all remained seared on my brain.

That said, the emergence in 2023 of the Spaniard, Carlos Alcaraz, was the perfect antidote to my twin states of infuriation and incarceration. Here was a young player out of the Rafael Nadal mould, well-rounded, family oriented, humble and an explosive presence on the court.

The entire ward was glued to the men's final, as Alcaraz took aim at the playing establishment in the form of Serbia's Novak Djokovic, a serial champion and someone to whom I had grown professionally close over the years.

Of the ward inhabitants, Bijay and I were the most animated during any sports broadcast. I was moved emotionally by the five-set victory for Alcaraz every bit as much as I would have been sitting in my old *Times'* seat on Centre Court.

Perhaps this had something to do with my dismal situation, where my brain was addled, reactions were unpredictable, and the mind could play roguish tricks. But I knew I had seen someone very special which was enough to assure me that – as of this day at least – my marbles were still in decent working order.

***

Bodily hygiene was vitally important to one marooned in relative isolation. I hated feeling unclean. Highclere Ward had a single cubicle shower room and by the time breakfast was completed, soon after 8am, it was time to pack my toiletries.

Ravi was customarily first in the queue to maintain his strikingly debonair persona. His clothes were arranged neatly in his wardrobe, and he would take himself on his walking aid to and from the shower, without the need for anyone's assistance, which I found truly remarkable.

I still required a plastic-throned mode of transport to get me there and back and in my early days I needed help to be washed, dried and then clothed to face the day.

On my daily task list then appeared 'OT/shower' which meant that once placed under the shower, I had to do everything on my own, from gauging and setting the water temperature, unscrewing the top of my shampoo bottle, finding the soap container, hopefully squeezing more of it on to a flannel than plopped on the floor and, after the rinsing process, at least begin to towel myself as dry as possible.

Ceri, my occupational therapist, handed me the emergency cord, drew the curtain, and closed the door which was just as well to protect the ears of the innocent outside as I began this fractured, frustrating task. Bloody hell, who knew taking a shower was so difficult?

The water seemed to go anywhere but over me, and when I finally turned the nozzle so that it was pointing in the right direction, it splashed me so hard in the eyes I couldn't see what I was attempting to do, and had to grope for a towel which was inevitably a couple of inches out of reach and by now sopping wet.

Remembering the daily admonition from Liz, my physio, to 'breathe Neil, breathe' I inhaled deeply, tried to recover my composure, and completed the task. When Ceri returned, she said I had done a pretty good job in the circumstances and now it would become part of my new life routine.

As I was pushed back to my bed, a cloth draped across me like some Roman consul, I waved at my chums while furiously attempting to prevent the edges of the towel becoming trapped in the spokes of the wheel, whence my naughties would have been laid bare for all to see.

The curtain would then be drawn around my bed so I could complete the formality of getting dressed in some degree of privacy. Once all that was done, it was time either to clamber back on to the bed or stay resplendent in my chair to take in what the day might hold in store.

Usually this meant two hour-long slots of physio, or the same of occupational therapy with periods of rest thrown in, which I tended to take with a mug of tea on the first-floor terrace now that summer had set in.

Blood tests were a regular inconvenience but entirely necessary to keep tabs on everything from cholesterol levels to prostate function. There was still a degree of concern about the potential for clotting in my left leg which could have serious implications. One evening after my bloods had been collected, I was dozing when my mobile phone buzzed with 'unknown number' flashing.

I usually ignored these but chose to answer this one. A male voice asked if this was Mr Harman and when I replied yes, he said he had my test results and wanted to discuss them. As it was gone 8pm, this felt very odd and became more alarming when he said the outcome had shown an increased susceptibility to clots, and that I should have a scan as soon as possible.

I asked him who the hell he was, and he said he was the locum on call. 'Should *you* be giving me this information?' I asked. 'Surely that news should come from one of the specialists I see here regularly rather than someone I don't know.'

I called for a nurse to take over the conversation as I was getting in a state that wasn't good for me. Frankly, she was astonished at such a call and after a restless night's sleep, when the breakfast medication came round, I told the morning staff in no uncertain terms that I thought this had been a shocking way to behave.

The outcome was that – though apologies were profuse – I had to be taken back to the Royal Berks for a scan for which, after a fitful day of roadworks en route, delays and much useless hanging around in corridors confined to my wheelchair, I was ushered into a room more suited to a Wendy House.

The man with the freezing gel and scanning device prodded around my calf and groin for five minutes and told me there was no sign of a clot, and he was surprised I'd been sent here in the first place. What a waste of everyone's time and dreadful for my blood pressure.

Not only that, but the ambulance got lost on the way back to Newbury when we went three times around a one-way system in operation in the town for major road works.

Strapped into my wheelchair, I could see out of the front window across the driver's shoulder and remonstrated when he attempted a shortcut.

'Didn't you see that sign for No Through Road?' I asked politely as we headed up a set of tracks towards a distant farmhouse, but he was far too busy cursing at his phone to have spotted it and probably wouldn't have known what it meant if he had.

I was bloody seething by now and wouldn't need additional zopiclone to find sleep that night.

I did harbour one medicinal grouse. On my daily list of pills was a smallish yellow one offered as a relaxant to be taken an hour before any night-time sleeping aid. When I asked what it was, the answer came back that it was my antidepressant. 'But I'm not depressed,' I argued. 'I don't need it.'

There followed a bit of a debate among the nurses before it was removed from my medication file. You should never let people assume you were depressed just because you'd had a stroke.

Now, if they had handed out anti-frustration pills, I'd have emptied an entire bottle (if it wasn't for the desperate difficulty I still had with swallowing).

***

One mid-morning, without warning, Ravi came walking into the ward unassisted. We had never seen him without his frame and an absolute silence descended on us all. The nurses and physios gathered around the entrance. It might have been more of a shuffle than a walk, but we didn't much care. I was astonished at Ravi's courage and balance.

My own determination was re-doubled there and then. A couple of weeks later, about to return to the ward from the gym, Liz told me to rest my stick against the wall, move to the middle of the corridor and start walking. 'You mean now?' I pleaded. 'Of course,' she said.

Liz held my hips from behind as a guide and a new young physio, on her first day on the ward – I can't recall her name – walked backwards in front of me with her arms outstretched, ready to break any forward plunge.

I sensed that, as in Ravi's case, all work in the nurses' area suddenly ceased. I would have to make my way past the desk where the staff did their computer work, enter the ward, deal with the onrush of peace, and potter to the last bed on the left.

My heart was pounding, I kept eye contact with the physio ahead of me – she was particularly pretty – rather than concern myself with foot placement and if the final steps were more of a falter, I made it to the edge of the mattress and slumped backwards. There was a spontaneous burst of applause, and I dabbed my eyes.

From next to nowhere, it felt as if I had taken a giant stride both literally and metaphorically.

The challenges were coming thick and fast now. Liz and Ceri had visited my home to check on what perils might need to be faced once I'd been given permission to leave hospital. A clear red flag was our flight of stairs, with a handrail on the left-hand side going up. Unless I wanted to spend the rest of my life on one floor, I had to practise both climbing and descent before they would consider a release.

A steel staircase that linked Highclere ward on the first floor of the West Berkshire Hospital to the reception area at ground level became the scene of several rehearsals. I had only used the lift before, and usually in a wheelchair. Now would come a decidedly frightening prospect.

The correct procedure was to lead with the bad leg going down the stairs and the good one coming up. I'd imagined being back at the top of a flight of stairs and staring down – something I'd obviously done many thousands of times – but nothing prepared you for seeing yourself going down head-first.

I grasped the handrail on the right tightly, my legs felt as if they weren't properly attached and as usual, Liz's first admonition was to take a deep breath and then not clench the rail but rather rest the palm of my right hand on top of it.

I really didn't think my left leg had enough strength in it to hold the rest of my body taking even one step down, let alone a dozen or more but after the longest of pauses, it was time to boldly go where every other stroke patient with my physical limitations had had to go before.

I needed a glass of water halfway down but made it to the bottom without calamity and enjoyed going back up, though the left leg felt as if an anchor had been attached to it while I wasn't looking. This was one of the weirdest sensations after stroke, how a leg could change so markedly from weak to strong and then back again.

But I had at least ticked another box on my recovery list and had persuaded the physio and OT that I could tackle one of the greatest challenges I'd face on a return to domestic life.

Another was to get in and out of the shower without risking a fall. I don't know how but Maureen had fixed a vertical steel bar on to the tiled surrounds of the shower cubicle in our bedroom's ensuite (the scene of my stroke) as an aid for stepping in and then backing out in reverse.

My DIY skills were non-existent but once Maureen set her heart on doing something, it always got done. When I got out of here, I would have something new to cling to.

A SPELL IN SOLITARY

THE WEATHER had turned a touch warmer in August and inside the ward, debate raged as to whether we should open the one glass door to the outside world. As the nearest patient to it, I preferred a natural breeze, but the communal vote went against me.

As a means of keeping the two sides happy, the staff wheeled an air conditioning unit into the gap where the door was prised slightly ajar. It spluttered into action.

My problem – expressed with one or two 'bloodys' for good measure – was that it blew unnatural air straight at me and I soon felt a chill coming on. Over a couple of days, this developed into a cough, disturbing enough for the nurses to decide I should have a COVID-19 test. You can probably work out the rest.

Like an overwhelming majority of the population, I had been vaccinated during the scary height of the 2020/21 pandemic, in my case with a double dose of the AstraZeneca variety as well as a booster six months after the initial two.

Could these vaccines have played a defining part in weakening my system and encouraging the onset of stroke? (A headline in the *Daily Mail* in October 2024 alleged thousands of Britons had been left 'permanently disabled' having taken this company's jabs. Legal actions against AstraZeneca were underway and the caseload was growing exponentially.)

I read articles both for and against this argument after my haemorrhage and so it was irresponsible to rule out the possibility entirely, but I'd willingly gone along with the medical propaganda at the time and had nothing but vague theorisation on which to base a judgement. I had neither contracted the virus, nor ever felt poorly.

Now here I was after three months in hospital with a positive result and, given the habitually laid-back atmosphere in Thatcham, it felt as if all hell had broken loose.

The staff donned complete body armour, in their case bright blue full-length protective clothing, face masks, shoe coverings and latex gloves. Anytime one of them came gingerly in my direction I felt as if I was about to be dragged into an operating theatre for something particularly hideous. I had to guess identities from eye colouring. Those pushing the tea trolley were dressed like something out of Armageddon.

It was decided for mine and everyone else's sanity that I should be transferred to solitary confinement, a spare room 50 yards or so away from the ward which was obviously where they usually sent the naughty children.

I appreciated, of course, that Covid was a horrendous plague that cost thousands their lives – often in unfathomable circumstances – but in my case, it was entirely liberating. The physio team took it a lot easier on me and in my detached living quarters I had my own TV, remote control, shower room, blinded window, armchair and, of course, complete peace and quiet.

The refreshment trolley came to me first, so I had the freshest brew. A minimal downside was that the cleaning crew used to gather in the corridor recess outside my door and natter on endlessly about their life and times – hardly a riveting expose – but which I could put up with.

Frankly, I barely felt rough at all but coughed outrageously for effect so that I'd be able to spend a bit more time in my own company. The nurses fussed over me rather splendidly, then beat hasty retreats, chit chat was cut to a minimum and I indulged in repeats of *Midsomer Murders* and *A Touch of Frost* with no one to argue if I wanted to change the channel.

Maureen wondered how I could possibly enjoy programmes when I knew the plot and the murderer within five minutes because I had seen them all before. It mattered not to me, I just laid back and spluttered with ever greater emphasis.

Such an idyll couldn't last indefinitely and after a week and a sodding negative test, I was told that I was being returned, not to my old bed, but to the piggy in the middle of three in the ward (Ronald's old home) which felt like the worst of all worlds.

Not only that, but the nurses' call system had malfunctioned, no one could find a handyman, so they had handed each patient a small bell with which to summon assistance.

The new occupant of Bijay's bed, an elderly gentleman named Aziz had taken this as an invitation to ring the bloody thing every couple of minutes, usually to complain his pillow was not fluffed up enough or his tea was a touch lukewarm.

He was going to get right on my nerves, which didn't take long.

***

My desire to spend as much time as possible on the first-floor terrace overlooking the garden where patients could indulge green-fingered hobbies, precipitated the worst incident of my eight weeks in neuro-rehab. It also made catching COVID seem like a breeze.

After a particularly strenuous exercise hour, I hadn't long settled back in my armchair when one of the psychologists came over to ask if this was an okay time for a session. I suggested we could go outside for greater privacy and with a nurse accompanying me for support, I chose to walk on my stick rather than be pushed in a wheelchair.

The entrance to the terrace was via two glass doors which swung outward from a metal base which inclined slightly on either side and required careful negotiation. A touch knackered after a thorough workout, I didn't lift my left foot high enough to carry the base, my big toe got stuck and I tumbled forwards, the stick going one way with me landing on the concrete on my bad elbow.

If that wasn't enough of a jolt, I then smacked my head on the ground because I had no means of stopping the fall. This could have been a back-to-square-one emergency.

The poor nurse was beside herself but given the non-space with one of the two doors closed, she had no means of preventing my fall even if she'd tried. The psychologist was equally distressed. Their cries for help brought several people running to the scene, where it needed four of them to haul me up before placing me gingerly in a wheelchair.

My pride hurt more than my elbow and most fortunately, the crack on the head was minor, though the doctors flocked around. Any blow to the skull in a stroke patient causes alarm but no damage seemed to have been done and no blood was spilled.

I was wheeled to the ward entrance but, ego bruised once, insisted I needed to get up and walk the last few steps, rather than be seen back in the chair. The minute I slumped on to my bed, a text from Kathleen, my daughter, arrived asking how I was doing today.

I'm afraid that was it, the waterworks began, my body shook and a couple of nurses, especially the wonderful Lucy, offered consoling gestures and a giant box of tissues.

If anything, this was a timely reminder not to take anything for granted and to learn to walk with some semblance of certainty before deciding you could run.

***

There was a chart on the wall next to my original bed in the corner on to which each morning was scrawled the local weather forecast in Sharpie pen with a nice illustration of the expected conditions for artistic effect.

The resident artist in question was Paula, an occupational therapist from Madrid, a sunshine presence in keeping with her nationality. I felt chastened that for all my many trips to Spain, most notably to the capital to report on both football and tennis, I had picked up so few words of the language.

But something had stuck in my mind. Travelling so often on the city's blessedly spotless metro – I'd get on at Sol near my lodgings on the Gran Via, disembarking at San-Fermin Orcasur for the Caja Magica tennis centre – the piped voice that intoned '*proxima estacion*' (next station), came bounding back to my brain. It would precipitate a somehow uplifting exchange between Paula and I to welcome each new day.

After a cheery '*buenos dias*' I would name a couple of metro stations followed by '*proxima estacion, correspondiente a la linea uno, dos*' or whatever number it was and then we reverted to English to complete our chat lines of the morning.

Whatever helped make any day a touch lighter was to any stroke victim's benefit. Well, Paula and I laughed at our silliness if nobody else had the slightest idea what we were gibbering on about – except Ravi who spoke fluent Spanish.

Paula was also terrifically upbeat at her job, continuously making me feel as if I'd accomplished something, however minor it may have seemed at the time.

Every nurse, physio and occupational therapist had their own special talent. Together, they formed a wonderful, patient group in whom I'd the utmost trust and respect. I would be very sorry when the time came to bid them farewell.

***

The two physical trainers at Thatcham, Shaun and Reuben, were the overtly sporty types, who oversaw most of the strengthening exercises necessary to get us poor debilitated folk to redevelop a muscle set or two.

Shaun was a stalwart Manchester United fan, often taking a transit van with his pals to Old Trafford on match days. When he learned that I knew (and had often crossed swords with) Alex Ferguson, we spoke of little else. Reuben followed Tottenham, so there was always plenty of opportunity for head shaking and commiserations when he wasn't aiding and abetting Shaun to turn what was left of my body to pulp.

They staged the sports days – we had a second occasion on the terrace that involved rigorous squats and other ungainly jerks and bends – and otherwise stretched and extended our bad arms and legs (i.e. generally pulverised us into submission). All for a good cause, I continually tried to reassure myself.

They would walk into the ward grinning from ear to ear and pointing to their prey, which always unnerved me greatly.

One afternoon, having restored poor Colin to his distant bed in a rather bedraggled state – shorts around his knees, hair untidy, forehead sweaty – Shaun said, 'I'll leave you in peace now.' 'Don't you mean pieces?' I shouted across the floor of the ward to much amusement. There was that bloody grin again.

***

The final days in Thatcham were a confusing mix of wanting to go home but worrying if I could possibly cope in a nurse-free world without instant, comforting supervision and basic security.

Lucy, one of the senior ward nurses, had shown me how to self-medicate, in other words to properly measure my daily intake and use my one good hand to extract the pills from their compartments and not spill them all over the floor.

Deep down I thought I'd cope okay, but it was frightening too – the world was an unsafe place for those blessed with all their physical faculties, but I was still incredibly unsteady on my feet and prone to emotional outbursts.

The moods and rhythms of the rehab centre had become so much a part of my new life, and I would miss them. For the last couple of days, the team had let me reoccupy the single room so that if I did get a bit uptight, it would be contained in private and no one else needed to know.

It was always nice to be serenaded anywhere and so it was that Jon, another senior member of the nursing staff, brought his ukulele into the room and sat himself in the corner on my penultimate day.

He would often burst into song to keep spirits up and was especially popular on the ladies' ward when he took out his instrument.

For my parting, he used his own lyrical twist to the tune of 'I Will Survive' by Gloria Gaynor,

'Before I came to Thatcham I was petrified, I couldn't move the arm or leg on my left side; I spent all day in bed, and I couldn't feed myself; I had a dodgy swallow and even dodgier mental health.

So they said go, see the OT; she taught me how to wash myself and make a cup of tea; she fashioned me a wrist splint and then she kept me calm; as I tried to put my T-shirt on with just one working arm.

It took all the strength I had just to stand up straight; they did the best they could to fix my wonky gait; they got me standing up, but I felt like such a fool; when I wore my Batman underpants into the hydro pool.

And they said go, see the speech therapist; I couldn't speak, my words were slurred as if completely pissed; she gave me swallow practise, I found out very soon; that I could drink my coffee normally and not eat it with a spoon.

So I will go, walk out the door; you can keep your Zimmer frame I don't need it anymore; you were the ones who got me back up on my feet; yes I can walk and talk now that my rehab is complete;

Yeah, yeah.'

LABOUR INTENSE

THURSDAY, 4 July 2024, was General Election day in the United Kingdom. It was also the day Andy Murray became the main event once more on Wimbledon's Centre Court. There was conspicuous national celebration at the demise of a tarnished Conservative government, but at the tennis the mood was of desolation.

And if the British still did one thing terribly well, it was full-on sentimentality. The date kept being shifted in the diary but Andy's career as a tennis professional was coming to an end and one evening, in a setting he hoped might be commensurate with the occasion, the curtain would officially be lowered.

I was quite euphoric that morning as after months of exasperating wait-and-see, I'd been notified by the DVLA that they considered me medically sound enough to drive again and after a strenuous morning physio session, Maureen unexpectedly handed me the keys.

I knew I could do it. I'd passed the mental aptitude test, my eyesight remained strong so all I had to do was steer the thing in the right direction and avoid oncoming traffic on roads that had, to my consternation, suddenly become inexplicably narrow.

Getting into the car required me, backside first and legs dangling outside, to dip my head, swivel, swing both legs up and then extricate my weaker left from where it had become trapped both by the steering column and underneath the brake pedal. Once I had managed that, and with a series of deep breaths, we were on our way.

My left arm was still given to moments of rigidity which meant, for the sake of comfort, it best remained in my lap while my right arm did all the work. The trouble would come when I needed to indicate.

Rather than this being an instinctive movement as it had been for the best part of 50 years, my arm shook a little and if I went looking for the indicator, the tendency was to take my eye off the road. I could sense Maureen gripping the sides of the passenger seat as I veered, albeit slowly and with plenty of time for recovery, to the left.

We made it home safely though, even managing to reverse into our driveway without so much as the need for any repeat manoeuvres.

Kathleen escorted me to the council offices so I could register my vote – her car was a manual, so I was back in the passenger seat – an extended process with much shuffling needed to pull the voter ID from my wallet, then hold the ballot paper still with a wobbly left arm while marking the X with my unnatural right. The ever-growing, muttering queue would just have to wait.

The rest of the day was taken up with tennis, watching Britain's second ranked players – Cameron Norrie and Harriet Dart – beating the number ones – Jack Draper and Katie Boulter – in the Wimbledon singles. Then the Murray brothers, Andy and Jamie, were ushered on to Centre Court to face an Aussie pair, Rinky Hijikata and John Peers.

The Murrays had never teamed together at Wimbledon before. I'd always had the sense Jamie didn't play with the same freedom when paired with Andy as he did with other partners. Inferiority perhaps; an inner need to play at his best under critical gaze, certainly. Andy's back was playing him up, restricting his movement, there was much characteristic clutching and grimacing, and the Aussies ultimately had too much craft for them.

Andy would not be allowed to simply walk off stage without some recognition of a phenomenal career. Wimbledon, as was its wont, laid it on thick – extravagant video, posse of famous players, Sue Barker summoned from her retirement to act as MC, all provoking the Murray family to various states of emotional upheaval.

I had never felt particularly comfortable with on-court interviews, saccharin overdoses and weepy relations. Sitting at home, knowing that I'd shared in many magical Murray moments and that my body still reacted oddly when sensations were ripe, I declined to watch.

It went off so spectacularly well that even Maureen, not given to unabashed sentimentality, said it was moving, but I preferred the Murray of my mind's eye, soaring above the best in the singles at Wimbledon and in the London Olympics of 2012 on Centre Court, recalling my own reactions from the press box as witness to such sporting hugeness.

In terms of personal achievement, it could not be bettered, and I wanted to leave it at that.

I supposed I did have some sense of what Andy was going through, well just a little. When your body didn't function as it used to, when pain lingered and nothing you did or took completely assuaged it, when routine became a chore, you coped as best you could, but nothing felt quite right.

In Andy's situation, it meant having to prepare to step into the shadows whereas in my case, I was desperate to emerge from them.

Still, I kept up with the reaction on the various social media channels, where celebration of his achievements was rightly colourful and unrestrained. For once I concurred with every message. Then the politics intervened and a momentous day in the UK left me too depressed for words.

In my time on the frontline of sportswriting, the closest you got to public admonition was if someone wrote to you (taking a deal of time and effort and usually deserving of a reply), knocked on the window of the press box and offered to debate you outside or recognised you as you collected your suitcase at an airport carousel and suggested, in front of your mates and his, that you were something of a twat.

These were usually non-threatening situations – though the letters could be spicy – which led to a reasoned discourse and an exchange of views. Whereas in those days the critics would just think your match reporting was hopeless and you might have an irrational dislike for one club/player or another, by now the major forms of abuse were misogynistic, on perceived sexual orientation, racism and cyber-stalking. It was horrible out there.

Still, I missed the nip and tuck of debate and let myself become entwined in many social media spats about politics I should have ignored, though I felt the need to defend my old profession (those who warranted defending). Had my condition made me more outrageous in my opinions and less bothered at who might be offended by them? I became angry at how the world was panning out and mortification at my own situation. When you were trapped in a body that did only half of what it used to, you felt 50 per cent less significant and 50 per cent more reactionary.

***

It was the stuff that had once been so basic and had become so infuriatingly bloody complex that made stroke recovery such a bastard.

I knew you shouldn't place your elbows on the table while you were eating – etiquette we learned from our parents. But when you'd had a brain infarction that severed the connect between shoulder blade and muscles and tried placing your bad forearm on a table while seated, it made up its own mind to slide back and come thrashing into your lap, threatening all manner of genital mayhem.

Just keeping my arm steady and balanced took all the strength I could muster and placed inordinate pressure on the top and front section of the shoulder, meaning I reluctantly let it slide to eat in some degree of comfort. Niceties would have to wait for less stressful times.

The same was true when I had done the considered number of steps to keep up an acceptable exercise regimen. Because the left leg was twice as heavy as the right – even with the aid of a strapping round the left ankle supposed to aid heel uplift – the shoulder, neck and hip felt the strain so every part of the body that was damaged combined to leave me mentally and physically imperfect.

Understandably, others may have thought I was taking too many breaks for the hell of it. More than once, I said out loud that if people picking up on my moments of insecurity had to endure for 15 minutes what I went through constantly, I might be treated with a greater degree of sympathy, though that too was a double-edged emotion.

Yes, I sought some degree of regard for my plight before that same sympathy became a bothersome inconvenience – one of the many paradoxes of the condition.

Someone wanted to raise you up, but you needed to do it – stand, walk, lift, cut – on your own and when seeking to explain why you declined offers of support, finding the right words wasn't easy. I'd make an indignant face and flap my right arm in a show of agitation and frustration. When Maureen aped these gestures, I found myself laughing rather than getting angry, a better way to be.

I wasn't alone, I knew that but equally no one who hadn't been in this state could properly appreciate the suffering and anxiety one felt, day in and day out.

Pauline, the NHS occupational therapist continuing my recovery at home, was insistent that I should use my uncooperative left hand to fulfil menial labour – picking up and using cutlery, turning on a tap, opening a cupboard, trying to prise a screw top from a carton of milk, to hold and control my electric toothbrush, wash, and brush my hair, do up a shirt button.

Only by repeating these tasks over and over with your bad 'un would the brain reconnect with the muscles, the muscles with the sinew, the sinew with the bone and all might one day be well. Sheer necessity and the desire not to spend half an hour slamming cupboard doors into your face, flailing at food in the fridge, dropping the toothbrush so that it buzzed around on the bathroom floor like a half-stunned insect and other potential disasters, often led one to take the easy way out and use the right.

It reached a stage where Pauline suggested I should put an oven mitt on my right hand simply to stop me trying to use it in the kitchen. Heaven forbid I was going to spend time walking around like Nigel Slater, a couple of breadsticks short of a picnic. I'd do it while Pauline was here but take it off the minute her car pulled out of the driveway.

My domestic arm and scapula improvement exercise programme consisted of straight arm pull downs using a resistance band, push-ups on a kitchen worktop, trying to get my left arm as straight as possible and put pressure on my wrist and shoulder proprioception, stretching my left arm straight and embedding the base of my palm on a ball against a wall to try to stop it from falling. Repeat and repeat and repeat.

I was poleaxed by a condition known as spasticity, a nasty side-effect of certain neurological conditions where the muscles contracted all at once. In my case, when my mouth, cheek and nose stiffened, my arm stiffened, when my arm stiffened, my leg stiffened and so on in a vicious circle.

This was triple infirmity, affecting movement and speech, the only cures for which were extensive physical therapy, certain medications and as something of a last resort, a range of Botox injections over an extended time frame.

These were designed to relax your rigid muscles and it was imperative to know which regions of the body required smaller or greater doses. The Botox usually took anywhere between ten days to a month to have any effect. To be honest, six weeks after my first round of ten injections around the shoulder, upper arm, leg and ankle in March 2024 I barely felt any benefit at all, which was a crushing setback.

The body was a remarkable thing but when it malfunctioned, especially after stroke, strange happenings did occur. For instance, if I had an itchy nose and could only rub it with my right hand, my left arm would spin up in rigid concert with the working hand. The same thing happened if I ran water on to my right hand: the left would spontaneously react as if it wanted some of the action.

There was something there, but it came at me in severe jolts, often accompanied by much cracking of joints in the shoulder blade area and stiffness of fingers and thumb where my knuckles would turn bright white and the hand acted like a claw, forming a death grip around anything I was attempting to hold on to.

And my left thumb would constantly want to turn inwards under the palm rather than extend itself fully so I could purchase properly when doing my standing or squatting press-ups. All that time in the hospital when my fingers and thumb wouldn't respond at all and now, they moved in dreaded concert at all the wrong times and into all the wrong places. It was like something out of a horror movie.

Manoeuvring my new stroller ought to have been reasonably easy but once more the left hand grabbed at the handle on that side, fixed itself into an uncomfortably rigid position and almost had to be prised off when I wanted a moment's relaxation.

My leg exercises, which included marching on the spot, were a doddle by comparison; the most acute physical pain I suffered was generated from the disconnected scapula through the elbow to the tips of my fingers. Of the three parts of my body I wanted to have back in painless service, the arm was the one that nagged the most.

The mouth still needed a lot of work as well. A speech therapist offered several tips, most of which involved stretching the skin away from my mouth, nose, and at the bottom of my eye to encourage a relaxation of the tightness across half of my face.

There were also exercises that largely encompassed sticking my tongue out at various angles, opening my eyes wide and at the same time grinning like a Cheshire cat. It was important to replicate the skin relaxing techniques on the working side of my face so the brain was reminded that the two parts should live in harmony.

I always did these tasks in private so as not to frighten the neighbours, the dog, or the horses from the stables at the bottom of the lane.

JOHN GORMAN

THE SCARS were varied and distinct. John Gorman pointed them out with a degree of pride mixed with resignation. The career signposts of this professional footballer were marked in the form of criss-crossing flesh wounds rather than anything you could regularly polish and display in a trophy cabinet.

Our conversation became a trifle more difficult when it came to discussing the blemishes you couldn't see but knew were there. That and the fact neither of us had the full cooperation of our mouth muscles and had to reach for a tissue after each slurp of coffee provided by the good people of the Hive Cafe, in Crowthorne.

'This bloody dribbling pisses you off, doesn't it?' John said. 'I'm like it all the fucking time.' We both got our noses covered in froth at that one.

John Gorman suffered his stroke six months after mine and had recovered more appreciably in the physical sense, even if he was eight years my senior. Like me, he had collapsed at home, upstairs, when he had just taken a shower. Like me, his left side was completely compromised.

His partner Denise was having breakfast downstairs and, upon hearing John yell something incomprehensible, called up, 'are you having a stroke?' She couldn't have been more prescient.

The flight of stairs was too narrow to manoeuvre a wheelchair, so the paramedics had to carry John down in their bare arms. The first stop was Frimley Park Hospital but the facilities there were not sufficient for his immediate needs, so he was taken to London for the requisite treatment. Like me, his recovery was steady but bloody tiresome.

When we met for the first time since his stroke, John was already cycling – despite one fall when his chain came loose – and was able to perform what passed as swimming, though he conceded it was more like floating balance sessions, but good for him. If I had tried to swim, I'd have sunk to the bottom in nanoseconds.

He suggested I seemed to be dealing with the emotional side a little better but perhaps I was more adept at hiding my concerns and hadn't had to otherwise deal with his resume of operations, repair jobs and general wear and tear from many years of football before being sideswiped by a stroke's destructive impact.

I had witnessed John's playing days as a left full-back of culture and dynamism, especially for Carlisle United during its brief flirtation with the big time, and at Tottenham Hotspur where he played in the same company as Glenn Hoddle, Osvaldo Ardiles, Ricardo Villa and Pat Jennings, to name but a few world-class performers.

We got to know each other well as he turned to coaching, firstly during his time at Swindon Town when the club was promoted to the Premier League with Hoddle as player/manager and Gorman running the operation from the bench. Glenn remained elegance personified on the pitch, the queen bee as the workers buzzed around.

When the idea of end-of-season play-offs in the Football League was first mooted in 1992, I used my considerable platform in the *Daily Mail* to vehemently oppose the suggestion that a team which completed the season in sixth place could ultimately be promoted when one finishing third would not. A season's entire labours should be the ultimate determination, not the lottery of a one-match shoot-out, was my firm contention.

Swindon's pulsating 4-3 victory over Leicester in the 1992/93 Wembley final (Swindon led 3-0 and were pegged back to 3-3, before Paul Bodin won a crazy match from the penalty spot), was persuasive evidence to the contrary.

I wouldn't be budged from my belief that the system should not reward a club with poorer results over nine months but accepted that occasions with the potential for a mass outbreak of destructive blood pressure ought to have a place in the sport's diary, and the play-offs became an annual enrichment to the football season.

Within days of Swindon's promotion, Hoddle agreed that the grass would be greener with Chelsea, he controversially departed, and Gorman was promoted to the manager's chair for what became an exacting, stressful season in the highest echelon.

Victories were few and far between, Swindon became everyone's favourite whipping boys and were eventually relegated – they did postpone the inevitable until the last two weeks of the season – having conceded 100 goals, an achievement unmatched in the competition's history. It was to their great credit that they didn't resort to nasty, niggling football even as their fate became inevitable.

When we reunited in the summer of 2024, John had recently returned to Swindon for a gathering of the boys of 1993 and was disappointed the emphasis on the occasion had been more on negative outcomes than cherishing the fact that a club of Swindon's limited resources had reached the Premier League at all.

'I told the MC that I wasn't too happy,' he said, and I suspected that in the circumstances, where anger at one's personal condition gave rise to uncharacteristic bouts of temper, the exchange had been deliciously fruity.

'It could have been much more upbeat, but it was great to see quite a few of the players from a time which meant so much to the club.'

When Hoddle was installed as England head coach in late 1996, he immediately called on Gorman to become his assistant once more, a job of pressure-cooker intensity. Trust in each other was vital as they utilised subtle differences in personality to draw the best from the nation's foremost talents in an unforgiving glare.

It may have been simplistic to suggest they were 'good cop, bad cop' though the players felt comfortable in John's company, believing he would not be as judgmental as Glenn, who was given to bouts of haughtiness that unnerved the hardiest professionals.

'I always knew how to approach Glenn and what to say to him, that was my great strength,' John said. 'I could almost twist him around my little finger. During a match, I'd make comments about certain players, he'd argue and then come round to my way of thinking. Tactically, Glenn was fantastic. He knew the game inside out.'

The most contentious moment of their three years with England came in the frenetic build-up to the 1998 World Cup in France. England had earned qualification with a redoubtable goalless draw in Italy and in the last of three friendlies before the tournament proper, drew 0-0 against Belgium.

At half time, brothers Gary and Phil Neville, the Manchester United full-backs were substituted and there was much nervous anticipation as the head coach prepared to announce who would be culled before the final 22-man squad was named.

As it turned out, Gary was selected and Phil omitted, though Phil subsequently insisted Gorman had told him he would be in the squad come what may, which aggravated his sense of grievance at being left out.

John refuted Phil's claim, clear in his mind he could not and would never have made such a promise and said only to the younger Neville that a good performance against the Belgians would almost certainly secure his place. As it was, he had a shocking 45 minutes.

Phil spent that evening in tears, while in the next room to his, Paul Gascoigne did rather more than simply cry when Hoddle told him he wasn't in the squad. He wrecked the joint.

The quarter-final loss to Argentina on penalties in the competition proper was a savage and controversial ending – David Beckham was sent off and endured horrific personal abuse for weeks on end – to a tournament which offered so much promise but left the nation unfulfilled.

When Hoddle was sacked from the England post over comments he was alleged to have made about people with disabilities, Gorman was told the FA wanted him to remain and help Howard Wilkinson as an interim partnership, but John's approach to football and that of the former Leeds manager were too markedly opposed for it to have worked for long.

And so began a peripatetic existence which saw him return to Tottenham (as Hoddle's assistant once more), before moves to Wycombe, Gillingham, Northampton, Southampton, Queens Park Rangers, Ipswich and MK Dons, when in 2012 he chose to retire – though you never officially 'retired' from football, you just didn't work in it full-time anymore.

And it was not as if John didn't have enough experience of tragedy, both in his personal and professional life before the seismic effects of a stroke clubbed him for six.

When he was trying to resuscitate Swindon after their Premier League relegation, the club's hugely popular physiotherapist Kevin Morris committed suicide – a loss that no one could properly fathom.

At Wycombe, where he was appointed manager in 2005, the club finished the season tenth in League Two, and embarked on a 21-match unbeaten run at the start of the following campaign. Behind the scenes, John's wife Myra was losing her battle with cancer and the club, which accepted £500,000 from Nottingham Forest for their star striker Nathan Tyson and offered only a fraction of it for him to spend, relieved him of his post, suggesting they were being compassionate. Naturally he didn't see it that way.

***

Like Noel Blake, the progress of John's protégés in professional football gave him immense satisfaction. He had loved coaching some of the finest players of the late 20th and early 21st centuries, recalling as an example, times when he would stay back after official England training and help Michael Owen perfect his finishing.

There were the training sessions he used to hold on an Astroturf pitch in north London attended by such wide-eyed kids as Declan Rice, now the heartbeat of Arsenal and England, and the Everton striker Dominic Calvert-Lewin.

When a 20-year-old Matt O'Riley was released by Fulham, John took him for one-to-one coaching sessions before recruiting him for MK Dons. He made 49 appearances in Buckinghamshire before being snapped up by Glasgow Celtic – John's first club and lifetime love – for £1.5 million where he won the Player of the Year,

Young Player of the Year and Players' Player of the Year awards at the end of the 2023/24 season.

He should have played for Denmark – the country of his mother's birth – in the 2024 European Championship but manager Kasper Hjulmand suggested Scottish football wasn't of an adequate standard in which to judge a prospective international and left O'Riley to kick his heels. (Hjulmand resigned after Denmark's defeat in the round of 16.)

'That was hugely disrespectful to the Scottish game,' John said. 'I know that Matt and his father especially were really upset. Matt is a terrifically gifted midfield player with a great left foot, much like Glenn [Hoddle]. When I told his dad that Matt reminded me of him, he loved that.'

O'Riley would move from Celtic to English Premier League Brighton & Hove Albion for £25 million in the close season, only for his career there to be crudely interrupted after two weeks by a brutal tackle in a League Cup tie against Crawley Town.

It was symptomatic of the relations that John Gorman had built with so many players down the years that the pair would text on a weekly basis to keep up with each other's progress on the medical front. The 50-year age gap made no difference.

In early November, after ankle surgery and extensive recuperation, O'Riley returned to the front line, was called on as a substitute against the champions Manchester City and, demonstrating that the period out had cost him none of his intuitive skill and poise, promptly scored the winning goal to inflict City's fourth consecutive defeat, an unwanted and historic blemish on Pep Guardiola's stewardship of the club which would soon become much worse.

***

Glenn Hoddle was, not unsurprisingly, head of the queue to call when news of John's stroke broke. 'It wasn't something I wanted the world to know about, well you didn't did you?' he said. 'But the football grapevine did its job and soon the messages were flooding in.'

That was not surprising as John had lost none of his cheerful approachability and players remembered the significant impact he had had on their careers. As he rummaged around at the Hive coffee shop for some cushions so I could perch more comfortably on the wooden benches, it struck me that a basic decency had been the hallmark of his man-management.

But beneath that soft Scottish lilt beat a determined heart. When he listed the cornucopia of injuries and operations necessary to keep him playing, I struggled to keep up, so I hope he might be forgiving if I missed a hernia op or two. I wasn't particularly surprised when he told me that as a ten-year-old in Glasgow he had once fallen from a building and was fortunate to survive the impact.

'I was always good at recovery because I'd had that many injuries I perfected it – and there were some terrible ones as well. At Carlisle I had stomach problems and did both my knees,' he recalled.

He suffered from Gilmore's groin, which is explained on the Top Doctors website as 'a condition that typically affected footballers who will get pain if they twist and turn and kick many long balls or dead balls. There could be pain after exercising and though they may recover temporarily the pattern will get worse and can come on suddenly during a game. The deterioration is gradual eventually resulting in the groin giving out'. John needed several injections to keep playing, probably more than he should have been given.

Soon after his move to Tottenham, he suffered a severely pulled muscle in his left leg 'I've still got the hole here,' which he proudly pointed out. He'd bend crosses in with the outside of his right foot rather than use his left – 'just to get through them'. He was patched up and sent out to play more times than management had a right to expect.

If John thought his later years may have afforded some relaxation, in 2015 he was told he needed a pacemaker fitted as every so often his heart would stop beating for ten to 15 seconds, something he had never known. Then came the biggest hit of the lot. 'I dealt with all those injuries for so many years and then this,' he said.

'The stroke was the worst because as long as the pacemaker still worked, I was alive. Stroke was so bloody wearing. It was something you needed great mental resilience to deal with. I needed to take so many pills, for blood pressure, then blood thinners which caused all sorts of bruising if I knocked into anything, and worst was the water tablets because they made you want to pee all the time.

'It was easy to become demoralised, but I was determined to stay as strong as possible. People assumed I was back to normal because I looked normal, but I wasn't really.'

***

Over the years, John had built up a considerable reputation as an artist and, thankfully, the effects of a stroke have not diminished his ability to draw with real panache. He specialises in caricatures, especially those of sporting personalities. His work has helped raise funds for several charities.

I mentioned on one coffee morning that I'd spoken to Noel Blake as part of this enterprise and by the time of our next date he presented me with a drawing of Noel which features in this book's photo assembly.

A YEAR BACK IN THE WILD

SUNDAY, 1 SEPTEMBER 2024, was the first anniversary of my hospital discharge. Most of the intervening days had passed without a deal of incident to the point of crushing boredom – I had better get used to that as improvement stalled, which provoked much fretting.

The goodwill messages had dried up, many of those who promised they would come and see me hadn't shown, and of those who had, one visit was obviously sufficient without the need for a follow-up. I got that. There was a fine line between doing a good turn and then over-egging the goodness.

The last thing I wanted to do was ring people in my contacts book to let them know how I was getting on, that was too much like a craving for attention. But there were names in there I had expected might have at least sent a note if nothing else. Maybe they simply hadn't heard of my dice with death.

On the plus side, only a single accident had befallen me in that year, not bad for a clod. When turning too sharply having prised the final three articles of clothing and their pegs from the washing line without dropping anything, I stubbed my left foot against a slightly raised paving stone in the back garden, flew sideways and ended up spreadeagled across the patio table, taking out a laundry basket full of clean clothes as I fell.

Maureen was at work and the dog was too busy trying to climb a tree to interrupt a couple of fornicating pigeons to take any notice. After much heaving, grunting and muttered expletives, I managed to haul myself to near vertical, regained my composure and wrote it off as an avoidable mishap. There were bound to be more in the future.

My exercise regime remained reasonably constant, though it was important to add bits and pieces to interrupt monotonous repetition (there were only so many ways you could replicate marching like a soldier on the parade ground while balancing your right hand on a kitchen top).

For the most part I had done away with the stick indoors. Walking barefoot remained treacherous as the toes on my left foot would often curl under and become trapped in the carpet pile, leading to forward stumbles with the potential for calamity.

Maureen had placed resistance bands on the wooden surrounds of the upstairs landing for my leg bends and stretches (no point trying to tiptoe past them as she spotted everything anyway), another at the bottom of the bannister for arm extensions and one by the side of the bed so that I could fully extend each leg before falling asleep in the hope it would reduce potential for night-time cramps.

These were agony enough when you could get to your feet properly but just imagine how awful they were to endure when one leg had little muscle strength to begin with and then began to seize up. I hopped around like Long John Silver on speed.

Maureen said from the start that I had to deal with any complications as best I could alone rather than take the easy way out of summoning assistance. Tough love perhaps but essential in forcing you to figure out how best to help yourself.

At my wife's insistence, too, the seat in the shower was returned to the NHS and I was able to reach 90 per cent of my body from a standing position (below the knees remained an impossible stretch).

This required planting both feet as solidly as possible on a wet surface, grasping the bar with my sometime rigid, sometime flapping left hand and both washing, rinsing and reaching for the towel on the floor outside with my right. The daily squat routines were coming in tremendously handy, but it was all a bloody inconvenience.

***

Even in the final days in Thatcham I had the cardboard urine receptacles lined up – like a fairground coconut shy – in case a bedtime accident loomed. They didn't leave me any to take home, but Maureen had thought ahead and bought a reusable plastic container to have at my own bedside.

It looked very chic by comparison to the 'here's one you can make with three sheets of brown paper and some sticky-back plastic' Blue Peter hospital variety, and even had a handle, which was very 21st century.

The basic requirements were the same, the minute you sensed a stirring, you lifted the receptacle into place, balanced it between your thighs, placed your willy inside as far as it would go and then did the business. The trouble would invariably arrive in the aftermath.

The bottle had a screw-on top, held into place by a plastic ring fixed around one of the grooves at its neck. Once you'd delivered, keeping legs tight together, there was a quick grab for the handle with your right hand to keep the thing upright. Then you had to reposition and replace the top with the same, lone good hand.

Unfortunately, the screw-on top had a mind of its own and would spring into action, threatening severe discomfort in the genitalia. If it missed your balls, your appendage was in danger, and woe betide if you hadn't yet shaken any excess pee into the bottle.

You couldn't do much other than pray splashes of supplementary urine weren't deposited across your legs or worse still, on to the bed clothes. All of this often occurred in the dark and with a full bottle still perched precariously between kneecaps that were prone to uncontrollable wobbles.

It didn't take long for us (Maureen) to decide that this contraption had to go and as happened in the final days in the neuro rehab ward, I had to learn to contain any initial urgings, unwind myself from the covers, grab my stick, stretch my legs (not too wide), totter the dozen or so strides to the toilet, slump down on to the invariably freezing seat and relieve myself like any normal human being.

***

A major downside of the faculty reorganisation was the staggering impact it had on your emotions, unseen by others but acutely felt by the patient.

One minute you were a placid mute, the next you raged at some minor inconvenience – someone slamming the fridge door, scraping a Brillo pad aggressively on a saucepan, the dog reacting to two pigeons going at it on a fence post – before breaking down for some reason or another you couldn't put your finger on.

I had always been a bit on the sensitive side, much like my mum, an East ender who yearned to be a singer until the Second World War intervened, the grimy block of flats she called home was bombed, her life was turned upside down and ambitions were brutally dashed.

She never quite had the life she *really* wanted and lived too much of it on an emotional precipice. She took everything to heart did Peggy and I was very much the same, never as self-confident as my rise on the journalistic ladder might have suggested.

Tears came easily, especially when it came to sentimental movies. I don't know how many times I'd watched *ET, the Extra-Terrestrial,* but when ET hugged Elliot before departing for his home planet, I felt them forming. The same was true when Henry Fonda embraced his daughter Jane (they were estranged in real life) at the climax to *On Golden Pond*. Best to keep me away from *It's a Wonderful Life* at Christmas.

Certain music pieces got me where it hurt, including everything by the master John Williams. I could have listened to his compositions all day. Any song performed by Clifford T Ward, James Taylor, David Gates, Crosby, Stills and Nash, Karen Carpenter or Beth Nielsen Chapman would elevate the spirits and send me into uncontainable emotional shudders.

***

The front patio, though recently re-cemented, still had enough kinks in the stonework to require careful planting of the stick to make sure it didn't suddenly jerk from my grasp.

And moving out for a regular walk up and down the lane meant pushing my stroller through the loose gravel of our drive – another assault course to be tackled with maximum concentration. The stroller had no suspension, the front wheels would twist and turn and if you happened to push it over a manhole cover, the shuddering felt as if you were trying to hold on to a pneumatic drill.

My daily step routine had increased to a minimum of 2,000 but late in July 2024, when the weather had taken a turn for the better and I ought to have preferred the shade, I managed consecutive days of over 3,000 and then a magical 5,000.

The latter was on the first occasion I'd driven myself to the gym in Wokingham and parked in one of its disabled bays which were, in an act of cruel perversion, located nearer to the entrance of an amusement arcade than the gymnasium itself. The din from inside – machine and human in discordant harmony – was an aggravating distraction when total concentration was required.

There were no helpful gradients so I could push my stroller along without having to lift it over a kerb. And why couldn't they find a level surface on which to place the disabled spots? All the paving work was absurdly uneven, perfect for trapping an unwieldy leg. Bloody stupid.

The Monday sessions in the wellbeing section of the gym were an hour effectively spent though. Each of us in the two o'clock group had a different reason for attending, be it breathing difficulties, a desire for greater energy, to ease mental discomfiture or in my case to generate increased strength and flexibility in my legs and arms.

This required at least a 20-minute spell on a treadmill, leg stretches, backward peddling on the exercise bike, and by yanking on a pulley, trying to replicate the arm movement a skier utilised when setting off on a slalom.

The first-floor treadmills overlooked the local Burger King and often Brian – who had to carry a small box across his shoulder attached to breathing tubes – and I offered a running commentary on the shapes and sizes of those who appeared unconcerned that huge brown parcels of fast food in the early afternoon may have hastened a descent into type two diabetes.

We spotted Whoppers a mile off. And why did they all wear ill-fitting track suits that were either sickly pink or lime green? Oh well, it helped the two of us to pass the time.

As punishment for these sins of sarcasm, the lift at the gym didn't work for the best part of three months in spring and summer, which meant that by the time we reached the first floor via two flights of stairs, most of us felt we'd completed a full session already.

On the first day of August, I decided on another first step, taking myself to Tesco to run a couple of errands. Loading and unloading my stroller was not an easy exercise, made more difficult by the tendency of the boot door to suddenly release upwards, threatening to knock me off my feet.

I had to sidestep my way to the side of the car and slowly lift the door off the latch at full stretch before stepping back the other way, and prising the stroller, one handed, out of the car.

It then required to be assembled into shape and I had to dance around the thing to get it pointed in the right direction. I needed some cash but just as I inserted my card into the machine – all this single-handed don't forget – the wallet slipped from my grasp and the other cards tumbled to the pavement. Was there a Good Samaritan in the vicinity? Not a chance.

I went into one of my deepest squats, leaning against the cash machine for extra purchase, managed to pick the cards up one by one and replaced them in their allotted slots in the wallet. My heart pounded, beads of sweat formed on my brow but at least I retrieved them all without anyone coshing me over the head.

I collected my prescription – a new batch of blood pressure pills was particularly timely – the Jakemans' cough and throat menthol lozenges which had become a daily indulgence to moisten my impossibly dry mouth and a couple of bags of treats for the dog, before repeating the rigmarole in the car park, chucking everything on to the passenger seat, folding up the stroller, picking it up and levering it back into the boot between huge intakes of breath as no one took a blind bit of notice.

I didn't think I'd be returning anytime soon.

Costco in Reading was a challenge, too. Whoever designed the traffic flow in these places needed a slap: cars came at you well above the speed limit from every direction, and pedestrian crossings were ignored or non-existent.

The one uptick was the height of the Costco trolleys, perfect for my stride pattern and I didn't have to lean forward like I had to reach the handles on my stroller but could stand tall, as the physios had instructed for improved general posture.

The only thing was, trying to replicate the left leg marching lift, my knee would consistently hit the wire surrounds of the trolley, causing much wincing but – unusually – I kept my emotions in decent check and didn't subject passing patrons to a fusillade of expletives.

***

One schoolboy error I committed early on after returning home was coming over a bit too smug about any minor domestic achievement.

Vacuum the downstairs rooms once, do the dusting or hang out and retrieve a load of washing (the clothes pegs had a mind of their own and it was a miracle I wasn't blinded as they pinged from my grasp), it was then (Maureen's) expectation that I could do them all the time.

The problem was each task was horribly exhausting. Therapeutically, these chores were meant to enhance a sense of accomplishment, but in the first instance I constantly struggled to lift my left foot high enough to prevent the vacuum cord becoming entangled around it, presenting all kinds of perspiration-inducing perils.

There was a foot pedal on the right-hand side of the vacuum cleaner I had to release for the middle section to be unlocked and allow me to push the thing around. But I couldn't simultaneously hold the vacuum and lift my right leg off the floor as that meant teetering backwards, so I had to move sidestep fashion for a wall to lean against to carry out a relatively straightforward function.

It wasn't so much that the dusting was difficult – but my left arm would still not fully extend, the fingers curled up when I wanted them to spread and the duster would become scrunched up instead of flat. Picking up and replacing picture frames and dusting beneath them with one hand was not the doddle it might have appeared to able-bodied brethren.

Maureen was soon fed up with the exaggerated sighing – my new favourite word 'buggeration' was earning considerable overtime – as I plodded around the house, so it became preferable to try to complete this menial labour as best I could when she was at work.

The same was true of the loading and unloading of the dishwasher. Here I was in my physio/OT pomp, all manner of carrying, bending, stretching, reaching and placing, though almost all of it with my good right hand. I wasn't brave or foolhardy enough to attempt any of this with my left, especially when glassware was involved.

I did use it to pull the various compartments from the machine which required squatting and shifting before leaning against the refrigerator for safety purposes. Of course, the minute I slumped sideways and brushed against the control panel on the fridge door, buzzing noises were emitted. I had inadvertently activated the Power Freeze or the Child Lock which now needed re-setting (if only I knew where the manual was).

Finally came the toughest bit, transporting the contents of an unpacked dishwasher to their various locations in the kitchen cabinets. I got my head around the fact that this would probably take a good ten trips, what with the dishwasher being in the conservatory, with a left and right turn before I could cross the kitchen floor.

The cutlery didn't pose much of a problem, but our plates and bowls were heavy and I couldn't carry more than two at one time, hence all the back and forth (manna for my daily step count).

The glasses were an accident waiting to shatter. I had a bit of a wheeze – placing them upside down on a carving board, which I slid towards me and picked up one handed, steadying myself, inhaling deeply, hoping I didn't kick the fridge with a flailing left foot, and setting off with pitter-pat strides towards the cabinets.

As of writing this chapter, I hadn't dropped a single glass, though what the entire process had done for my blood pressure, God alone knew.

As the ironing board and iron were set up in the living room and my shirts placed across the top, I naturally assumed my wife was about to burst into action. Her ironing skill was legendary. When the whole shebang was still there the next day and the one after, the penny dropped.

'But I'm bound to scald myself,' I wailed. 'Get on with it,' came the response. So, I did. Nowhere near perfect, needing to lean across the board to keep the shirts from riding up, leaving too many unsightly creases, but at least I got there. The next time, the number of shirts had trebled. Bloody domestics.

***

Maureen said she was going to leave me. Not permanently I hasten to add (though the thought had probably crossed her mind more than once!) but for a three-day work conference in the west country. That would leave just me and the dog to mooch around in the house. The lingering fear was obviously that I might fall and be unable to get myself up again.

I had eschewed the purchase of one of those alarms you could wear around your neck or wrist, thinking that they looked ridiculous and only served to emphasise my embarrassment at infirmity.

I was now able to shower, shave and dress myself so long as I took my time, I owned a pair of sturdy Skechers which were fastened with straps rather than laces and I could attach my ankle harness to them without too much stress.

We had long advanced from the days when Maureen would oversee my rise and descent on the stairs, so all I really needed was a decent food supply, the key to the gin cabinet, the TV remote and Bob was your uncle.

A couple of meals for one were sufficient, and my only concern was the bending and retrieving of them from the oven, which necessitated extravagant sideways shuffling around the door and much concern over dropping the contents on the floor, but I made it and the house was still standing upon my wife's return.

I counted this as a particularly notable achievement, that in certain circumstances I could reasonably take care of myself.

***

Arlo developed an infection between the first and second toes of his front right paw and was constantly licking it. Initially, I administered apple cider vinegar diluted in water but that didn't work – mostly because I couldn't hold his paw in the bowl with my shaking left hand – and next some antiseptic skin care which failed to prevent further licking.

I took myself off to Pets at Home to purchase a protective shoe to cover the paw so at least the wound might settle. Now came a task for which I was patently ill equipped, unwrapping the Velcro from round the shoe, trying to insert his paw into it with one hand and reattaching the Velcro into place so that it would stay on for a while at least.

What a palaver. Once more, my left arm was not stable enough to hold on to the paw he kept trying to drag away from me. After about ten minutes of struggle, I got enough of his furry leg inside to attempt to fasten it into place. The Velcro had a mind of its own and kept sticking either to my skin hair or bits of the shoe it wasn't meant to.

By this time, I had to get on to the floor to try to get some purchase but that failed as my left leg buckled and kneed him twice on the side of his face. I just yanked the thing off and threw it across the living room. And yes, I swore.

At least I was down on the ground so I could go through my regular floor exercise programme, which was nothing like Olga Korbut's in 1972. It involved bridges, knee rolls, leg stretches, left arm pointing upwards with elbow straight (if possible) and as far behind me as was bearable and, lastly, laughable attempts at push-ups because the fingers of my left hand kept curling under, causing me to lose balance and list heavily to port.

Once the regime was completed to a general state of exhaustion, then came the arduous task of getting myself back up on to the sofa. I had to climb to my knees in a position perfect for prayer (head buried in the sitting cushion for purchase) draw my right leg to a 45° angle and then push up for all my worth, at the same time spinning my body around so when (if) I landed on the cushion, I was facing in the right direction.

The dog was limping around me, desperately trying to pull his paw out of the protective shoe that Maureen had since managed to attach to his leg. Even with her two hands it required much grunting and exasperation.

The noise of the Velcro brought back a memory of life on the ward I thought I'd buried in my darker recesses.

I was one of the fortunate ones who had never been incontinent and thus was spared the night-time visits from nurses with lamps attached to their headgear who would shuffle between beds seeking out those who had wet themselves. There was nothing a startled patient could do about it, as the Velcro was ripped apart, the nappy removed, a new one attached, he was settled and tried to fall back to sleep. But it was the noise, that awful noise that resounded. I didn't think I'd ever be able to hear it without thinking of men who pissed in the night.

***

Evening meal time became rather predictable when it came to the choice of food. So much depended on what I could properly swallow and ingest. Maureen and I had enjoyed the occasional fillet steak (medium rare) pre-stroke but that was when I was able to relish the flavour.

Now, I would first need it to be cut into chewable pieces. Then I'd have to play around with it in my mouth and swallow – usually with an enormous gulp – without being able to appreciate the tenderness of the meat. This was a sacrilegious waste of prime, pricey food.

I attempted the cutting bit myself, but my left arm was still largely unbalanced, and my fingers would so manically grip the knife (I was left-handed, remember)

I couldn't turn my wrist into a position where I could successfully slice through anything that required a degree of to-and-fro effort.

I couldn't bear the thought of someone else having to cut up meals for me for the foreseeable future so we'd plump for the easier options – a piece of fish or pasta (though not spaghetti because I couldn't suck it properly with half a mouth and refused to have it chopped – culinary barbarism). Chicken was relatively chewable. Anything with eggs usually went down a treat.

Even green salads posed a problem because lettuce, rocket or any other leaf would get lodged in the back of my throat, causing a wild coughing explosion at the dinner table.

The upside was I didn't put away as much as I had done before and thus dropped the weight I'd gained during the months I took out the frustrations of unemployment by eating significantly greater portions than I should. I didn't snack as much either so even from bad situations, good things could happen.

If we went out socially, I'd choose the menu option that would cause me least distress and spare us the embarrassment of restaurant patrons staring at this apparently sane man getting in such a bloody state eating a simple meal.

I'm afraid they had to get used to the sound of cutlery clanging on the floor when I tried to pick up a knife or fork with my left hand and usually sent one or other and often both spinning through the air.

***

It dawned on me around the time of this special being-at-home anniversary that I'd completely forgotten what it felt like to walk properly. Imagine that. My brain had still not mended well enough for me to be able to place one foot in front of the other as a natural movement.

Everything was contrived, having to use an armrest, to reach back for a wall to pull myself up, then balance, choose which foot I should place forward first (it should have been the right, but sometimes I'd cheat) before setting off with a general sense of direction towards my target.

There were the days when my left foot felt impossibly heavy, it got stuck and I momentarily panicked. These were difficult moments, the dread that I had peaked and wouldn't get much better. I was doing all the physio, the marching, the knee-lifting, the bending, the toe uncurling and yet nothing felt different.

Trying to get my left arm to straighten at the elbow took every ounce of my willpower and it refused point blank to cooperate, or at least I could keep it there for a few seconds before it was too painful and landed sharply back in my lap. My left wrist kept wanting to adopt the Larry Grayson position, which was not the desired look.

My left hand was permanently darker and more purplish in appearance than my right; and the tips of the fingers of that hand were unremittingly cold, as if the blood flow stopped at the knuckles. My left foot was forever puffed up (especially at night) and its toes stubbornly refused to straighten. It seemed to me that stroke had me in a grip it wouldn't loosen.

Come on brain, I was doing my bit, now it was your turn. Have some pity on me, offer me a break, show me a sign this wouldn't go on forever. I couldn't face that.

I tried not to let anyone in on my self-flagellation because it wouldn't have done any good. It was best to keep any demons where they couldn't be seen. Even writing this stuff was getting bloody hard, a contemplation of more miserable days to come, the extended hopelessness of physical infirmity.

One day maybe it would all fall back into place and this insufferable misery would be over.

***

While trying to restore some sense of normality to your life, all the time lurked a real fear of a second stroke and how that would completely poleaxe you. Anytime I sensed the onset of a headache, I rushed as quickly as I could to fetch a couple of paracetamols. I would just sit and close my eyes, praying that it would go away.

If the right-hand side of my body kept up a decent degree of functionality, I could at least live a tolerable existence.

But what if I should pull a muscle – such as they were – in my right leg, overtax my right arm or hurt my right cheek? I needed to be extra vigilant to protect the parts of my body which still retained some vigour and flexibility otherwise I'd be at a complete loss.

My oft-blinking left eye occasionally misted over so that vision became impaired and irregular, much to my consternation. I was doing all I could to lead a more simplistic existence to avoid potential accidents, but I needed to press on with vigour or face inevitable and damaging stagnation.

This meant living a partial life, neither quite one thing nor the other. It was horrendous, but if it remained my truth, there was no other recourse but to accept it and endeavour to fight on.

JUSTIN TIME

SOUTHEND-ON-SEA. THE very name evoked something mystical, of childhood, adolescence, newspaper rounds, swims in the sea, pink rock, Rossi's ice cream, cockles, winkles, first dates, first rejections, first alcohol, packs of five Park Drive cigarettes, work and play. There were no such emotions in a hospital ward, only striving, frustration and a horrifying state of inconsequence.

Shut away for four months, one's mind pondered many things, most of them from the dim and distant past, where everything had seemed so colourful and ultimately rewarding. Faces from those days would return very clearly, working relationships, atmospheres and the joys of being whole.

For me, this meant periods spent reflecting on Southend United, my hometown football club. I had been back to the old place (about to become a city) three months before my stroke, to attend a reunion of the Dave Smith boys of 1977, when the team played bold and stylish football and friendships were formed which time apart had not diminished.

A few of us had been to a ramshackle Roots Hall that afternoon, to watch the current team play rather poorly and then reconvened in the evening at a bowls club (showing our age) to distil old memories, tell each other how good we looked and believe it, before insisting we would do it all again one day.

There was a particular picture from that night of four of us, Micky Laverick, Colin Morris, and Derrick Parker – players from that era, all northern lads – and myself, the cub reporter and local boy, which particularly resonated and not just because I was standing up.

We formed a WhatsApp group, and it was a horrible moment to have to tell them a few weeks later that I was now confined to a hospital bed. Their messages were full of the kind of inspirational support I desperately needed. They were good lads, the sort of sturdy, resolute people in which their part of the country specialised.

I wondered if the Southend United of today could boast such characters and I was hopeful it could, albeit that the club had fallen on depressing times, so much so I likened it to a stroke victim, for it had clearly suffered a brain bleed and its future was about as unpredictable as any human with the condition.

Those many decades ago, though the club had to function as a legitimate entity, I recalled scant focus in the paper on its finances save for usual player sales and purchases, ticket prices, the annual general meeting, or bargains to be found on washing machines and refrigerators at well-heeled director Howard Stone's electrical stores on the London Road.

United seemed to run itself astutely, offered stability, paid its bills and avoided confrontation with the tax man. As the years had passed, a decline and fall gathered such inexorable pace I wondered if it might lose all functionality before I did. The talk seemed of nothing else but stalled property development plans, unpaid wages, players flitting in and out, dangerous brinkmanship.

A pocket summation of the story was told in a fine piece in *The Guardian* by Tim Burrows published exactly a year after my collapse.

'I first heard the roar of the Roots Hall crowd from my nan's back garden two streets from the ground,' Burrows wrote. 'By 1998, when I was old enough to take myself to matches, there was an air of apathy after consecutive relegations, but in the following decade, the club briefly climbed back up to the Championship.

'In November 2006, Southend played Manchester United in the League Cup [a match that I covered for *The Times,* coincidentally]. Unbelievably, they won – beating a team that included Wayne Rooney and Cristiano Ronaldo – 1-0 thanks to a sublime free-kick from 25 yards out by Freddy Eastwood.

'For many fans, it remains the greatest day in the club's history and many still boast of Southend's 100 per cent record against United, that being the first and only time the two teams met.'

Burrows then explained that Southend chairman Ron Martin came up with a plan to move the club from Roots Hall to Fossetts Farm. The first planning application for the new 22,000-seater stadium, with hotel, conference facilities, restaurants, shops and residences, was made in 2000 but wasn't approved by the local council until January 2007.

'Fans packed the council's public gallery and sang with joy after 13 of 16 committee members voted for the move. When Martin appeared outside the chamber where the meeting had been held, they started singing in unison, "There's only one Ron Martin." That euphoric feeling did not last.'

Indeed, it did not. The Fossetts plan seemed trapped in permanent abeyance, Martin remained as chairman through a protracted period of on-field stagnation and off-field atrophy. Every year the levels of hatred towards him in the club's fanbase grew more menacing. There were protests outside his home. After innumerable High Court appearances, last-ditch rescues and stays of execution, one day something would have to give. I felt their pain.

The team somehow managed, under head coach Kevin Maher, to keep the good ship Shrimper afloat, but it was severely listing and while Martin stayed on the bridge, appeared ultimately doomed. He clung on limpet fashion. What could prise him away?

***

I was born in Rochford, lived in Leigh-on-Sea my first 21 years and joined the *Southend Evening Echo* as a trainee sports reporter in 1974, at the age of 16. As I gained experience, I was let loose covering Southend, first at youth team and reserve level and eventually the first team, then in the old Fourth Division of the Football League.

Never had I imagined that the club would disappear from the league as happened in 2021 when they were relegated to what became known as the National League (it used to be the Conference).

I hadn't been involved intimately with United for many years but that didn't stop me from caring. Many hours of boredom in isolation were spent picking through the club's litany of misadventure. A rescue mission was required but did anyone (or group of people) have the finance, daring and savvy to rid the club of its owner and point it towards a sustainable future? A group called COSU (Custodians of Southend United) stepped forward.

Justin Rees was the front man and hardly your anticipated superhero: an Australian raised in the Blue Mountains west of Sydney, New South Wales – about as far removed in breathtaking beauty as Sydney Opera House was from Southend Pier. Justin's desire for a low profile was never likely to be successful, given that, in Southend at least, he was venerated as a dragon slayer. A dinkum St George.

And yet until he read a short piece on the BBC website in 2022, he'd never heard of the place. 'It was an impulse, pure and simple,' he said. 'It wasn't like "hey I want to buy a football team". I read the piece, was intrigued and decided to go down the rabbit hole. I contacted the broker listed in the article, left a message and three days later my phone rang. It was like "oh shit, he's called back".

'I wasn't aware of the club's history and how far it had fallen. I'd been living back in Australia for the past 13 years, so it wasn't as though the story was on the news every day. I hadn't looked at any other clubs and didn't even know if I wanted to go through with it, but I was in Spain for a break and three days later I caught a flight to Southend, met with Ron Martin, and John Still (United's head of football) and I was hooked.

'I knew then that this was definitely what I wanted to do but it needed quite a while to figure out how to do it and whether I could afford to do it. I just fell into it. I didn't look around to see if any other clubs were available, I sized up the opportunity, fell for it and became fixated on how to save Southend. And I knew it needed to be saved.

'Time wasn't necessarily the problem, I'd sold a previous business, I wasn't working; in my head I was retired – I wasn't going to work anymore, just live a more relaxed life at home. I was enjoying it, I was present in conversations and being the best version of myself whereas in my previous work life I was always distracted and not really there.

'I was happier, healthier, I was reading classic books and now, since the Southend business began, I'd read probably four pages of a book because I couldn't concentrate. It became very evident how important the club was. I really felt that, but I couldn't figure out financially how to do it without risking being bankrupt myself. There was no point in saving it and then being in the same position Ron [Martin] was three years later. I knew I couldn't go into it if I couldn't see a way out of it which ultimately led to the consortium being formed.

'It was a "heart first" process so it took several months to figure out how to do it [save the club] and part of that process was to recognise I couldn't do it by myself and wouldn't want to. It was a new industry for me, so the consortium was the answer, doing it with help from a bunch of people who shared the same vision.

'I didn't want the story to centre on me but because the takeover process was so long, I became the focus. If we'd made our offer on one day, Ron had accepted it the next and signed on the dotted line there and then, there wouldn't have been all this stress. But we trod water for a year.

'During that period, we weren't really transforming the place, but just paid the wages and kept the lights on. And because the process was so prolonged and involved, I developed a real bond with the fans, they realised we had gone the extra mile just to get the deal done. Since the takeover, we had been a lot quieter, trying to give everyone space to breathe. Then of course we were criticised for not communicating well enough.

'The longer we were in the process the tougher it was to stay in, but it would have been equally tough to walk away. Some people thought we were idiots and just paying Ron's bills for him but if we'd walked, a year of my life and a lot of my money would have gone down the drain. At least we achieved our purpose.

'As soon as my name got out there, fans were reaching out saying "please, please, please save us". It was always going to be hard once they knew who you were. Only if you believed in the value of saving a football club, did anything else make any sense.

'Once I'd started to meet people, the motivation to help simply increased. Southend as a club was big enough that we could dream of promotion and days at Wembley, but small enough to feel very much like a local community club. I felt viscerally connected to the town. I knew lots of the fans by name, knew the local landlords, the local coffee shops, the charities. We were not a club like Wealdstone or Maidenhead, with every respect. We could dream of bigger days ahead.'

On the *Shrimpercast* podcast with another former *Echo* reporter Bernie Friend in October 2024, Justin joined Tom Arnold, a fellow COSU member and offered insight as to their motivation, something they never believed was misplaced. 'We bought the club with lots of old debt, but we knew that that was part of the deal,' Justin said. 'The club had lost about £2 million a season and we think we'll lose £1.7million this year.

'We had assumed around 7,300 average crowds, right now that's looking pretty good, but bizarre for the National League [where the 2024 average was 2,400]. We felt there would be a post-transaction bounce in attendance levels, but it's been higher than we expected and allowed us to put more money into the playing squad. But there's still a long way to go. At the first board meeting someone said, "Let's try to lose £1.6 million this year." My response was, "What sort of bloody business is this?"'

***

So, Southend United would be bleeding for some while yet. 'We came into this with our eyes open,' Tom Arnold said. 'It was our intention to reduce losses slowly to a stage where the club would be sustainable and run itself, but that was going to take a lot of work and external revenue. Where we are now is where we thought we would be.

'The fans were doing their bit, it wasn't as if we could say "let's get to 13,000 crowds" and all our problems would be solved. The real dents would be made when we could bring on services like 4G pitches that could be rented out to the public, ultimately a new East Stand would be a real game-changer, spending money to make truly new money. We wanted to drive towards breaking even but not all of that could come from the same match-going fans, there was only so much you could ask of them.

'We were trying to maximise our appeal to local business which was going well because it helped us pay for improvements that obviously we would have been paying for otherwise.

'Who knew what could happen in the future, but we were prepared for each one of the three or four scenarios we had painted. What hadn't changed was that we needed £20 million to do what we wanted at Roots Hall and at the training ground.

'When we first signed this deal in October 2023, we looked at each other and said, "Do we have the money to cover the initial £1.7 million losses every year?" Now we had to find another £8 million – we needed to be creative and not be running around simply looking for pots of gold from the bank.'

What also mattered was the owners seeing beyond each Saturday's result as either the start of another crisis or the end of the last one. Of course, supporters lived from week to week, emotions soared and fell in equal part but this was an extended process, one which might take years to complete.

At least there was now a genuine sense of leadership and hope. Kieran Maguire, one of the foremost authorities on finance in British football posted a tweet on 24 July, when the ownership finally changed hands, which said, 'It's official. The 'Wrong' Martin reign of brinkmanship and appalling management at Southend United is now ended per Companies House filings today. Good luck to the new owners and hats off to all Shrimpers who fought the good fight.'

***

The machinations of the football club aside, Southend as a place to live was by several accounts degenerating at an alarming rate. The downfall was encapsulated in October 2021 when Sir David Amess, the MP for Southend West, was stabbed to death at a constituency surgery less than 200 yards from my first home.

How could this outrage have happened in the road where I played hopscotch, did my bit for Bob-a-Job week, climbed trees, delivered papers, worked mornings and evenings across two newsagents and caught the No.29 bus to school?

It hadn't seemed real. The murderer was 25-year-old Ali Harbi Ali, an Islamic fundamentalist who, seven years earlier, had been reported to Prevent, the Home Office's de-radicalisation scheme, but only had one meeting before his case was closed. This was failure of a catastrophic order. According to an article in the *Sunday Times* with the late MP's daughter Katherine, Ali had plotted a 'lone wolf' attack and chose to kill an MP because they were 'easy, accessible, and numerous'.

Sir David was believed to have been singled out because of his voting record on Syria. Ali was sentenced to a whole-life order in 2022 and Katherine Amess spoke heart-wrenchingly of 'the most unbearable, unspeakable pain' that never left her. Her father had been a brilliant, one-off, real man-of-the-people, community MP.

Through the summer of 2024 I was struck by the posting of persistent images of gangs of youths running through Southend's streets, many armed to the teeth with knives, scattering day trippers and locals alike. The once devil-may-care High Street was regularly plagued by devils.

In September, a video landed of a masked man brandishing a sword like something out of the Pirate Boat, a former seafront attraction in *Peter Pan's Playground* (the swords were made of wood back then). I had never seen anything like it or wanted to again.

There was no mention of this on any TV news bulletin or in any papers the following day. They were more concerned about who was paying for the Prime Minister's glasses, suits, and his wife's clothes (a bloody liberty if you asked me) and the wording of 40th birthday wishes to Prince Harry from his family.

Watching this unfold, seeing my old home desecrated, the fortunes of the local football club were momentarily relegated – not a word I enjoyed contemplating where Southend United was concerned.

WHO WAS THERE FOR US?

DIGGING AROUND for reassurance that something might turn up for the better, I was brought to a jarring halt when I discovered that having a brain haemorrhage on average knocked 7.3 years from a life. Bloody hell. That was a lot of living wiped away.

My form of stroke was also regarded as the most difficult from which to make a significant recovery, so I had a decent decade to play with if He was merciful. I'd already been robbed of ten years by being made redundant. Now this.

Sometimes, perhaps, it was better for one's peace of mind to stay in the dark. The light could be too blinding. I'd confronted a lot of tough days and knowing there would be more ahead hadn't (yet) diminished my resolve to stay as strong as possible. Knowing I wasn't alone in suffering was some small consolation, but not a lot.

For the record, I am among 1.3 million stroke survivors in the UK where, per annum, 100,000 people (the capacity at the old Empire Stadium, Wembley) will be struck down in one form or another. Almost 40,000 are killed by stroke every year, many before they had a clue what was happening to them. Two thirds of those who survived the initial impact find themselves having to live with a permanent disability.

Finding solace in recovery isn't easy, though good people are on your side. The Stroke Association is an underrated but not undervalued charity which does much-appreciated work on behalf of all victims of this affliction, largely without wide-scale acknowledgement.

My initial interaction with them was within a couple of weeks of my collapse: two ladies in bright purple shirts who arrived at my bedside blessed with a cheery manner and saying a lot more than I then had the capacity to take in. It was clear they had my best interest at heart and promised to be at the end of a phone if ever I needed a friendly voice.

Their boss was Juliet Bouverie, the Stroke Association's chief executive officer. We spoke at the end of 2024, as I was trying to come to terms with another spell of stagnation in my recovery and she had calculated that the new Labour government's first budget would cost the charity £700,000 p.a. to meet the rise in National Insurance employer's contributions. What sort of government was it that plundered a charity's good works to waste on Net Zero fanaticism, and the concreting of precious farmland among other fallacious policies?

There was to be a huge push across the charity world to try to persuade Rachel Reeves, the hapless chancellor, to think anew. Between the completion of this book and its publication date, there may have been a change of heart, but I wasn't going to be holding my breath.

As Juliet said, 'That £700,000 was money we wanted spend on direct intervention for stroke survivors, not paying government tax bills. It also increased the cost of our local services, and we were worried that local NHS and local authority commissioners wouldn't be prepared to pay that increase.

'It was an additional burden for us, meaning that more of a percentage of the money that either our donors or supporters gave so generously had to go to the government and not on support for stroke survivors. We, along with 8,000 charities, signed a letter to the chancellor asking for an exemption from the NI increase. The NHS and the public sector were exempt, and we said that a lot of our services were delivered in partnership with the NHS or commissioned by them so as we were in effect delivering public services, we should be exempt as well.'

Perhaps Ms Reeves and some of her colleagues might undertake to have a greater understanding of stroke and the devastating impact it has on so many of their constituents. And where would many of those have been without the Stroke Association, who tried as best they could to bring this condition to a wider public audience?

'There were two relevant pieces of research,' Juliet said. 'The first was that when we asked the public about the health conditions they were most frightened of, they said cancer, heart attacks and dementia but very rarely stroke. If they did mention it, it was probably because they'd had either somebody in their family who suffered or a direct experience of stroke through a friend or colleague.

'Then, we tried to understand in more detail the public's perception and awareness of stroke and discovered more recognised that it was a medical emergency because they'd heard of the F.A.S.T. (Face, Arms, Speech, Time) campaign and knew some of the symptoms but after that their understanding completely stopped.

'They assumed it's something you either died from or lived with, a bit like breaking a leg, you just got over it. It was a stroke, it was traumatic, it happened but then it was over.

'The public had little knowledge of the concept of recovery and that that journey was long, gruelling and needed an awful lot of strength. We launched our TV awareness campaign (in October 2024) based on a lot of insight, to try to create a new cultural narrative around stroke, that recovery was possible, but it was really tough and that's why stroke survivors needed support.

'We focused on the "wake up" moments after a stroke, showing that it could happen to people of any age, had a massive traumatic effect on the family and caused a lot of disability, with the survivors initially not able to move, swallow, see, speak. We did it deliberately to surprise and slightly shock people because they had no idea about the depth and breadth of the side effects associated with a stroke.

'There was a lot more media attention, clicks through to our website, where people stayed for longer, through an appreciation of the stories and identifying with the videos, because we captured the real lived experience of stroke, with stories that were emotionally compelling. This new attention on us was something we intended to sustain by keeping the message fresh, relevant, memorable, to hopefully increase engagement and help us to influence governments and other decision-makers to prioritise stroke.

'It really does turn lives upside down, and there are ongoing psychological and emotional impacts. There are all sorts of invisible effects like fatigue – incredibly common among stroke survivors – but also those who struggle with processing, numbers, cognition with sight, hearing, one in three survivors suffers from aphasia, and that is apart from the various physical challenges.'

***

The revelation that Sir Chris Hoy, clearly one of the nicest of men as well as an astonishing athlete, should be living with a terminal cancer diagnosis, poleaxed the nation. He had so much to live for: beautiful wife, gorgeous children, the opportunity to do so much good and, with a degree of fortune, plenty of time in which to do it.

Cancer is a thoroughly nasty business, and one reads about its malignant effect on so many lives on an almost daily basis. In the male population, prostate cancer is among the most prolific, as the case of the multi gold-medal winning 48-year-old Olympian vividly identified.

During a season spent undercover to write a book on Wycombe Wanderers five years ago, I had garnered a great affection for Bill Turnbull, the former *BBC Breakfast* presenter, who fought a long, courageous campaign against the same form of cancer, before he succumbed in 2022.

Bill was a Wycombe fanatic, whom I had sat alongside at a deserted Wembley two years earlier when his team were promoted to the Championship during the frightening frenzy of the Covid pandemic. He knew then that his time was short, but it hadn't stopped him glorying in every minute of an improbable tale.

These stories drove high-profile recognition and raised thousands of pounds for cancer charities. Rightly so. By contrast, there is very little such awareness-raising about stroke, which means the condition is often lost in the maelstrom of charitable demands. Too many stroke survivors live their lives in the shadows. Many prefer it that way.

The task for Juliet and her team is to shed more light on our plight. 'One of the reasons that cancer is such a public, political priority is partly because it is so prevalent but also because of a huge lobby of survivors now who happily shout loud and proud and deliver a big cancer-patient voice,' she said.

'One of my theories is that poor old stroke survivors so often just struggle with their day-to-day living that they don't have the time to advocate, to share their stories, their pain, and step up in the way that cancer survivors do.

'Another is that there have been incredible medical advances in the last 30 years so stroke mortality has been cut by half but I'm not sure people understand that stroke is treatable and recoverable. Many people assume it is something that happens only to older people and an "oh well, they're going to die anyway" attitude prevails.

'There is a kind of fatalism that there is nothing that can be done about a stroke but the message I regularly take to government ministers and decision makers is that it is preventable, treatable and recoverable.

'Fifty per cent of strokes are caused by high blood pressure which can be prevented and managed, as can cholesterol levels and atrial fibrillation – other major risk factors. If you have a clot-related stroke, thrombolysis and thrombectomy are absolutely life-changing and disability-reducing treatments. And recovery is possible, but for that you need access to high dose, high intensity stroke specialist rehabilitation and unfortunately none of those three elements are being managed well across the UK.

'You see pockets of great practise but a lot of it is quite poor. Across most indicators of stroke care in the last ten years things have deteriorated, in areas like the time from onset to hospital, and from access to hospital to getting into a stroke unit: all of that has sadly been slipping back. Though there are parts of the country that perform brilliantly, it isn't universal.

'Inequalities are huge. We've been campaigning strongly for access to a thrombectomy. If you have a blood clot there is a procedure that involves a stent that goes through the groin, into the main artery and up into the brain, it clips on to the clot and physically sucks it out of the brain.

'It is the most remarkable treatment with incredible outcomes, very cost effective and global trials proved its efficacy, but the UK has been desperately slow to adopt it. There are massive variations in terms of who can get access to it 24/7.

'If you live in London, you have a very good chance of having one if you need it in the middle of the night, but if you are in Norfolk or Yorkshire, say, your chances are very low. It shouldn't be like that.'

***

Its 'Online Community' allows Stroke Association members the opportunity to chat anonymously, share miseries and misadventures and occasionally enjoy a mental uplift. Sometimes I wept, laughed now and again and there were the times when I tuned out because the stories were unremittingly sad and reading other's testimonies depressed me because I was living them too.

I offer the following assortment of examples as poignant evidence of the battles stroke victims and their families face after the shock of being side-swiped by the onrush of brain damage.

One contributor wrote, 'Every day I wake, and I say to myself, "right, I have 24 hours", and that is the sum of my life until the next 24 hours. The symptoms are milder but not any easier. The idea of kicking back and relaxing is a luxury to me. I have moments of reprieve, and that's what I seek. Delicious moments where I feel as if I hadn't any troubles at all.

'These occur at odd times, mainly in the morning when my brain hasn't properly started communicating with my central nervous system. Other times, it's after a few beers or when completely immersed in company. It's a strange and uncomfortable existence, peppered with thoughts of further complications or a plateau of a dysfunctional last leg of my life's journey.

'When symptoms are acute, it's a bit like how I imagine bungee jumping is, I don't want to backtrack and let fear stop me from stepping forward, but it is still exhausting. In theory, everyday movement should be rehabilitating my symptoms, and still I'm creeping along with progress, but I suspect certain psychological obstructions may impede this process a little.

'The cerebellum is a complex and under-studied part of the brain; I imagine my cerebellum is like a city that got blitzed. The two strokes left and right, the left disrupting transport facilities and observational units, and the right hitting libraries and assemblies. What a mess. What a clean-up.

'The ongoing complication with it all is that four years ago, I was a younger, fitter fellow and subsequently have aged, no doubt with deterioration associated with aging, other bodily erosion, and the weakened state of my corporeal being. Not to mention the challenge to my mental state, which has defended its sanity like the Black Knight from *Monty Python and The Holy Grail*, "Tis but a scratch." – "A scratch? Your arm's off." – "No, it isn't." – "Well, what's that then?" – "I've had worse".'

I read these evidence-based cries from the heart with a desire to know more but also not to invade private agonies. That people were happy to offer up personal purgatories for discussion took immense courage. For instance, 'My husband had an eye stroke a month ago, he is only 41. He has no vision in one eye and has post-stroke fatigue so can only do things for about 15 minutes and then needs to rest for half an hour or more.

'He is now on medication for blood pressure, cholesterol and blood thinners so I feel reassured he is safe. He has no medical conditions, or family history of strokes and leads a mostly healthy lifestyle (could do more exercise and lose a little bit of weight).

'The last month has been a whirlwind of hospital visits, tests, doctors' visits, etc, as they are trying to find the cause and to look at the damage to the eye. I don't think my husband has taken this all in and may be in denial as he hasn't cried or shown any emotion and just says he feels like a fraud because people look at him and say he looks fine.

'I am being strong for him and our little one and doing more to help him and around the house and trying to have as much normal for our son [as I can]. I'm working full time in a management job which is quite stressful and this week I had to take time off work sick as I feel overwhelmed with everything. I just feel everything has been turned upside down and don't know how to find a new normal or what our new normal will be.'

I tended to be drawn to forum entries that most closely mirrored my own situation and how it affected Maureen especially. As an example, one forum member, feeling the immense strain of supporting a loved-one, wrote, 'My husband had a big stroke just before his 65th birthday. He was feeling well and working beforehand so this has utterly changed our lives. He was in hospital and rehab for seven weeks – a very hard time.

'I was exhausted as I'd wake at night and couldn't go back to sleep. I became very tearful. I discussed it with the doctor who started me on a course of anti-depressants – a serotonin lifter. He explained that under stress our natural serotonin levels depleted quickly and I needed to boost mine, so I was able to support my husband's recovery.

'My husband is being a pessimist. He is having problems with aspiration. They [the doctors] are not sure if this is from eating and drinking or some other reason, so he had another video scan to see if there have been any changes to his swallowing.

'His mental capacity was tested a few days ago. He can understand basic instructions and information but has trouble processing anything more or retaining information so they say he hasn't got the capacity to make important decisions about his care so it will be down to doctors, myself, etc, to decide. He has been going through so many emotions, understandably. Anger, frustration and now tears.'

It was a familiar refrain, lives changed in a split second and little reassurance they could ever be put back together again. The responses on the website were as positive as they could be. There was anger, sadness and anxiety, but also positivity, support and kindness.

And there was certainly a heck of a lot of us out there, willing to offer what we could, while at the same time crying out for help ourselves.

***

It took five exhausting months of phone call upon phone call to secure a second round of Botox treatment, eight injections plunged into my resolutely stiff left arm and leg muscles on Christmas Eve, 2024. The idea was that once the muscles relaxed, the brain's messages would more easily get through to them, and they could start to respond to what it was asking them to do. We'd see.

It was therefore with a still pathetic shoulder shrug (the best I could manage with a misbehaving scapula) that I discovered that in 2023/24, the Stroke Association secured a record income of £42.1 million, an increase of four per cent in the year.

For a charity which did so much of its work under the radar, this was a remarkable achievement. They also grew expenditure on charitable activities by 16 per cent from £30.5 million to £35.2 million, allowing a rise from £18 million to £20.6 million to be spent on direct services to stroke survivors.

Who funded the association? Juliet Bouverie said, 'We received a small amount of public sector money from either local NHS or local authorities but that only represented 28 per cent of our total income. The remaining 72 per cent came from the public. We were lucky to receive a healthy proportion from legacies, people gave very generously in their wills (£16 million in 2023). The remaining £12 million was raised from companies, trusts and foundations, individuals giving to us on a regular basis through direct debits, from raffles or lotteries.

'There were those who raised money running the London Marathon and the Great North Run: we had quite a mix of different income sources and deliberately had a diverse portfolio so we could spread the risk which gave people a variety of choices about ways they supported us.

'Our major ambition was to reach and add value to the lives of every single newly diagnosed stroke survivor. We currently reached only one third and we wanted to be there for everybody. That meant needing to increase public awareness of stroke, of our services and provide personalised support so that everybody was supported by us with their recovery in whatever way they wanted.

'Stroke didn't discriminate, and people thought it was only a condition for older people but sadly it wasn't. We'd known for a long time that one in four strokes happened in people under the age of 65 but we were seeing new data emerging that there was a stark increase in strokes in middle age, people from 40 to 55, a rapid increase and nobody yet understood what the reasons were.'

Anyone affected by stroke can visit stroke.org.uk or call the dedicated stroke support helpline on 0303 3033 100 for information, guidance or a chat when times are tough.

JUDE, GAZZA, COLE AND DESMOND

IT WAS a beautiful paradox of football writing that arguably the most cut-throat of all the roles in journalism should engender such long-lasting friendships based on mutual respect and – one hoped – an admiration for each other's endeavours over many years.

Most hours of working days and sleepless nights were spent attempting to get one over the opposition, at the same time as there were the myriad joys to be found in each other's company.

The thick end of three decades had passed since my career as a frontline football correspondent closed, yet invitations to a lunch or awards ceremony still dropped – there was nothing from tennis which spoke volumes about the quality of many of the people associated with it. Or maybe they just didn't want me around, which was perfectly understandable. I wasn't missing them either.

At a crucial stage of my recovery, when I earnestly needed public rehabilitation, a call arrived from Alex Montgomery who had been chief football writer of *The Sun* when I landed the same post on the *Daily Mail* in 1990. Would I be interested in meeting up with a group of ex No.1 writers for lunch in London?

In social terms I hadn't strayed far since my discharge, cognisant of my physical limitations, and unwilling to put them under unnecessary strain. How would I get to London, how might I fare around so many people and when (if) I made it to the restaurant, would I have the energy to engage and what if I was suddenly caught short and the toilet might be either up or down a flight of stairs?

What would be insignificances to an able-bodied person preyed on the insecurities of someone with a disability. I desperately wanted to go and see my old chums, but I had to be as sure as I could that I would neither embarrass myself nor disconcert them.

Maureen came to the rescue once more, saying she would take me from door to door, spend a couple of hours looking in shop windows and then pick me up – not literally I hoped – to bring me home.

Getting dressed into something smart was a sod of a chore. As the days passed in my recovery, I dropped a significant amount of weight to the extent that suits which once clung too tightly, now seemed more appropriate for Gulliver's big brother.

Pulling a shirt over my head and aiming my arms through the sleeves was one thing, doing up the buttons something else entirely. As the left arm still tended to swing around with a mind of its own, it was completely useless when it came to my attempt to widen the hole enough to squeeze the button through. An onrush of incandescence brought Maureen dashing upstairs to fasten them in place.

What exacerbated my frustration was that in the desire to get the shirt fitted properly, my trousers kept falling below my knees because I couldn't fasten them quickly enough. This, of course, meant much bending and retrieving, which remained a painful trial.

'If you practised your squats more often that would be much easier,' Maureen said, and she was right of course. My glutes had long since given up the ghost and I had to strengthen them if I wasn't to spend the rest of my days giving passable imitations of the former US President Joe Biden reaching back for a chair that wasn't there.

By this time too, just over a year after my stroke, Maureen had taken away the raised toilet covers which had aided my standing and sitting, saying I had to re-learn the old style. It was ridiculous how low toilet seats were, especially when you had to reach and balance with your right hand twisted behind your back on the cistern before you could lower into position.

Getting back up was equally treacherous, because the left leg was not sufficiently strong to take its share of body weight, so there was much swivelling and cursing as you attempted to stand tall while heaving your boxers back into position without a fumble that would send them tumbling back to the floor, whereupon you had to start again from scratch. I presumed my lack of buttock muscles meant toilet seats seemed 20° colder than I remembered.

I slid easily into my size 36in waist trousers and threaded the belt through single-handedly to much fluster, though the next trial was attempting to hold myself up to insert the belt catch into one of the holes and pull it tight without losing balance. I found the best way was to lean against a wall so that I had a solid support before attempting the fiddly bits. There was no way I could tie a tie on my own, so the missus stepped in there, too.

All dressed up – but extremely frazzled – it was time to meet my old mates at Motcombs, a very pleasant restaurant a stone's throw from Harrods which had been a favoured haunt of Terry Venables, when the former England head coach held court with his favoured journalists. Suffice to say it was my first time there.

The last time I'd seen Terry a few years back he was not his old chirpy self; something was clearly amiss. Those who knew him better than I told me that he had become increasingly vague and forgetful, a tragic circumstance for someone with such a vibrant, lively personality and brilliant mind.

When he passed away in November 2023 his loss was deeply felt across the football world as a hugely talented player who became a gifted coach and raised the hopes of a nation when England came so close to landing the Euro '96 Championship.

Six months on from his death, five of us scribes – me, Alex, Bob Harris, Patrick Collins and Paddy Barclay – gathered in the private section of the restaurant which had been Terry's chosen space to debate the football landscape. He may not have picked some of us as first-choice companions, but I doubted he'd have denied us this small celebration of all things football-writing brotherhood.

The initial toast was to absent friends of whom there were too many to mention. Faces and places flashed momentarily through my mind, initially evoking sadness soon replaced by a sense of gratitude that I had known them and was still here with mates to celebrate them.

Then, for three hours I was able to forget stiff joints and partially operating mouth to relish fine food and (expensive) wine, good company, and even better storytelling. I wish I remembered all the best lines, but one tale stuck in my mind.

Alex was a young reporter sent by the *Daily Mail* to cover a match in the west country – he was pretty sure it was Exeter – and arrived in the press box to ask the local freelance which was his phone.

In those days, freelancers would effectively 'own' each phone on their patch and could dictate how much they charged and how long each paper was allotted for their use. Alex was told he had to share with three other reporters who would have to fit in with each other's good nature and timing of composition to send their copy.

The No.1 football writer on the *Daily Express* in those days was the famous Desmond Hackett, whose trademark was the bowler hat he would doff to all and sundry as he walked to his seat in the box.

The fawning freelance told Hackett, who arrived a few minutes late as was his wont, he could have a phone for his personal use and that the home team were already a goal to the good, scored by a player whose father happened to be a local taxi driver. He dutifully described the goal to the most famous occupant of his press box.

The other reporters breathlessly filed their copy – the goal Hackett missed turned out to be the match winner – in time to listen to the legendary reporter's pearls of wisdom.

The *Express* man lifted the receiver, asked for the copytaker, and began to dictate, 'Arriving from Paddington to this beautiful west country town for last night's cup tie I was collected at the station by a taxi driver who informed me that his son would score the winning goal. John Smith [the name is made up] duly delivered.'

No one of course would raise a word of dissent, but Hackett had made up the whole, 'being picked up by the taxi driver' and their subsequent conversation stuff. *Express* readers the next morning would simply believe that their man had been in the know all along, which merely added to his level of mystique.

The story, enhanced by Alex's lyrical storytelling style, had the rest of us in fits. The days when such characters abounded in sportswriting had long gone, and more was the pity in many respects. Like hot metal, typewriters, long lunches and reporters wearing bowler hats, we were yesterday's scribes, but our memories were sharp and our delight in a fun story undiminished.

We remained in love with our industry, though much of it had changed beyond all recognition. The relationships we were able to forge with players and managers alike were long-lasting and strong. I put a picture of the occasion on LinkedIn and was chuffed that several respected football people commented on our qualities both as writers and human beings.

To me, it simply meant that I had tried to do the job to the best of my ability which was reward enough – had I been seeking one.

Having something positive to hang your hat on was one of the imperatives for long-term healing from stroke. It could be a simple word, a gesture, an ambition, a spark, anything that made a day go by with a little less worrying about your condition and distracted from the shroud-like negativity.

There was an inevitable concentration on your rehabilitation because that was really all that mattered, but if you thought of nothing else, the days would drag and the nights were interminably uncomfortable.

***

The day after the Motcombs lunch, the European Championship began in Germany with England among the favoured nations. It was time to expand on my football reading too.

In days of yore, I'd have devoured every word of Barclay and Collins with especial veracity. The torch had been passed to a new generation of which old pals Ollie Holt – an early bedside solace, remember – and Martin Samuel were my pick of the crop. I had seen both guys rise through the ranks to become the sports heartbeat of the *Daily Mail* and *The Times*. They – like me – had worked for both papers which underscored their ability to change styles without pause to satisfy the nuances of a different readership.

In the days immediately preceding England's opening match against Serbia, many eyes fixed on our generational talent, Jude Bellingham. This young man commanded matches. I was taken back to my time writing about England when Paul Gascoigne was in what became his pomp.

Gazza was a dominant personality too; he could shape a match in his image, thumping into tackles, shaking up the opposition, spreading the play, running with the ball as if superglued to his feet and he was bloody courageous as well.

I remembered reporting on a far-post header he scored for Tottenham at Fratton Park, Portsmouth in an FA Cup tie in 1991, flying into the boots and bodies, not worried for himself, just a determination to get to the ball first.

That image flashed through my head when Bellingham scored the only goal of the game against the Serbs, showing not a moment's concern for his own safety but playing by instinct. Where the ball was, he wanted to be. Just like Gazza.

Sadly, for Paul, an inclination for recklessness would bring about the decline of a great talent. His lunge at Gary Charles of Nottingham Forest in the 1991 Cup Final tore his knee to shreds and its aftermath would prevent him fulfilling all he should have achieved. I just hoped Bellingham was a more sensible lad all round.

Originally from Stourbridge in the West Midlands, he joined Birmingham City, storming their ramparts to such an extent that Borussia Dortmund succeeded in tempting him to the Bundesliga from where he had joined Real Madrid, the forefather of European dominance. Real had won the Champions League a month before the tournament began and Bellingham was their princely motif.

After the initial surge against Serbia, his contribution waned in subsequent group matches, England played fitfully but did enough to emerge on top, securing a place in the round of 16 where they would meet Slovakia. Here again, Bellingham's instinct and bravado proved decisive.

A goal down and five minutes into injury time, seemingly defeated, an England long throw was nudged on and with his back to goal, young Jude spun in the air to connect perfectly with an overhead kick that wrong-footed the Slovak goalkeeper. England were saved and a minute into extra time, captain Harry Kane would score the decisive goal. I was tempted to take an extra Ramipril just in case my blood pressure required coming down a degree or two.

A further supply was needed for the quarter-final against Switzerland. Twenty-eight years earlier, the Swiss had proved redoubtable as our first group opponents in Euro '96, and their talents had flourished in the meantime. It needed a fizzing left-footed equaliser from Arsenal's Bukayo Saka for England to reach extra time and subsequently a penalty shoot-out, where Trent Alexander-Arnold scored the decisive eighth to secure a place in the semis.

Either discouraged by my current condition or years of press box deflation, I had become fatalistic about our chances of winning the tournament, especially as the Netherlands were the opposition, and I'd been at both Wembley and in Rotterdam in 1993 when Graham Taylor's England should have beaten them twice and secured a place in the World Cup finals in the USA.

The sight of Ronald Koeman in the Dutch dugout brought me out in a bit of a funk. Nothing against the man personally, but he had been the prime culprit in arguably the most controversial moment of Taylor's international management, a foul on David Platt which ought to have been punished by dismissal, only for him to pop up and score the free kick which effectively settled our elimination from the competition in the penultimate qualifier.

I was gratified when England were awarded a dubious penalty after a VAR review when a defender was adjudged to have fouled Harry Kane, whose ankle-grabbing agony was excessive given the minimal level of contact. I shouted something like 'up yours Ronnie' at the TV when Kane used his injured right foot to equalise.

In the final minutes of the match, the avenging of Koeman's crimes was complete when Aston Villa's Ollie Watkins, a recent substitute, scored a stunning winner and England were in the final to play the favourites, Spain. This, I felt in my gut, would only end one way.

I wasn't the only one in the country staggered at England manager Gareth Southgate's reluctance to give Cole Palmer of Chelsea more minutes in the tournament. Here was a mercurial talent, largely skin and bone but balanced, supremely athletic and possessing an innate ability to win a game. And that, the last time I checked, was still what it was all about.

What had changed since my working days in football was the number of substitutions allowed in a single game. I thought it had gone nuts, great swathes of comings and goings throughout the second-half, incessant interruptions to balance and strategy, constant panic-measures celebrated as tactical genius (if a team won).

Palmer said he was readily accepted by the more experienced players in the squad but kept asking himself why he wasn't starting matches. In the final he was again among the substitutes and within three minutes of being brought on with England a goal down, scored an exquisite equaliser to deliver momentary hope.

Spain, of course, would score a late winner to win the Championship, leaving English football to turn in on itself once more and provoke more intense examination as to why major events continued to elude us. A head coach not picking his best players and retreating to tactical conservatism usually had something to do with it.

Jude Bellingham said a couple of weeks after the Championship that he had felt unfairly scapegoated for England's 'failure'. I hoped he might learn over time that such emotions were self-defeating. The perceived harshness of any criticism was in its way a back-handed compliment to his myriad talents and importance to his country's hope of success.

***

From my experience, football writers did not make the best armchair viewers. Nothing could replicate the thrill of being there live and the challenge of finding the appropriate words to describe the match in the time allotted before deadline.

I found myself wanting to get up and wander (limp) around the living room during matches, dismayed at the quality of both commentary and studio analysis.

Not for the first time I yearned to be transported to my press days when John Motson, Brian Moore, Gerald Sindstadt and Hugh Johns (all of whom became friends) were masters of their art. They never buried you beneath tiresome tactical mumbo jumbo, or a running commentary on formations, as those to whom they passed on the microphones did while fighting to persuade us how bloody smart they were.

And everyone felt the need to shout – Sky Sports' new lead commentator Peter Drury was exhibit A in the station's increasingly tiresome Premier League coverage. For someone whose brain reacted now with pronounced discomfort to excessive noise, this manifestation was particularly unwelcome.

Drury was not alone in the contemporary scream stakes. Sam Matterface, Steve Wilson and the consistently aggravating Jamie Carragher and Gary Neville needed to learn that not all their audience were audio-challenged dimwits. We knew a bit about the game.

Alan Shearer had become a co-commentator on the BBC and didn't spare the rod when it came to criticism of England's performances. That was all well and good, and he was handsomely paid for his services, but the Shearer I remembered as a player was monosyllabic and prickly in the extreme when it came to any criticism of his performances.

There was no doubt that at Southampton, Blackburn, Newcastle and when he was fit for England – sadly not often enough – he was the complete centre-forward: courageous, strong, with a firecracker of a right foot and extremely self-possessed as all good strikers had to be. But find fault either with him personally or a team display in which he participated, and he was no fun to run into.

That was his prerogative of course but I did find it rather amusing to watch him taking aim at the current crop of international players with such relish. The boot really was on the other foot.

***

How would I cope in a football crowd, a phalanx of people not often remaining in their own space, noisy, distracted, quaffing beer as they went and hardly likely to pay much attention to an old fella stumbling around on a stick?

It didn't take long into the 2024/25 season for me to find out – and I survived. Five years earlier I had been introduced to the glories of Wycombe Wanderers, becoming the club's fly-on-the-wall reporter, to pen what I considered my best work to date.

The book was called *Close Quarters* (it pulled in an overwhelming majority of five-star reviews on Amazon, I was humbled to see). The idea was to chronicle the story of the League One club with the lowest budget and run by a Supporters' Trust to a veritable pauper's existence.

Wycombe went along with my overtures, but none could have foreseen that within a month of the journey beginning, the club would be taken over by a lawyer from Louisiana with no background in English football, to understandable head-shaking and trepidation.

From there, the investment of Rob Couhig and family was such that a decent squad was formed by the push-me-pull-you management duo of Gareth Ainsworth and Richard Dobson, the players discovered an inner belief they probably didn't know they possessed and a month into the season were top of the league.

They were still there or thereabouts when the COVID pandemic descended like a 21st century plague in early 2020. A controversial algorithm was used by Football League bosses to determine places in the play-offs, Wycombe sneaked in and would compete in a two-legged semi-final against Fleetwood Town.

A couple more astonishing performances later and we were at Wembley Stadium for the final with cardboard cut-out fans and zero atmosphere as no crowds above a gaggle were allowed to assemble under the government's strict lockdown enforcement (unless you popped in for a beer in the garden of 10 Downing Street).

Wycombe would have three chances and score twice; opponents Oxford United a dozen and score once – a fluke cross that sailed in over the goalkeeper – and the most improbable of stories ended with the Buckinghamshire town celebrating a place in the Championship. All completely nonsensical.

The entire management team, the US owners, the medical staff and all but three of the players had departed for pastures new by the time August 2024 rolled around but the club still looked upon me kindly and a ticket and car park pass at OAP rates were offered for the first home league match of the season against relegated Birmingham City.

I met some former associates, including ex-Wycombe manager Martin O'Neill, with whom I'd had a couple of ding dongs in my reporting career, and his old Nottingham Forest team-mate and England international, Tony Woodcock. Both looked fit enough to be playing now.

I hung around in the main corridor area for five minutes but once Birmingham's players had arrived and decamped to their dressing room, I was shooed away because I didn't have the appropriate pass and wasn't allowed to take a shortcut up the tunnel and around the pitch to my front row seat in the opposite stand.

What did they think I was going to do? A lone pitch invader with one half-decent leg, a walking stick, a penchant for tripping up steps and wobbling wildly every couple of strides wouldn't have escaped even the dumbest of stewards.

I wailed 'I'm being thrown out' to no avail, limped back outside, managed to squeeze through a small gap past the Birmingham coach and after several pauses to catch my breath under a blazing sun, reached my allotted spot decently before kick-off.

Half-way there I was offered a wheelchair by a St John Ambulance man and politely declined. I was determined to make it under my own steam. A friendly steward at gate eight said he would walk me to the seat, which was very decent of him.

At least where I was seated, I could fully extend my left leg and not be stuck with the same uncomfortable body position for 90 minutes, plus the ludicrous amount of additional time they added on these days. My unbending, stiffened frame wouldn't have taken too kindly to that.

The match did not live up to expectations, or perhaps it did, given they were limited. There was a different sensation around the ground from 2019/20 I couldn't quite put my finger on. It wouldn't have been the first time the arrival of new club ownership had brought about a change in the entire dynamic.

Something didn't feel quite right, either, about Wycombe's levels of commitment, or the lack of full-throated endeavour that had been the shining hallmark of the old squad. Wycombe were too often second to the ball, offered scant control and on the vital commodities of ball possession and individual quality, Birmingham merited their 3-2 victory.

I was reminded more than once that City's spending on two players – including £1 million for goalkeeper Ryan Allsop, a strong feature in Wycombe's promotion year who couldn't get into the Birmingham team this afternoon – was roughly twice the home club's total player outlay. Thus, I shouldn't have been too surprised at the result.

That was all well and good, but Birmingham were not exactly startling, though they did demonstrate the advantages of stretching a game the full width of the pitch. Getting to the byline and turning defenders was not vogue anymore – and yet Birmingham excelled at it. Even so, with more poise at critical moments, Wycombe might easily have collected a point, perhaps all three.

This was the club's second consecutive league defeat so I left hoping that something would click soon, and Wanderers would be spared an uphill battle before we had reached September. We would see. It was not as if the club hadn't been underwhelming before and lived to see brighter days. I'd been privy to quite a few of them. Things would turn, there were too many good people at the club for them not to.

All in all, I was chuffed to have driven to and from home, negotiating motorway traffic for the first time, survived a teeming Marlow High Street, parked within the white lines of my appointed space, half circumnavigated Adams Park without assistance and then become so emotionally attached to a football match.

Having spent my entire professional life as an objective observer, the freedom to shout, 'what the fucking hell was that?' at a referee and really mean it while not running the risk of being escorted from the premises was entirely invigorating.

Those within earshot of me in the stand, noting my demeanour, nearby walking aid and stumbling attempts at standing up, probably passed me off as halfway round the twist anyway. They weren't far wrong.

***

Why was it that I found it impossible to watch the Paralympics on TV in late summer?

'You could do that,' Maureen said as people without arms splashed through the water of the swimming pool as if radar-guided. 'But I've got one arm, so I'd simply go round and round in circles and probably sink to the bottom,' I replied. We agreed to disagree that getting back into the swimming pool was a good idea, for now.

I was a member of the Infirmity Club, had had plenty of wheelchair practice, and still possessed one working arm and leg so ought to have had a special affiliation with those contestants in Paris who put their frailties to one side and competed with remarkable bravery.

Most of these athletes were, of course, 30 or 40 years my junior and had strength I could no longer muster. Maybe in watching them I saw an unwelcome reflection of my own inadequacy and couldn't face it. Maybe it was the sight of Italy's transgender athlete Valentina Petrillo running in women's races, and people pretending it was okay.

Put it down as part and parcel of the psychological damage stroke had caused, a mind that went haywire, a working body suddenly impaired and as things were standing, only minimal hope of all being restored.

Whatever the reason, I simply couldn't bear to watch – Clare Balding's saccharine-laced presentation didn't help either – and much preferred seeing able-bodied sportsmen going about their business – that was until it came to watching Manchester United trying to play decent football by which time, I abandoned hope.

***

It was uplifting to see the BBC TV interview with Sir Alex Ferguson, broadcast in the autumn of 2024, in which he talked of his love of music and how important it was as a comfort and inspiration in his later years.

Alex was speaking on behalf of National Playlist Day, a charity that helped dementia patients get through lonely spells by listening to their favourite tunes. It could just as easily have been a reference point for those seeking mental stimulation after a stroke.

I had mentioned my love of Boom Radio at one of my physio sessions at the clinic and it became the resident background music. Treadmill walking was far more tolerable while marching to disco or Motown, and the attempts to straighten my left elbow before indulging in press ups (or what passed for them) were helped if Doris Day or Dusty Springfield was the lyrical accompaniment.

Alex looked terrific for a man soon to turn 83, and in keeping with the mood of memory-jerking, I couldn't help but be reminded of those halcyon days in the 1990s when he formed Manchester United into a remarkable winning unit and ran the club on his own, inimitable terms.

Anyone he regarded as an obstacle to the master plan – and I was one such individual – soon learned that it was not a desirable place to be.

We had both travelled far from May 1993, when United won their first league title for 26 years and Alex was invited by the No.1 football writers of the day to a celebratory lunch at a London hotel. He initially declined unless I was removed from the guest list (I can't think why) and was talked around on the distinct proviso that I was to keep my mouth shut during the festivities.

As the group rose to leave at the end of a convivial meal, fortified by a significant amount of (expensive) red wine, Alex asked (told) me to remain where I was as he wanted a private word.

I learned, hardly to my surprise, that he liked neither me nor my written work and he insisted that I had allowed my friendship with Ron Atkinson, his predecessor, to cloud my judgement when writing about the current team. I summoned enough courage to say I didn't particularly like him either and that his comments about Ron were patently ridiculous.

Over the years Alex mellowed (a little) and we increasingly saw eye to eye on many subjects, but he never lost the ability to make my hair stand on end if he took affront to any article he regarded as lacking coherence and much worse, as being critical of United for the sake of stirring controversy.

I was reminded watching him now that he had suffered a brain haemorrhage in 2018 and had worried, mostly, that his mind would be irreversibly harmed. He was terrified when he couldn't get a single word out that made sense. 'Is my memory going to come back? Will I ever speak again?' were his two most pressing concerns.

Hours of speech therapy were required to return one of the most unforgettable voices of his time to somewhere approaching its former ferocity. One of his exercises was to recall every member of his many United teams and they proved to be as unforgettable to their old boss as they were to anyone who witnessed them. After ten days repeating 'Schmeichel, Parker, Irwin, Bruce, Pallister, etc,' he was well on the way to his old self.

His all-time musical favourites were 'Dirty Old Town' by The Pogues, 'Moon River' sung by Audrey Hepburn from the soundtrack to *Breakfast at Tiffany's*, and 'My Own True Love', a lyrical adaption of Nino Rota's theme from the multi-Oscar winning *Gone with the Wind.*

These were classical choices, made the more poignant by the faraway look in Alex's eyes as he listened to them (he had lost his wife and rock, Lady Cathy, a year earlier). The old boy really had a heart.

***

At Thorpes Neuro Rehab unit in Eversley to where I decamped every other Friday, my physio Charlotte Eley would constantly mix up the physical regime, making things just that little bit harder each time, so that I was never in what might be described as a comfort zone.

In late October 2024, a new dimension was added when she rolled a football in my direction. Now came the tricky bit. My balance was still corrupted, though the left leg felt stronger than it had at any stage through the recovery process.

For me to focus on a steady pivot, Charlotte didn't tell me in advance which foot she would send the ball towards. As such I had to reach back and grab for the bar behind me so as not to fall flat on my face. But that wasn't in the rules, so I had to let go. I wanted to use my instep in the manner of the coaching manual but trying to turn either foot outwards caused all manner of flailing gestures. Craig Revel-Horwood would have slaughtered me.

Eventually, after the ball had flown in every direction bar straight, the instructions were simply, 'left' then 'right' and I was reduced to toe-poking it back to her. The important part was to swing my left leg through as quickly as possible to replicate a proper walking step.

Rather, I was reminded of those pub table-football games where the ball is tossed between rows of figures attached to a steel rod that the players spin in the relevant direction. I must have looked like one of those wooden men, stabbing at the ball for all my worth, while my head was spinning.

That said, the sense of achievement when I would direct it back straight into Charlotte's clutches, was inwardly rewarding. Who knew that kicking a ball like a three-year-old again could be so much fun?

CAMERON McKINNELL

IN THE summer of 2004, as I scurried across the hinterland of Royal Troon GC as the junior member of *The Times* squad reporting on the Open Golf Championship, young Cameron McKinnell was on work experience in the media, ferrying camera film to American networks from their troops stomping the fairways.

Cameron recalled the uproar when an unknown American, Todd Hamilton, came from nowhere – well Oquawka, Illinois to be fair – and won the title in a play-off with South African Ernie Els. He loved the thrill of negotiating the humps and hollows of Troon on a buggy inside the ropes, with the evidence of Hamilton's unlikely success in his possession.

Twenty years on, he lived in a house not a quarter of a mile from the front gate of the club of which he was now a member, content with his handicap of 12, though still preferring to play well within himself because of an incident that happened nearby, on another sporting field altogether.

At the age of 28, Cameron had been captain of Troon FC, leading them in an Ayrshire derby against Kilwinning on a particularly biting west-of-Scotland morning. It was nil-nil at half time and in the Troon dressing room he would normally have been at his most vocal, urging his team to greater effort in the second half.

Instead, he took himself off to the toilet where, he would later be reminded, though he had no recollection of it at the time, he threw up.

'I had begun to feel a little strange in the first half, colder than I ever used to be, even though it was quite cold anyway,' he said. 'I didn't really take in anything at half-time when I'd normally be right in the boys' faces.'

In the opening moments of the second half, the ball came towards Cameron who swung a leg at it, took an air shot and collapsed on to his right side. 'I'd probably been running around like a lunatic for the first 45 minutes,' he said. 'There was a decent sized crowd and when I went to control the ball and completely missed it, I was told there was a good load of banter from the opposition fans.

'Fortunately, there were enough observant people watching who realised quickly that something wasn't right. I came off the pitch very reluctantly and the next thing I was in my father-in-law's car being driven to hospital [Crosshouse in Kilmarnock].

'My dad would normally have been there, but he was at a funeral that day and my father-in-law said I refused to take an ambulance – there was no way I was leaving a local derby like that. I didn't want to go to hospital at all, but I was persuaded, and he said he just talked rubbish all the way there to keep me awake and occupied.

'I think back now and realise how fortunate I was to have been where I was at the time. The previous six weeks I'd been driving all over Europe for work [as an IT specialist for a healthcare company]. I was unluckily lucky. What if it had happened abroad somewhere?'

The 'it' in question was an ischaemic stroke that occurs when a blockage interrupts the blood supply to your brain and surrounding cells are killed off. Damage to these cells affects how the body works, including how you think and feel. This is the most common type of stroke, the cause of 85 per cent of such attacks in the United Kingdom.

The doctors in Kilmarnock, confronted by an obviously fit fellow in his 20s, wondered amongst themselves if he had indeed had a stroke. 'I wasn't sure they were convinced, especially given the age factor,' Cameron said. 'I was told I was showing all the symptoms of a stroke, but it was as if they couldn't quite believe it.

'"You're only 28, you're very young," was their initial reaction. 'I said "does that mean I can't have a stroke?" "No, that's not the case," one said. I went for a scan and the result of that was confirmation. On the one hand it was a reassurance but on the other it was scary – a real contrast of emotions.

'I struggled with the age element because if not indestructible, you were able to control most things and it was a real eye-opener to find myself in hospital. What made it worse was I was put in a ward full of geriatrics. That was such a depressing experience. I had to sign myself out after nine days.'

In his subsequent work on behalf of the Stroke Association, Cameron was astonished to discover that 20 per cent of strokes in the UK happened to people under the age of 30.

'I came to understand that age was almost irrelevant and attacks on your body could happen at any age, but I do think the mindset of age could play a huge part in your attitude towards recovery.

'I observed individuals at what I might call the back end of life who just accepted where they were. I was young and fit, and my mantra was "just get on with it". I never liked being beaten – at football, golf or a game of cards – and it was important to carry that sense throughout my rehabilitation.

'Someone from the Stroke Association said, "it's the new you". That was a far better way of thinking of it rather than dwell on not being what you were. You had to find a way of accepting this new person and other people had to do the same. I'm sure my wife would agree I was more than a bit grumpy at times but that was just the frustration inside bubbling to the surface.'

But like so many in this position, what concerned Cameron most was the void of uncertainty. He knew something wasn't right but couldn't find anyone to put their finger on the nub of the matter. Victims of stroke probably stay in the dark longer than anyone with a life-altering condition, expanding the degrees of helplessness.

'The Stroke Association were a fantastic help with what I should expect from my emotions, when I got back to driving, what to expect with financial assistance: there were so many avenues where they were straight to the point with insight that always concentrated on my potential,' he said.

'That was massive for me on my journey. I was concentrating more on getting back physically because I didn't want to be seen as weak in the eyes of friends, but the association gave me a different impetus, to realise I wasn't on my own, I just needed to find a way to navigate the changes I'd be facing.'

As an eloquent advocate for those in his (our) position, Cameron's message was a common one, that at the first suspicion something might be wrong, prevarication was your worst enemy. 'It might seem a cliché, but it was so important to act quickly because things could go downhill fast,' he said. Acceptance of stroke was tricky too, especially for someone as young as he was when taken down.

***

Recovery was a continuous journey. There was a rapid initial burst (of improvement), then you reached the intersection when you needed to be careful that you didn't suddenly go downhill, become a bit delusional and didn't accept the reality of the situation.

'I found it to be a rollercoaster experience,' Cameron said. 'I didn't find the natural change in the curve we talk about in business; my recovery meandered quite a bit for the first three or four years and then the meanders shortened.'

Ten years on from the day he whiffed at a football, and having to deal with his limitations – while he acknowledged them – remained a tall order. 'I didn't like people fussing over me and that became an easy "out" when I didn't really want to talk about it (the stroke),' he said.

'The physical aspect came out in various forms, there was a weakness in my right arm which prevented me doing any DIY which I liked to do and now struggled with. Also, when I got really tired my right eye tended to droop a little.

'I had to go through quite a bit of speech therapy, learning how to speak more slowly and clearly which really helped, with my Scottish accent and working for a global company. It also made me slow down when speaking overall. When I became tired, I could sound quite slurry and that was a real mental challenge because people commented on the accent at work all the time, saying they couldn't understand me. That would rile me.

'I often felt I held myself back from being the full me in certain scenarios but that was just a confidence thing. When you didn't feel 100 per cent physically, the speech might go a little bit, the eye might go a little, it could be in a work session, a pub session, even sitting at the dinner table with the family and you could come across as being drunk or incapable, but it was just me.

'I liked to dress smartly and look good, but these things took a mental toll. Everyone had battles on their own journey, some people came through them fully but being honest with myself, there was always something holding me back from being 100 per cent and I just had to deal with it.'

One of those drawbacks was a loss of peripheral vision which meant stringent tests before he was allowed back behind the wheel of a car. That day of independence, he recalled, felt as if he had got his life back. 'Being able to go somewhere on my own and having the confidence to do it was a definite game changer,' he said.

'I found the stroke made me more determined in various ways, in what mattered to me because it put a different perspective on things, it made me sharpen up my idea of what my career should look like and doing what I really wanted to do. The recovery phases were interesting, to say the least.

'There were quite a number of lows but looking back ten years and it was – and I never thought I'd hear myself say this – a positive intersect in my life to have re-calibrated and focused on myself and my family [a wife and two children under the age of ten] more.

'We lived in a time of such rapid change, where everything was instant and digital and what happened to me meant I could choose my own pace and direction. The journey has allowed me to think differently.'

Very little on this earth could beat the opportunity to live a few hundred yards from one of nature's most beautiful expanses of golfing ground and 20 years on from being a kid in a buggy at Royal Troon, he could now play the course when the mood took him, which was usually with people he knew who understood his personal battle.

'I played much better pre-stroke, which was another reality check, but I'm back doing something I really enjoy,' he said. He once played to a handicap of eight which went up to 18 post-stroke and was now back to a very creditable 12, especially on a mentally taxing links.

'I only play socially and when I have some control over the environment, I play more relaxed,' he said. 'You could do that if you were playing with friends, but I tended to be more nervous if I was in a competition and drew someone random I didn't know. Then I'd get anxious and didn't do myself justice.

'My pals joked that I needed an extra stroke a hole these days, but maybe not in that way!'

BETWEEN A LIFE AND DEATH

IF YOU skimmed the leader-board at the conclusion of the 2024 Open – staged those few hundred paces from Cameron McKinnell's front door – Gary Woodland was to be found in a tie for 50th place.

I had not seen a single shot of Woodland's figure in British TV coverage and completing the championship 18 strokes behind eventual champion, his fellow American Xander Schauffele, would not have been in his mind's eye as he played his first tee shot on Thursday afternoon.

But of all those who lasted the four rounds, few deserved more acknowledgement than the 40-year-old from Kansas who only a year earlier feared he might never swing a club again, either professionally or for nickels and dimes at his local club. Woodland's 2023 was about as frightening as mine, one spent staring into a depressing abyss.

He explained it in an article for *Golf Digest* early in 2024 that opened with the awful spectre of a grown man clinging to the mattress on his bed, fearing that if he let go, he would spin into oblivion. He said that he had played in the 2023 US PGA Championship at Oak Hill, New York despite constantly feeling sick with worry.

Eventually, Gary visited his GP who insisted he took an MRI scan, in the hope that it could rule out the onset of Parkinson's disease. Instead, the scan discovered a lesion on Woodland's brain, located on the part of the cranium that 'controlled fear and anxiety'. It was no wonder the man was scared all the time.

Woodland began a course of medication for anxiety but when he played in the final PGA tournament of the year, he would decide what club to use and then ask his caddie for a different one. He had no concentration on the greens and as his confidence deteriorated, his doctors suggested he should undergo surgery.

They would remove what was described as a baseball-sized section from the left side of his skull and a tumorous growth that, if left untreated, could have seriously impacted on his eyesight. Woodland's scalp was reattached with titanium plates and screws.

'It was a horrible experience,' he said. 'All I wanted to do was go to sleep and not think about it, when going to sleep was the worst part. That is when all the seizures happened – it was a horrible five months.

'I learned a lot about myself. When I was struggling, if my doctor had just given me medication to calm me down and not ordered that MRI who knows how much larger the lesion could have grown. More than anything, that saved me.

'At the end of the day I just want to prove you can do hard things. I want to prove to my kids that nobody can tell you that you can't do anything. You can overcome scary places in your life; not everything is easy but I'm not going to let it stop me. I'm here because I believed this was what I was born to do – play great golf. I wanted this to be not a bump in the road for me, but a jump start in my career.'

For some folks on the pro golf tour, 50th place in a major golf championship might have seemed like a so-so happening. For Gary Woodland, it was something very different and more than enough reason to have uncorked a bottle of expensive wine and celebrated.

***

I was well beyond my athletic zenith – if I ever had one – and all I prayed for was a reasonable standard of living in the winding-down years. I fully respected those younger than me who took stroke on as a means of resetting their lives. When you reached your mid-60s, however, the scene was different.

I supposed that that was why I remained so crabby as signs of progress waned, the more so when I was consistently told how much better I was looking. Then there were moments that jolted you back to a sense that your suffering was as naught compared to many others in the world.

The thought of ending it all never seriously crossed my mind, the 'single to Beachy Head' comment notwithstanding. I wouldn't have had the first clue how to do it anyway, nor the courage to go through with it and life, even a painstaking one, was ultimately too precious to be given away voluntarily.

One Sunday morning in August, Canon Simon asked at Mass that the congregation should keep a parishioner in our prayers as she had recently taken her own life. It shook me to the core.

Next morning, my former colleague, *The Times* cricket correspondent Mike Atherton, revealed that Graham Thorpe, an England team-mate of his from yesteryear who had recently passed away, had spent years suffering from depression that would ultimately culminate in his suicide. He was only 55 years old.

This was a ghastly revelation, handled with typical sensitivity by Mike in what must have been a brutally difficult article to write.

Kitty, Graham's daughter, told Mike that her father, 'loved life, he loved us, but he just couldn't see a way out. It was heartbreaking to see how withdrawn he had become – he was not the same person. It was strange to see this person trapped in the body of Dad and that's why we've been so happy that the many reflections were about his life before this illness took over'.

I hadn't known Graham Thorpe, had never met him, but my memory was of a pugnacious batsman who took on and beat off some of the most intimidating bowling attacks in international cricket, most especially the Aussies in Australia. He epitomised dogged determination and entrenchment.

Sadly, his life had been one of continuous struggle against mental demons that would not let him be. The brain could play awful tricks.

***

Graham Thorpe would have taken serious evasive measures if, while at the crease, a ball had been coming at his head, but in football, the use of that part of your anatomy was part-and-parcel of the game – the only one I could think of in which this ability was a prized asset. Being 'good in the air' meant any player could be worth an extra few bob.

Over the years, though, evidence increased that repetitive use of head against ball had particularly life-changing consequences. In boxing, punches to the head were not only habitual knockout blows but had potentially life-ending consequences. Falling off a horse and landing on your head was not recommended.

It was football, grand old football, that was the meanest of all, but romanticism trumped best practice, the subject was sidestepped in the George Best manner, alarms were raised but ignored, the concern of relatives for loved ones was lost in the mists of their own recollection and brought scant, if any, recognition.

I was sent a video by Derrick Parker, on our Southend Legends WhatsApp group, which featured disturbing and undeniable proof that CTE (Chronic Traumatic Encephalopathy), was running rife through the later lives of ex-players and nobody in power appeared prepared to take much notice.

One of the interviewees was Wendy Ormsby, wife of Brendan, the former Aston Villa and Leeds United defender mentioned in his own story by Noel Blake. Brendan suffered a severe stroke in 2017, the ramifications of which were two types of epilepsy, a heart attack, cancer and aphasia.

He had begun to lose his memory and CTE was the probable cause (CTE can only be diagnosed post-mortem). 'For his carers, life was very stressful,' Wendy said. 'We would love it to go back to the way it was but unfortunately we can't so all we were asking for was some help. As we were caring, we hoped others would care.'

My 'Legends' mates, Derrick, Colin Morris and Micky Laverick were distraught to see Jimmy Robson featured in the message. Jimmy had passed away in 2021 at the age of 82, his final years defined by the scourge of Alzheimer's. In his prime, he was a member of the Burnley side that won the First Division title in 1960 and scored their goal in the 3-1 FA Cup final loss to Tottenham in 1962.

He joined the coaching staff at Turf Moor and Colin remembered 'a lovely, lovely guy. He had a VW seven-seater van and used to do his milk round in it'. Micky recalled Jimmy's time as reserve team manager at Huddersfield when he was a player there. 'The nicest man you could meet,' he said.

Dany, Jimmy's daughter, had pleaded for more financial help from the Professional Footballers Association (PFA) so that his final days could have been spent in greater comfort. Four years on, and with CTE case studies piling high, there remained a dispiriting lack of awareness from football authorities about its impact, past, present and future.

John Stiles, son of the great Nobby of Manchester United, and 1966 World Cup fame, had taken up the ravages of the illness as a *cause celebre* and banged the drum loudly for greater exposure to what he regarded as an epidemic in football.

Those who wanted the story to go away would insist that the 'old' balls from bygone eras absorbed a great deal more water and therefore delivered a heavier impact; Stiles retorted with evidence that today's footballs travelled so much faster through the air and landed against the skull (and thus brain) with almost the full smack of a boxing punch.

'I know of players who had begun to show the symptoms in their 40s and 50s and they were absolutely terrified,' John said on the *Common Sense* podcast with former player and manager Joey Barton in 2024. 'I calculated that in my father's career he probably headed the ball between 70,000 and 100,000 times which was a frightening statistic.

'I wrote about this to all 92 league clubs and none of them would let me in to talk to players about it. I stood in the car park at my old club Doncaster Rovers handing out leaflets and they told me to go away.'

***

Maureen was clearing the loft out in the autumn and came across some of my old cuttings, one of which was a picture from 1980 in the *Birmingham Post & Mail* office featuring myself, the former editor of *Sports Argus,* Ian 'Jonce' Johnson, its chief writer, Peter White and a fresh-faced Gary Shaw, the Aston Villa striker who had come in to write his weekly column with Whitey.

Young Gary was already press-savvy, realising that to have his name attached to the (now defunct) Saturday *Pink 'un* that was devoured across the West Midlands back then, would enhance his growing status as one of the standout young players in the First Division.

He was about to help inspire Villa to the First Division title and extraordinarily, a year later, they would win the European Cup, a feat that remained one of the most underrated of the past 70 years of football anywhere. This was a team built in his image by sergeant-major manager Ron Saunders, and which was perhaps unfairly described as drill-like in its efficiency.

Ron and I had our differences, he was never quite my cup of tea, nor I his, but my admiration for what he had achieved with a group of only 14 selected players all of whom were British, was total. Gary was the team's lone Brummie.

Every team was possessed of an individual who stood out from the crowd. It may have been his flaxen locks, the boy-next-door accent, his cheery persona but more importantly the remarkable eye for goal, innate flair and unquenchable stamina which made Gary Shaw its undeniable superstar.

The lad had such talent, but it rested easily on him. He bore no airs and graces, no arrogance, and accepted the adulation and all else that fell at his feet with an endearingly gracious and humble demeanour.

In the intervening years, he had suffered enduring pain from the knee problems that cut short his career, an undeserved legacy. After ten days in a coma following a fall outside his home in September 2024, Gary passed away at the age of 63.

By now, I had learned to treat the extent of certain news that reached me by how much my muscles stiffened, fingers shook and left eye began to quiver. The minute I heard of Gary's death, all three happened at once, uncontrollably, swiftly.

At that morning's Mass, Canon Simon had mentioned the word 'suffering' at least a dozen times. Gary's suffering – for far too long as it had been for him – had now been lifted.

***

Peter Withe was first to the casket and touched it lovingly. The service in Sutton Coldfield to send Gary Shaw on his way was ending and his striking partner from those Villa glory days could not part without a loving remembrance.

Big Peter, Scouse voice cracking, had spoken of the teenager who was not marked down as his original team-mate in the Villa forward line when Saunders made him the club's record signing in a £500,000 deal from Newcastle United, but earned his spurs when Brian Little was ruled out with an injury.

'Life had another plan and instead I was lucky enough to be paired with Gary,' Peter told the congregation. 'When we first met, I thought he was very shy, quiet and reserved but you didn't need to spend very long with him to see his immense talent. From that first meeting I knew I was in the presence of someone special.

'On the field, something incredible happened, it was as if we could reach into each other's minds, an unspoken connection. Together we became a feared duo, one that other teams didn't want to face. Gary was 19 and still finding his way in the world and as a 29-year-old, I naturally became his minder and his mentor. And certainly, his protector.

'I was proud to take on that role, not only because he was my team-mate but because he was my friend as well. He was still young, and on the field opposition centre-halves would try to intimidate him. I just had to remind them that if they wanted to get to Gary, they had to come through me first.

'The very first game of that title season was at Leeds United, we were drawing 1-1, when Tony [Morley] and Dennis [Mortimer] made surging runs down the right-hand side and for once, I don't know why, but I went to the near post for once and took everyone with me. The ball was played into me, I dummied it, and Gary was there to roll it into an empty net. The lads would probably say I missed it, and maybe they're right.

'Gary would score 18 goals (in 40 appearances) that season, and we won the title for the first time since 1910. His contribution was immense. I remembered he was so proud as he went from watching Villa from the terraces to becoming an idol on the pitch.

'Tony Morley scored the [BBC TV] goal of that season [against Everton at Villa Park]. Gary Williams played the ball up to Gary who made a remarkable turn on the halfway line [leaving Everton defender Billy Wright spinning like a top] and released Tony who ran 30 yards before rocketing the ball into the top of the net. But my vivid memory of that goal was the way Gary turned the defender; it was phenomenal the way he rolled him before passing to Tony.'

Reflections were inevitable, too, on the 1-0 victory over Bayern Munich in the 1982 European Cup Final, and Gary's contribution to the only goal in Rotterdam, once more gliding past a midfield challenge, feeding Morley who reached the byline and crossed for Withe to scramble the ball across the line. It remained the single most important goal in the club's history – unlikely ever to be topped.

Gary could just as easily have been a professional cricketer – he moved to the Birmingham suburb of Harborne in his early 20s to be closer to Edgbaston cricket ground – and it was revealed that his sporting hero was not a footballer like Ray Graydon or Chico Hamilton but the former Warwickshire and England opening bat, Dennis Amiss.

His cousin Michael reflected that Gary was, 'a strong person, a private person, and what I remembered most throughout his life, he was well-mannered, respectable and incredibly kind'.

As a montage of the most fulfilling moments of Gary Shaw's life were shown, 'The Way We Were' by Barbra Streisand ('scattered pictures of the smiles we left behind') was played to the unfolding of handkerchiefs and stirring of emotions. Musical contributions from UB40, Prince and Sting also formed part of the service that ended with these poignant lyrics from the American songwriter Jimmy Scott:

'If tears could build a stairway
And memories a lane
We'd walk right up to heaven
And bring you back again.

It broke our hearts to lose you
But you did not go alone
For part of us went with you
The day God called you home.

God looked around his garden
And he found an empty place
Then he looked down upon the earth
And he saw your precious face.

He put his arms around you
And he lifted you to rest
God's garden must be beautiful
He always takes the best.

Yes, he always takes the best.'

WHAT WAS AROUND THE CORNER?

SPORTSWRITERS WEREN'T supposed to be too wistful and maudlin.

It was our great good fortune – allied to some degree of talent for seeking truth, appreciating perspective, having a distinct feel for the game and stringing the odd decent sentence together – to be sent out to chart noble deeds with notebook and pen ('the tools of our trade,' Brian Clough once told an assembly of football hacks, having asked us none-too-politely to take our brandished tape recorders out of his face).

I had heard of a particular sports desk referred to by the other reporters in the office as 'the groin strain department'. We had a good laugh at that. There was the well-thumbed football manager's press conference opening gambit, 'any injuries Ron/Alex/Jose?' In-depth medical analyses were left for, well, the medical correspondent and the ever-multiplying army of doctors-cum-journalists.

We sports boys suffered our share of aches and pains – usually brought on by a surfeit of self-indulgence at our employer's expense – but our old landscape was being rapidly filled with articles on cancer, MS, MND, CTE and early-onset dementia (as per the previous chapter).

I knew nothing of stroke before my own fall and was taken aback at just how prevalent this perilous affliction was. This would only have been half a book (and less than half as interesting, naturally) were it not for the wonderful help I was freely given by Noel Blake, John Gorman, Michael Johnson, Michael Lynagh, Cameron McKinnell and Ali Turpie*.

They were all truly inspirational people who fought to get their lives back on track after so much anguish and foreboding. They told their stories bravely and fulsomely.

My own suffering, limited as it was, was nowhere near over. Yes, I was up on my feet, there was increasing movement in my affected arm, leg, and mouth, but I was way short of the 90 per cent of the former Neil I would gladly have accepted. Whether that would happen, not even the brightest specialist could tell.

My wish for this book was that it might act as an inspiration to those afflicted by stroke and to show that there could be a way out. I hope not to have offended anyone by finding a lighter side to my unwanted and unexpected descent into infirmity. For many people, there was no levity in stroke, it was a serious, unhappy, unremitting hardship that delivered little but anguish.

It was important not to retreat into self-pity or wallow in sadness. Yes of course I wished it had never happened, but it had, there was no escaping it. Life lessons didn't come much harder. How you responded was the key.

**In December 2024 at the NEC in Birmingham, Ali was a gold medallist in the British Indoor Rowing Championships 4000m relay with his team-mates Frazer Brent, Rhys Westall and Elliot Awin (who was fitted with a pacemaker). The four competitors leapt on and off the rowing machines you find in your local gym and rowed for all their worth. It was an astonishing feat of strength and endurance.*

***

Even the sunniest optimist among stroke survivors went through dark periods. A mind that was not entirely as it once was, threw up horrible images. And so, in late

November 2024, I watched the parliamentary debate on assisted dying with more than uncommon interest.

Entirely well-intentioned MPs in favour of the bill spoke with persuasive force but the more literate and compassionate speeches were made by those who saw great danger, both moral and mortal, in such legislation. I sided unequivocally with them. I had been treated with such devoted care and appreciated, as time went on, that I would need more of it as greater physical decline set in.

My condition was not my burden alone, it was shared. Death would be shared as well, but the sanctity of life was immensely precious, God's gift, something not to be given – or taken – away.

In a letter to all his parishioners, Philip Egan, bishop of our diocese of Portsmouth wrote, 'Campaigners argue that the terminally ill fear severe pain, loss of dignity and poor quality of life whereas assisted suicide would offer a quick end to physical suffering and emotional distress. Yet, modern medicine means that no one need die without dignity. Britain is a leader in palliative care with methods and drugs that have the capability to manage pain right to the end. Care is the answer, not suicide.

'Caring shows real love for the terminally ill, acknowledging their eternal value. Some argue that euthanasia for those with little hope of recovery would ease the pressure on health services but legalising assisted suicide only opens the door to abuse. If we love and care for someone, efficiency and cost-saving is irrelevant. How could helping someone to kill themselves be compassionate? It is evil, masquerading as kindness.'

Hopefully, I remained some way off from this being of personal relevance. But the whole concept of agreeing to death by means anything other than the natural course of events really was too much to bear.

***

To what was I looking forward in 2025? Setting aside a desire for a speedier recovery, extended health, the welfare of all my family and friends, and a bit of peace and quiet in the world, on the sporting front I had been as gobsmacked as anyone at the news that Andy Murray would coach Novak Djokovic, initially at the Australian Open but perhaps he'd be granted an extension.

Neither man had been particularly tolerant of those who occupied the coach's seats when they were performing (an understatement if ever there was one), and it would have been delicious to see Andy on the receiving end of much of what he had delivered during his playing days. Sport had lost none of its ability to shock and surprise.

Like anyone with a keen interest in the future of British tennis, who might take on Murray's mantle was foremost in my thoughts. Emma Raducanu and Jack Draper were names to be reckoned with and though in the case of Raducanu, she was already a Grand Slam champion, a sense of unfulfilled promise remained.

She said that in the past, she and her myriad advisors hadn't planned properly. There was too much short-termism. 'Now I just want to see how good I can be,' she added. Bring on the future, young lady.

If I still pinched myself that I'd both seen and reported on a British male winning the Wimbledon singles title in the flesh, I hadn't thought I'd live to see the day that a German would manage the England football team.

Some of the comments when Thomas Tuchel was awarded the post in the autumn of 2024 were appalling, the worst kind of xenophobic intolerance. Deep down, I would have preferred an Englishman to assume the post but some of the expressions of disgust at his appointment went far too far.

Maybe when you had survived a near-death experience, things like where a manager was born didn't matter as much. For goodness' sake, our nation possessed enough quality players to challenge strongly for the 2026 World Cup, and it was Tuchel's job to blend them into a winning force. Let him get on with it. And don't get me started on all that anthem malarkey.

Meeting up with old writing mates remained a much-needed social rejuvenation and so in the first week of December it was invigorating to lunch at The Dog and Fox on Wimbledon High Street, with Mike Calvin and Chris Davies, two *Daily Telegraph* stalwarts. That morning had come sad news from afar that Neale Fraser, the 1960 men's singles champion, had passed away at the age of 91.

'Frase' and I had enjoyed each other's company for the best part of 30 years, golfed in his home city of Melbourne and he'd always stopped at my desk in tennis press rooms for a back-slap and some gentle Pommie ribbing. As I clung to a pavement bollard for stability and glanced around the village, my thoughts turned to those champions who had passed this way in the mists of time.

The present day's weather was inclined to mistiness, but the lunch table conversation was warming, especially the subject of our national game where Mike, Chris and I had crossed paths and press boxes for longer than I had known 'Frase'.

We were at our most urgent – with bouts of dissent – about the current state of football and if Chris believed the Premier League to be in rude health, Mike and I shared expressions of lament bordering on angst.

Our woes were the absence of credible and moral leadership – domestically and internationally – the values of those who plundered clubs on behalf of nation states or hedge funds which crudely distorted any sense of purpose and fairness but most imperatively, a stultifying absence of variety in the game.

A superb article in the *Sunday Times* the following weekend by the always excellent Jonathan Northcroft caught my eye. It was as if he had distilled a flavour of our pub discourse, and was a compelling piece about what was wrong with a game now at the mercy of the mad scientists of data.

'If you look at the Premier League's all-time scorers from outside the penalty area, the top 15 are a pure nostalgia-fest,' Northcroft wrote. 'The only present players (in sixth and 12th) are old-timers, Kevin De Bruyne and Christian Eriksen. Don't see many screamers anymore, do you? The reason is data. Analysts say attempts from too far out are "inefficient" and players should be in the "golden zone" (the area inside the penalty box within the width of the six-yard box where most goals are scored), before shooting.

'It's one example of where agency is being removed from players. Another is dribbling which is also "inefficient" unless in the "right" circumstances ... Clubs want to nurture street players and then, once they're in the first team, knock all the street out of them ...

'A dearth of long shots. A dearth of dribbles ... Almost no tackling. Virtually every pass short unless it is a choreographed cross-field ball or long pass to feed a rehearsed fast break.'

This was enough for me to ask the pharmacist on Monday morning for an increased dosage in my blood pressure medication.

And we hadn't even started on VAR, on which we did concur. Chris had been a long-time friend and confidant of many officials, I had refereed to a decent level and Mike was a prescient writer of his time. None of us would give VAR house room. 'The handball law used to extend to about 11 words,' Chris said. 'Now it's first phase this, second phase that, unnatural arm positions. It's unfathomable.'

Mike said, 'The organisations that control the sport are appalling. What is the PGMOL [the referees' professional body] other than a bunch of blokes protecting their own arses? That's all they are. And TV has become far too proprietorial. Its attitude is "we own the game" and promotes the myth that it [the Premier League] is the best in the world. Really? I get more out of watching the Championship, the purity, the endeavour, but even that's becoming a bit soured.

'Chris, you're a Bromley season-ticket holder, correct? I bet you see football that is more instantly recognisable to the likes of us than the Premier League, which becomes more alien week after week.' Chris nodded assent.

I could understand the raising of youthful hackles against the judgement of three stuffed-shirts who had long bade 60 a fond farewell. But the three of us felt we were trustees of the game with a century of combined experience covering football at every level, in newspapers, books and often leading public debate.

There was little we hadn't seen or experienced. I stood (if a trifle wobbly) with us.

***

After my unrewarding visit to Adams Park in August, Wycombe Wanderers became a team and club transformed. Nearing the end of their period in control, the American Couhig family were placed under intense pressure to dispense with the services of Matt Bloomfield, who they had brought back to the club to take over as manager from Gareth Ainsworth, after Blooms's brief spell in charge of Colchester United.

Loyalty had become a byword at Wycombe, the Couhigs knew it and saw something in a novice manager that the strident voices on social media couldn't appreciate. The new owner, a billionaire Georgian chappie who lived in Kazakhstan, was seeking to build on that and determined that long-term sustainability required a credible hand on the tiller.

The programme started to click into place from September onwards. In an excellent article on The Coaches' Voice website in November 2024 'Blooms' articulated his coaching principles and I understood from it why he had a chance to become one of the most talented young managers in the game.

'I want my teams to play fast, convincing football and not have possession for possession's sake,' he said. 'I want to know *why* we are moving the ball around the pitch, what is the purpose and what is the move we are building towards. I'm not trying to reinvent the wheel or be the cleverest manager in the Football League. What I'm trying to do is what's right for my group at any given moment.'

He said that ten years ago, when he was playing in League One, the tactical side of the game was quite basic, but it was easier to appreciate what was happening during a match as a player, than as someone standing on the sidelines.

'Playing in midfield, I was always in among the action. I could sense quite quickly if the opposition was doing something slightly different to what we'd been expecting, or what they'd been doing [previously]. That fed into my love of the tactical side of the game …

'These days I have a video analyst on the bench with me, coding the game live. We have an aerial view where the spacing can be seen so much more easily compared to being on the pitch or the sidelines. Anything the analysts can see quicker, they can feed back to me. We can then adjust things on the pitch before it gets to half-time.'

As the second half of the 2024/25 season approached, Wycombe embarked on an 11-match winning run that took them to the top of League One, earning plaudits for Bloomfield, who was being celebrated as one of the bright young things of English management. The club's unbeaten spell of 19 matches that ended on the final weekend of the year was the best across the entire Football League in 2024.

These were heady days indeed in Buckinghamshire. It felt to me as if another dramatic corner had been turned in the history of a club that didn't do dull.

***

The date had been in the diary for months. Missing the Manchester *Daily Mail* sports desk Christmas reunion in 2023 had been an immense blow. I still wasn't self-assured enough to make the 2024 journey by train, but could I drive 200 miles, get safely to a hotel, find a place to park and reach the front door of the Old Wellington near the cathedral, eat, drink and be merry and return home the following day without causing an accident?

Maureen said she would share the load, driving to a service station on the M6 toll road where I urged her to let me take the wheel. 'Are you sure?' she asked. 'Of course I am.' I knew the journey from there like the back of my hand and negotiated it dextrously until we reached the outskirts of the city where unfamiliar ring roads, a plethora of road works and one way traffic flow caused much consternation and unchecked outbursts.

The last little bit, less than 50 yards, was perhaps the most perilous: a cobbled pavement made greasy by a thin Manchester drizzle required careful planting of my stick and a couple of pauses to avoid clattering into distracted pedestrians. But I made it into a packed pub and the bosom of old colleagues and hearty welcomes.

Reaching our table required climbing three flights of stairs but the lads kept the one high-backed chair for the youngest of the group who suddenly felt – but didn't look, I hoped – the oldest. I did get the sense that an occasion which for over three decades had been a celebration of comradely life, had become an annual thanksgiving of avoiding death.

We were still over double figures (just) in attendance which was astonishing given the geographical spread of our homes and the advancing years. To my immediate right sat Doug Weatherall, now the group's elder statesman at 92 years of age. Okay, so he told me the same story four times and I had to shout back because of his hearing deficiencies but the fellow was a bloody marvel.

The *Mail*'s north-east football reporter for donkey's years regaled me with his love of Raich Carter and Len Shackleton and how he missed the single most replayed moment in his beloved Sunderland's history, Jim Montgomery's incredible fingertip save from Peter Lorimer of Leeds in the 1973 FA Cup Final.

'When Lorimer went to shoot, I was certain he'd score and closed my eyes, so I didn't have to see it go in,' Doug recalled. 'When I opened them and the ball was back in play, I assumed he'd hit the bar.

'It wasn't until I was in the dressing room after the match [Sunderland from the Second Division defeated the overwhelming favourites 1-0], that Dick Malone, the right-back, said, "What a magnificent save that was by Monty." "What save was that?"'

These were the memories we strove to stay alive for, interspersed as they were with the oft-repeated question, 'Why couldn't so-and-so make it, is he dead?' Some of our long-distance travellers had been trapped by the damage inflicted by Storm Darragh, others were too ill to attend, and a few had dropped off the invitation list because they hadn't responded for some reason, though we assumed they were still alive.

Those who lived to tell great tales were Derick 'Dino' Allsop, David Bowman, Peter Boyle, David Burke, Ray Clarkin, Arnold Critchley, Peter Ferguson, Brian Scott, David Shaw, Doug Weatherall and yours truly. We said we'd do it all again in 2025, with God's help and so long as Labour hadn't trousered any more of our pension pots.

Returning home the following day, Maureen wanted to stop at Bicester Village, the outlet centre just off the M40. The place was packed and so were the disabled parking bays, filled with a slew of 4x4s which possessed barely a hint of a blue badge between them.

The distracted security guard I'd beckoned over to point out the offenders shrugged his shoulders and said he wouldn't enforce the law as he'd had his fill of being verbally abused.

This was red rag time for me. I stumbled out of the car, remonstrated with a couple of drivers who were still in their seats, waved my stick in a menacing manner at their windscreens shouting, 'where's your badge?' When a couple of windows were wound down, they didn't argue when the penny dropped that I was properly infirm, enraged (probably deranged), and prepared to stand my ground – albeit tottering like young Mr Grace in *Are You Being Served?*

Two cars, one a highly polished black Roller, immediately backed out; a third was initially defiant but when I shuffled off to collect my mobile phone, turned around to brandish it and threaten to take an image of his licence plate, he was off as well.

I really did feel rather pleased with myself. Maureen couldn't believe it when she returned to find out all the fun she'd missed – and she hadn't bought anything anyway.

AND FINALLY…

THIS HAS been the hardest and yet unquestionably most satisfying of the many books I have written, for obvious reasons. What made it more challenging was that I couldn't type properly, well not with my left, dominant hand, and typing with one weak hand was an unremitting frustration.

I hadn't known that there was a facility on my laptop that used dictation as a writing assistant and even when it was pointed out by my daughters, because of the inconsistent working of my mouth, the words I meant to say often came out all wrong.

If Arlo barked during the process (often), the words 'be quiet' would appear in rapid succession across the page before I could switch the blasted thing off. I spent more time correcting inadvertent errors and typos than I did trying to pull up my nappies in hospital.

There are so many people I need to thank. Family, of course, takes precedence. My wife Maureen had to put up with more than her fair share of trial and tribulation in our first 34 years of marriage, but from 8 May 2023, our lives took on a new, extraordinary, frightening dimension when she first saw me lying across the floor of our bedroom.

Talk about picking up the pieces, she's done that every day since and on most long before that. I love and admire her more than I ever tell her. Of course, we had our difficult moments. It was hard accepting infirmity, and probably just as hard for someone close to live with it.

My daughters Elizabeth and Kathleen also shouldered their fair share of my anxieties and anger which often gave way to argumentative outbursts I immediately regretted. I am grateful they are still speaking to me and repeat how proud of me they are. It is reciprocated in full.

On 31 October 2023, a new light shone on my life in the form of our first granddaughter Amelie June who I hoped to be able to hold without fear of dropping before she grew too heavy to pick up. Kathleen and her husband James were already proving naturals as parents. James's dad Paul had a sticky year health wise in 2024 but came through it with typical Scottish defiance. Sending love to him and wife Karen.

The nursing staff both in Reading and Thatcham were beyond caring and brilliant but if I try to mention them all by name, I will be bound to miss one out which would be an unforgiveable shame. I do want to wish Callum Fraser, who was on work experience upon my arrival in ward D at the Royal Berks (giving the phrase a whole new meaning), the very best in his medical studies in Birmingham and for work beyond.

I know I would have raised my voice if I'd had me as a patient, but none did – though what they said about me at the nurses' station, who knew?

Dealing with stroke patients has to be the most gruelling of all assignments because we were all so unpredictable. They took care of me and sustained me in equal part. When Labour – God save us – won the 2024 election and kept saying the NHS was broken, I'd shout at the television, 'oh no it's not'.

On my discharge, the bulk of my physical rehabilitation was undertaken by Charlotte Eley in Eversley, who was a constant source of bloody hard work, though I could have done without that kneeling on my fingers to try to keep them flat! But thank you for everything, Charlotte. The NHS community staff did me proud: Helen, Pauline, Caroline and Sarah (I know I shouldn't have talked so much while I should have been concentrating on my stride pattern!) were terrifically understanding.

In the Wellness Gym in Wokingham, Lauren, Rachel and Shane watched over us, and even laughed at some of our inaner comments. Brian, Charlie, and Jen were the Monday two o'clock crew, inspiring each other as best we could. I wish them better tomorrows.

I am extremely grateful for the time Justin Rees, the leader of the consortium that completed the purchase of Southend United in 2024 gave me. I'm firmly of the opinion that the future of my hometown football club is in safe hands.

Sincere thanks to those friends and former press colleagues who took time out of their busy lives and either sat at my hospital bedside, on the Thatcham terrace or came to my home.

They were, in alphabetical order: Bassam Alchi, Jeremy Best, John and Vyvyenne Bingham, Tom Clarke, Doug and Nicola Cleary, David Davies, the late Mike Dickson, Peter Dixon, Dan Evans (journalist, not tennis player), David Felgate, Harry Findlay, Barry Flatman, Malcolm Folley, Paul and Rose Francis, Brian Hanlon, Dawn Hardiman, Oliver Holt, Richard Hughes, Richard Keys, David Lloyd, Jonathan Overend, Alan Parry, Colin Pearce, Sean Rafter, John Robins, George Salmon, Gordon Siviter, Mike and Ursula Skrakowski and David Walker.

An appreciative nod to the Skrakowskis and the Clearys, who formed the WhatsApp group 'Neil's Wheels' and took it in turns to transport me to and from Mass on Sunday and our Wednesday evening choir practice before I could get back behind the wheel. To all those who held me in their prayers – and I know there were many – I felt extremely humbled.

Blessings to the members of the Corpus Christi choir for sustaining my spirits each week: Bassam, Gordon, John, Rose and Ursula (from the previous list), Terry Crees, Celestina Ndubuisi, Barbara Robins, Una Smith, our organist David 'Maestro' Lumsden, and leader, the indefatigable Susan Vosser.

As we entered the autumn of 2024, our choir numbers had dwindled but in the space of a couple of weeks in mid-October, they suddenly flourished. In a remarkable coincidence I was introduced after one Mass to Hilary and Yasmin Morjaria. Hilary's husband Sanjay had suffered a stroke in July and, like me, was first in the Royal Berks, before a transfer to Thatcham, and the same Highclere Ward where I did my rehab. They showed an interest in swelling our numbers and were soon joined by sisters Juana and Anetra Gnanraj, lovely personalities who significantly reduced our average age!

Then I summoned the courage to try again on the psalms, which was both stimulating and fretful in equal measure. Whatever the prevailing headwinds, I believed that – in the words of Padre Pio – blessed was the crisis that made me grow.

***

Without a supportive publisher I wouldn't get far in this business, so I gratefully acknowledge Jane Camillin and the fine people of Pitch Publishing for giving me the chance to put pen to paper again, Katie Field for her skilful editing and Duncan Olner for once more coming up with a wonderful cover. This is the third book for which I have partnered Pitch and I hope it may lead to the odd one or two more after I've taken a few deep breaths.

To all those who shared the stroke wards with me in my four months of hospitalisation – the majority of whom

I neither talked to nor knew their name – I send prayers for continued recovery and relative peace of mind.

I changed the Christian names of those I noted prominently in here to protect their anonymity (except Marc and Anthony), but everything I wrote of really did happen.

When a stroke strikes, the victim deals with the consequences in a variety of ways. None of us knew what it was all about and if we'd survive for long; there was no upside and so we had to keep believing that the worst had passed and then get on with trying to put one unsteady foot back in front of the other.

Sir Alex Ferguson once made a memorable speech about confronting failure, to take it head on, refuse to accept it, and to come back stronger. He said he was a better manager the day *after* a defeat. I supposed stroke wasn't a defeat, not really. It wasn't a failure either. It was a challenge, perhaps the toughest of all. With resolve, you could live with it. And that's what I intend to do. To the best of my ability.